THE UNIVERSE THAT ISN'T

Does the vast—enormous—gigantic—stupendous universe
put before us by Modern Science
really and truly
exist?

The improver of natural knowledge absolutely refuses to acknowledge authority, as such. For him, skepticism is the highest of duties, blind faith the one unpardonable sin.

>
> Thomas Henry Huxley
> *On the Advisableness of Improving Natural Knowledge* (1868)

THE UNIVERSE THAT ISN'T
The Reality That Is.

by
J. H. Hacsi

CHAMPAGNE PRESS
P.O. Box 631
West Covina, CA 91793

Excerpts from COSMIC DAWN by Eric Chaisson. Copyright © 1981 by Eric Chaisson. Reprinted by permission of Little, Brown and Company.

Excerpts from COSMOS by Carl Sagan. Copyright © 1980 by Carl Sagan Productions, Inc. Reprinted by permission of Random House, Inc.

Dictionary definitions quoted in this book by permission from the RANDOM HOUSE COLLEGE DICTIONARY, Revised edition, © 1975, 1984 by Random House, Inc.

Thanks to my good friend Rae Hamilton for giving me my title.

THE UNIVERSE THAT ISN'T
Copyright © 1985 by J. H. Hacsi
All Rights Reserved.

ISBN 0-9612146-1-9

To those of open, inquiring mind,
ready to question, ponder and debate,
this book is gratefully dedicated.

PREFACE

Modern Science, with its recent discoveries, has placed before us a vast and ancient universe. Mankind's Earthly residence has been reduced to a very minor speck in this amazing universe, a universe said to contain billions and billions of stars clustered into billions and billions of galaxies.

The life that sprang into being on Earth did so entirely by chance, Scientists tell us, out of random happenings, fortuitously, in a universe indifferent to it, a universe geared to much bigger and better things.

Is this version of life and the universe a valid one?

The scientific universe is built upon a foundation not of fact but of faith.

The laws of nature—unvarying through time—are the same throughout the universe.

This is the premise—the article of faith—upon which Science has built its universe.

How much proof does Science have for this premise?

It has none. There is no proof at all, of any kind.

This fundamental premise is not only entirely unproved, at our current level of attainment it is absolutely and unconditionally unprovable. Yet within the hallowed halls of Science, it remains unquestioned.

The laws of nature remain unchanged through time and space.

Who says so?

Science says so. But what if Science is wrong?

If the Scientists are right, if Science has put its faith in an assumption that eventually proves to be correct, then the vast, old universe they have constructed on this premise may be a valid one; it may in fact exist.

If the scientific universe exists, if Man truly lives in an almost inconceivably vast, ten to twenty billion year old universe in which he accidentally emerged very recently, it becomes extremely difficult to believe that human life has much if any universal significance.

On the other hand, if human life *is* significant, it becomes extremely difficult to believe it emerged by accident in an inconceivably vast, ten to twenty billion year old universe.

The laws of nature, unvarying through time, are the same throughout the universe. —Science has built its universe on this premise, on this unproved and unprovable article of faith.

This book discards this unproven and currently unprovable assumption and substitutes an unproven and unprovable assumption of its own, to wit:

Man has significance; human life holds the key to the Creation; the Creation was created for Woman (a generic term which includes the male sex).

Using this as our foundation, can we arrive at a rational explanation for the universe—*and explain all the currently known facts about the universe*—building upon this premise?

We can most certainly give it a try.

TABLE OF CONTENTS

1 - ANCIENT GODS IN MODERN DRESS
   *What's in a Name? Call a Weed a Rose,
   Does it Smell Any Sweeter?* 1
2 - RESTORATION COMEDY
   *If Man Is An Accidental Nothing, How Can
   We Pretend He's Something?* 18
3 - LAW VERSUS CUSTOM
   *The Law Is The Law Is The Law—Or Is It
   Merely Custom?* 34
4 - LIGHT: THE CORPUSCULAR WAVE
   *Star Light, Star Bright, You've Traveled
   How Far To Get Here?* 56
5 - INTERACTION
   Does Consciousness Warp Space Time? 78
6 - FUN HOUSE MIRROR
   *Do We Quake in Fear or Bow Down in Awe
   Before Our Own Shadow?* 97
7 - WATER, WATER EVERYWHERE
   *Why Are We the Only Ones in the System
   With Plenty to Drink?* 114
8 - THE BREATH OF LIFE
   *Where Would We Be, What Would We Be,
   Without Oxygen?* 134
9 - THE FOUR FORCES
   *What Does Impersonal Nature Know of the
   Personal Heart?* 149
10 - THE ATOMIC WONDERLAND
   *Who Would Have Thought the Tiny Old
   Atom Had So Much Stuff In It?* 166
11 - SHADOW AND SUBSTANCE
   A Shadow Is—Does It Have Substance? 187
12 - A LOOKING GLASS WORLD
   *Mirror, Mirror in the Sky,
   Aren't You Proof We'll Never Die?* 209

1
ANCIENT GODS IN MODERN DRESS
What's in a Name? Call a Weed a Rose, Does it Smell Any Sweeter?

> The more things change, the more they remain the same.
> Alphonse Karr (1808-1890)

In the dim and distant past primitive Man huddled in caves—so the scholars tell us—his continued existence as a species far from certain.

Today modern Man huddles in his cities, his towns, his villages, his continued existence as a species—so we fear—far from certain.

Things *do* change, or we'd still be huddling in our caves.

Things not only change, of late the rate of change in industrial/technological societies has been so rapid as to be mind boggling. We are surrounded on all sides by innovation to where we are all but literally drowning in a sea of invention.

We all know from whence cometh this spectacular, awe inspiring array of ever new products. Necessity may be the Mother of invention, but proud Science is the Father.

In the last three centuries, since the dawning of the Modern Age, Science has brought us an unprecedented mastery of our physical environment. During this same period, as though exacting a proper payment for its efforts (a just retribution?), scientific thought has inexorably reduced the perceived significance of Man in the cosmic scheme of things.

For most of our history, our species—*Homo sapiens*—lived on an Earth believed to be flat, an Earth confidently assumed to be at the center of Creation. The Sun circled over our heads days to bring us light and warmth and the night was made enchanting not only by a big silver ball that waxed and waned but also by a magnificent display of sparkling stars. The universe had been created for us, and we were at the warm, pulsating heart of it all.

Then Science began its curiosity-propelled probing into the structure of the cosmos, and as it did so we got bumped, step by rude step, from this preeminent position. The geocentric view (Earth at the center), unchallenged or rarely challenged for millennia, was swept aside and replaced by the heliocentric (Sun at the center). All too soon this too was swept aside, our Sun unceremoniously demoted to the status of minor star on the outer fringes of a run-of-the-mill galaxy. Currently Science has us living in a universe so vast it is almost beyond imagining, a universe in which billions of stars in various stages of birth, aging and decay cluster together in billions of galaxies, the space surrounding them so boundless that if the matter of all these billions of stars, in these billions of galaxies, were uniformly distributed throughout the vastness of space, there would be only about one atom of hydrogen per cubic meter of space. Meanwhile the universe is expanding at an almost inconceivable rate, according to the Cosmologists: every four seconds it adds to itself a volume equal to the size of our Milky Way, creating ever new boundless reaches.

As the universe, in the eyes of Science, has been perceived as ever larger and grander, in inverse ratio we have shrunk. In the cosmic scheme of things, we have now been reduced to almost total insignificance, an accidental pimple of consciousness on a chunk of matter that just happened to come into existence in a low rent district around a mediocre star in the outlying regions of an unspectacular galaxy. As we rush forward in our mastery of the Earth, learning how to communicate at lightning speed, reproduce images of distant events on our TV screens, talk to each other over wires, make almost any happening on Earth *here* and *now* for a worldwide audience of viewers, transport ourselves under the sea, on the sea, up in the air, even beyond our atmosphere as far as our larger-than-average satellite, the Moon, even as we are achieving all these wondrous things, Science is forcing us to contemplate and reevaluate our overall ranking in the Creation.

Modern Science has not only reduced our Earthly residence to a very minor speck in the newly discovered gigantic universe, it has also, with recent discoveries, reduced the human race to near absurdity, as something that just happened to evolve as the tag end of a meaningless series of accidents.

Life on Earth came into being entirely by chance, we are told, out of random happenings, fortuitously, in a universe indifferent to us, a universe geared to much bigger and better things.

If the Learned Ones are right, if we truly live in a universe ten to twenty billion years old in which we have evolved by chance out of accidental life, in a universe so vast that light, traveling at the fantastic speed of 186,000 miles per second, hasn't yet had time, in twenty billion years, to circumnavigate it, it becomes extremely difficult if not impossible to justify any notion that Man has significance, that he is in truth, as we love to think, lord and master of all he surveys. We must, possibly, either relinquish this fond belief in our own significance or reject the universe the Learned Ones have placed before us.

In effect, we face a dilemma and may be logically forced to choose between these two positions:

1. Man lives in an almost inconceivably vast, ten to twenty billion year old universe, one in which he accidentally emerged very recently; therefore he cannot possibly have much if any universal significance.

2. Man *is* significant; therefore it is difficult—nay, in truth it is impossible—to believe he lives in an almost inconceivably vast universe, one which existed for several billions of years before life accidentally happened onto the scene.

Science, or many Scientists, have opted for number one above and have happily or reluctantly relinquished the notion that Man has importance, that human life holds the key to the Creation, that the Creation was made for Man, and that any rational construct of the universe has to start with this premise or it departs hopelessly from the real.

In this book, we will opt for number two above and head down the road the Scientists have abandoned. We will start from the premise that Man has significance, that the Creation exists for him, and see if we can arrive at a rational explanation for the universe, and all the currently known facts about the universe, built upon this premise.

Blessed with vision, Man has always looked around. Trying to make sense of his own existence, he has constructed stories to explain what he sees. The Scientists of our century are no different; they too are weaving narratives based upon their perceptions. Man has always had such stories; it is only right that we have ours. But there is no reason to suppose that the Scientific Tales of the late 20th Century have, for the first time in history, cornered Truth, the whole of it and nothing but. Rather the chances are overwhelming that the Scientific Stories of the 20th Century have the same amount of truth, and the same lack of validity, as the myths of earlier centuries.

It is only because the current myths are put forth so unblinkingly by Science—that Science seems so sure it has not only nailed down just about all the facts but is interpreting them correctly—that this book mounts a challenge against them. If Scientists were ready to acknowledge what in truth they are doing—spinning one more in an endless series of creation myths—their tales could be smiled at and enjoyed. But Science does not see itself as doing this at all: it sees itself as setting before us not only facts but Truth, built into an immense, elaborate, consistent, *proven* structure.

A structure which this book challenges and intends to do its best to bring down.

Before attempting to bring any structure down, the wrecker, or would-be wrecker, should walk around and through the building to get a sound idea of its dimensions, its method of construction, its strengths, its weaknesses, so that when it is brought down, its demolition can be accomplished in an orderly fashion without anyone's getting accidentally smashed or flattened in the process.

Therefore we will start by taking a close layman's look at the Scientific Edifice.

Ancient Man saw himself as at the mercy of capricious power. Malevolent spirits—demons, devils, gods—hid behind every bush, occupied every tree. Then the dawn of Science broke, and on Christmas Day 1642, Isaac Newton was born. In his masterwork, *Principia Mathematica,* Newton banished Caprice and gave us the great World Machine, a world ruled by Natural Law.

In the three centuries since Newton's time, Science has added to and refined its understanding of Natural Law. There are the Three Laws of Motion, the Three Laws of Thermodynamics dealing with the effects of heat and temperature, and the four relationships postulated in Maxwell's Equations which cover the workings of electricity and magnetism. These ten laws are said by Science to cover everything that happens in the macroscopic (visible) universe. In the world of the microscopic (invisible), the laws governing quantum mechanics are still being formulated, but the expectation is that eventually all quantum behavior will be covered by a small number of equally simple, unbreakable laws. In formulating all these immutable laws, Science repeatedly reconfirmed the banishment of Caprice, rendering the universe comprehensible.

But not for long.

If we take a close look at this century's scientific discoveries, we will note that despite the heroic efforts of the brilliant Newton and others who preceded and followed him, Caprice was not permanently routed after all. Modern Science has not only allowed her back in, it has insisted that she once again triumphantly resume her throne center stage, surrounded by her next of kin. While clinging stubbornly to these same ancient gods, Science has of course dressed them a bit differently in hopes of disguising them.

Naturally enough, our modern gods—presented to us by modern Science—have modern names. There is the Great God Chance, more familiarly known as By Chance, with his consort Lady Random, or, more affectionately, Randomly, with their offspring Fortuitous, or Fortuitously. (There are those among us, of course, myself included, who do not see these three as separate entities; rather we see them as three aspects of the One and Only God, but as this is a Tract on Science and Reason, not on Religion and Superstition, this is a point best left undiscussed.)

Since the dawn of the Science Age, vast amounts of knowledge have been accumulated and vast strides made in understanding the origin of the universe and the origin of life. The account given in Genesis in the Christian Bible—"In the beginning God created the heaven and the earth"—failed to satisfy everyone's thirst for understanding and knowledge. (Who or What is God and How-Why-When Did She-He-It Do These Things?) Fortunately, the biblical account left ample room for Science to charge into the breach in an attempt to amplify and elucidate this simple (some would say simple minded) and straightforward account.

The scenario (fairy-tale?) that most Cosmologists accept today runs something like this:

Once upon a time—originally—at the origin of everything—there was a singularity, a "cosmic egg." This egg exploded, in an event known as The Big Bang, creating space, starting time on its unidimensional flow.

If the Bang was big enough, and if matter is sparse enough, the universe will continue to expand forever, approaching infinity, and we live in an "open universe." This "open universe" will cool over time—a great deal of time—and in the end this open universe and all its contents will die of cold.

If the Bang wasn't quite that large, and if there is sufficient matter, with its attractive force or gravitational pull, to stop the expansion, we live in a "closed universe." Given enough time, our "closed universe" will stop expanding, will reverse itself and start contracting, will fall in on itself, growing hotter and hotter as its shrinks into a blazing egg similar to the original egg, and this universe will in time die from its own internal heat.

Or possibly it won't die. Possibly, after gathering back into the original singularity, it will again explode and start the process all over again. If this is how it is, then we live in an "oscillating universe" and the Big Bang that started our universe on its way was only one Bang in what may possibly be an infinite series of Bangs.

At the moment of the Bang, according to the current scenario, that which existed was incredibly, perhaps infinitely hot, and incredibly, perhaps infinitely compressed. "Most numerical experiments suggest that in the beginning, there was chaos!" writes Eric Chaisson in his highly entertaining book *Cosmic Dawn* (Little, Brown and Company, Boston, Toronto: 1981). At 10^{-43} seconds (.0000000000000000000000000000000000000000001 seconds) after the Bang—*Planck time* after the Bang—the explosion had brought the universe to a size equivalent to one-thousandth of a centimeter, which is smaller than the size of one atomic nucleus. Quicker than a flash, energy created matter. The newly created microscopic bits of matter, existing in extremely great density, collided with each other, annihilating into radiation, creating a brilliant fireball. "Whatever matter managed to exist did so as an inconspicuous precipitate suspended in a sea of dense, brilliant radiation." (Eric Chaisson, *Cosmic Dawn*.)

As time rushed forward, the universe continued to expand, cooling and thinning as it did so. The annihilation of matter slowed down to where it virtually ceased. Charged elementary particles, pulled together by electromagnetic forces, began to assemble, and the Era of Radiation gradually gave way to the Era in which we live, the Matter Era.

Single negatively charged electrons became attached to single positively charged protons, forming the first atoms, atoms of hydrogen, the simplest of all atoms, and hydrogen became the common ancestral element for all matter in our universe.

Some tens of millions of years after the Bang, the galaxies began to form. "Aside from the creation of atoms, the formation of galaxies was the first great accomplishment of the Matter Era." (Eric Chaisson, *Cosmic Dawn*.)

How this great accomplishment came about is still a matter of speculation. One suggested script goes like this:

In the early universe, "the initially homogeneous cloud would have surely experienced occasional fluctuations—small local irregularities in the gas density that came and went at random. No cloud, whether a terrestrial fluffy cloud in Earth's atmosphere, a tenuous interstellar cloud in our Milky Way Galaxy, or the primordial cloud. . . . , can remain completely homogeneous indefinitely. Each of the cloud's atoms is sure to have some motion, largely because of heat. Eventually, one atom somewhere in the cloud will accidentally move closer to another, making that part of the cloud just a little denser than the rest. The atoms may then separate, dispersing this density fluctuation, or they may act together to attract a third atom to enhance it. In this way, small pockets of gas can arise anywhere in a cloud simply by virtue of random atomic motion." (Eric Chaisson, *Cosmic Dawn*.)

There is a problem in this creation scenario, however. When Nature creates through random motion, it takes time. For the creation of anything as stupendous as a galaxy, with its billions of stars, calculations indicate it would take almost twenty billion years. As this is the estimated age of the universe itself, the galaxies should just now be forming whereas they are already in existence. This poses a problem for the scientific script of genesis that has not yet been solved.

The creation of stars presents far fewer problems.

The accepted scenario for star formation goes something like this:

Matter in space fluctuates. Atoms move around at random. Random motion leads to accidental collisions. In the course of such collisions the atoms may coalesce briefly, then the cluster disperses again.

There is more random motion, leading to more frequent collisions. Frequent collisions cause friction and an increase in heat. With increased heat, random motion increases, resulting in even more collisions. Pockets of gas form. When a sufficient number of atoms—estimated at nearly a thousand billion billion billion billion billion billion atoms, according to Eric Chaisson in *Cosmic Dawn*—accumulate into a gaseous cloud, the gravitational pull of the atoms on each other keeps the gas from dispersing again and a star is born.

Fortunately stars are not only born, they also age and die. Out of the debris of dead stars—we are told—planets are born, for only within the cores of high mass stars are conditions right for the manufacture of the heavier elements.

The currently accepted hypothesis for the creation of the Solar System goes something like this:

Through random motion, a dusty interstellar cloud fragment formed measuring about a light-year across. "Intermingled with the usual plentitude of hydrogen and helium atoms, the cloud harbors some heavy-element gas and dust, an accumulation of ejected matter from many past supernovae. Gravitational instabilities start the fragment contracting. . . . , after which dense protoplanetary eddies form of their own accord." (Eric Chaisson, *Cosmic Dawn*.)

What caused the instabilities that triggered the contractions? Current theory favors the notion that a supernova, an extremely bright star bursting into a last hurrah before fading away, exploded nearby. The explosion caused shock waves through the interstellar cloud which piled up matter before it. As Eric Chaisson explains it in his clear and informative book, *Cosmic Dawn:*

"Once the shock wave passed, turbulent gas eddies would appear naturally at various locations throughout the primitive, rotating Solar System, the bulk of which, by this time, would have flattened into a Frisbee-shaped disk. As in earlier cases of galaxy and star formation, these eddies would be nothing more than gas density fluctuations that come and go at random. Provided an eddy was able to sweep up enough matter while orbiting the protosun, including a rich enough mixture of dust to cool it, then gravity alone would ensure the formation of a planet. . .

"The natural satellites or moons of the planets presumably formed in similar fashion, as still smaller eddies condensed in the vicinity of their parent planets."

Once our Solar System had formed, we were ready for the emergence of life.

Again—according to the Scientists—Chance ruled. Water was essential for our particular form of life. "Only a fortuitous combination of temperature and pressure, unlike that of any other known planet, allows large quantities of water, enough to cover three-quarters of our planet's surface, to remain in the liquid phase." (Eric Chaisson, *Cosmic Dawn.*)

The atmosphere and surface of the primordial Earth were vastly different from the atmosphere and surface of today's Earth. The gases swirling around the prelife Earth—believed to be a mixture of ammonia, methane, hydrogen and carbon dioxide—did not react spontaneously with each other. For chemical interactions to occur, external energy was needed. That energy was supplied by the Sun. Solar radiation poured down, with no ozone layer surrounding the primordial Earth to screen out ultraviolet rays. This radiation was sufficiently energetic to stimulate chemical changes in the molecules. The liberated atoms and molecular fragments reformed into more complex molecules.

With random movement of molecules, random collisions, random reformation, ever more complex molecules were formed. In time—after half a billion years or so—non living molecules gave rise, through random chemical change, to living cells.

Once the first living cells came into being, they multiplied rapidly while, with changing Earthly conditions, the food source diminished. Starvation threatened, but once again Chance stepped in to ensure survival. Protoplant cells developed the process known as photosynthesis and began feeding themselves directly on sunlight, a change brought on, the Scientists suggest, By Chance mutation. Chance variations followed, and eventually life evolved into us, *Homo sapiens*.

For a clear, simple and straightforward Scientific Genesis, here is how Carl Sagan explains it all in his beautiful book *Cosmos* (Random House, New York: 1980.

> The Earth condensed out of interstellar gas and dust some 4.6 billion years ago. We know from the fossil record that the origin of life happened soon after, perhaps around 4.0 billions of years ago, in the ponds and oceans of the primitive earth. The first living things were not anything so complex as a one-celled organism, already a highly sophisticated form of life. The first stirrings were much more humble. In those early days, lightning and ultraviolet light from the Sun were breaking apart the simple hydrogen-rich molecules of the primitive atmosphere, the fragments spontaneously recombining into more and more complex molecules. The products of this early chemistry were dissolved in the oceans, forming a kind of organic soup of gradually increasing complexity, until one day, quite by accident, a molecule arose that was able to make crude copies of itself, using as building blocks other molecules in the soup.

Chance mutations followed, allowing the newly formed life to adapt and survive. With further beneficial mutations, By Chance, life grew ever more complex. Eventually the great primates evolved, about a million years ago our ancestors came on the scene, and, as Chance would have it, in time there was Modern Man.

There we have, in extremely condensed form, the history of the Cosmos as offered by Scientists of the late 20th Century.

To recap briefly:

Once upon a time there was a Cosmic Egg which exploded, following which the universe as we know it today was created By Chance, out of Random movement, Fortuitously.

Reading this script we find, possibly to our relief, possibly to our dismay, that we are still living in the same kind of universe our most distant ancestors lived in. The capricious gods they feared, before whom they bowed and scraped, are still very much alive and in charge today, wrapped in lovely new robes, of course, and under new names. But Caprice still rules: The Great God Chance, with his beloved spouse Randomly, aided by their offspring Fortuitously.

For the most part Science concerns itself with the *Whats,* the *Whens* and the *Hows,* not with philosophical *Whys.* Therefore it may not be sporting to demand of Science any answer as to why there was, in the beginning, a singularity, a Cosmic Egg to explode, starting the universe on its way.

Besides, if the Scientists are right and everything happened By Chance, out of Random movement, then the *Why* would seem to be answered too. If it all happened By Chance, Fortuitously, then surely it must have happened for no reason at all, at least for no reason pertaining to Man. The Cosmos and everything in it would seem to be, from Man's viewpoint, ultimately meaningless, and to seek for *Why?* answers an exercise in futility. When Man has been reduced in significance to where he is nothing but an accidental excrescence on a chunk of matter that just happened to coalesce due to a shock wave in a universe of stars and galaxies that formed themselves Randomly—with such a script it seems ridiculous to seek for meaning. Surely any meaning that did exist would not be meaningful to Man.

However, Man *is.* He *does* exist. He *does* have consciousness. He is after all the Scientist who is busily exploring the universe and discovering all these ego-blasting "truths." So let's forget the *Why?,* drop any search for a nonexistent meaning in life, and settle for what we know and have. We are and we know. Surely that is enough.

For many people this is not only enough, it is the most exciting script they can conceive for themselves. Self-made men often take extreme pride in being self-made, in not feeling beholden to anyone. If Man lives in a universe ruled not by a loving, omnipotent God who knows everything and keeps His eye on every sparrow, but lives instead in a universe ruled By Chance, a universe completely indifferent to the accidental emergence of life, then Man is the ultimate in self-madeness.

Man has already conquered the Earth, has made it to the Moon, and now has dreams of going beyond, of traveling to the other planets and eventually reaching out to the very stars. If he accomplishes all of this in a universe ruled By Chance, in which life emerged entirely by accident, in which he just happened to come into being by Random molecular recombinations—God, what a magnificent success story! Far more magnificent, surely, than if Man is simply the dearly beloved ward of an Omnipotent Spirit Who created the universe expressly for him, fostered his emergence, and now embraces him with love while watching over him, guiding him, earning his gratitude—some men by nature don't want to feel grateful or to share the credit.

Not everyone thrills to the thought that an Omnipotent Spirit, an Overseer, exists. Some thrill to the notion that Man in his accomplishments, even more in his hoped for accomplishments, is not beholden to any outside Force or Good. It's a mind-expanding, thrilling notion: Man the accidental gnat growing up to explore, discover, travel, take ultimate charge not only of his home planet but of the entire Solar System and even the universe beyond. What a dream of power and glory! David with little more than a slingshot of his own devising—David an orphan of the storm—David who sprouted accidentally in the primeval soup—against a Goliath vast beyond imagining, hard, cruel, impersonal. What a marvelous challenge! Who needs God? Who wants God? A universe ruled by Chance, with no one watching over Man—some of us revel in this. And will fight like angry children to make sure this thrilling notion is not snatched away.

Others, however, are uneasy with the notion that the universe is vast, that it evolved By Chance out of Randomly, that everything, including the emergence of life, was accidental. They find this Scientific Scenario of Creation belittling and depressing. How can Man have any stature, dignity or importance if he's little more than a bit of scum on the face of a tiny speck of matter in the vast ocean of the

Cosmos? These people don't want to accept Genesis as propounded by Science. They want to toss out the old, capricious gods, no matter by what name they are currently called, no matter in what gorgeous robes they are currently dressed, and cling to a newer, loving God of Purpose, a God who had something in mind for Man when Man was created. Is there any way to challenge Science and restore Design and Purpose to the universe?

Is there any chink at all in the armor of endless facts and figures welded together by 20th Century Science? any small crack in the edifice in which we might insert a tiny stick of dynamite to blow up the whole construction?

The plot of the Scientific Genesis seems so smooth, so nearly seamless, it's hard to see how one can grab hold anywhere in an attempt to tear it down. Nevertheless, with a closer look possibly we can spot a *deus ex machina* we can drag into the Great World Machine to do battle with Chance.

In *A Connecticut Yankee in King Arthur's Court,* Mark Twain saved his hero by having him "magically" spring a solar eclipse on his captors. (The Yankee was from the future, of course, and fortunately knew that a solar eclipse was scheduled to occur in this past time into which he had been thrust.)

Let's take a look at what is known about solar eclipses to see if we can use the same phenomenon to save modern day Yankees from the Chance-ruled universe of the Scientists.

As all of us know, Earth has a giant satellite, the Moon, the largest satellite in the Solar System relative to its parent planet except for distant Pluto with its companion moon, Charon.

Solar eclipses occur when our satellite, the Moon, moves in between Earth and the Sun, blocking out the Sun as the lunar shadow is cast onto the Earth.

Solar eclipses can be total, partial or annular. Total eclipses are visible somewhere on Earth about twice every three years. Partial eclipses occur more frequently. Annular eclipses occur when the Moon, in its eccentric orbit around the Earth, is too far away for its shadow to reach the Earth's surface. When the Moon moves in front of the Sun at this distance, its disc is not quite large enough to blot out the Sun entirely and a rim of the Sun can be seen as a bright ring around the obscuring Moon.

Eclipses give us immediate information about the relative sizes of the Sun and Moon as perceived from the surface of our planet. That total solar eclipses can occur tells us that the Moon must be, as viewed in our sky, at least as large as the Sun, while annular eclipses, eclipses in which the rim of the Sun can be seen encircling the Moon, tell us that the Moon at a slightly greater distance away from us is not quite as large as the Sun after all. In effect, eclipses confirm what our untrained eye has already told us: as viewed from our planet home, the two largest objects in our sky, the Sun and the Moon, are almost identical in size.

Astronomical measurement of these two large discs in our sky confirms this everyday observational knowledge. The Sun, as a disc in our sky, measures a little over one-half degree, or 31' 59" of arc. The Moon, moving around us in an eccentric orbit, varies in its disc size from 29' 21" to 33' 30", for an average very close to 32'. From our vantage point on Earth, these two bright and awe inspiring objects in our sky share the same gigantic size.

How curious. Especially when we consider the manner in which the Solar System, according to the Scientists, came into being. The Solar System, you will recall, formed out of a dusty interstellar cloud fragment, according to the Scientists. A shock wave from an unspecified source caused gravitational instabilities so that gas eddies came into being, the eddies managed to sweep up enough matter for gravity to come into play, and in this way the Sun, the planets and the satellites were formed. And in this Accidental or Fortuitous way, through Random motion and Random accumulation of particles, three bodies were formed—the three we are concerned with—in such a way that from the surface of one the other two, though at vastly different distances, share a common disc size in our sky.

How fantastic. What a coincidence. In truth, it sends a shock wave through me as I consider the enormity of it.

Surely the odds against such a coincidental equation of size must be more than staggering, they must be all but inconceivable.

In the center of this original interstellar cloud fragment, a large eddy formed, gathered material unto itself, and the Sun was born. Some 93,000,000 miles away another, much smaller eddy formed, gathered material unto itself, and the Earth was born. Some 240,000 miles from the soon-to-be Earth another even smaller eddy formed, gathered material unto itself, and the Moon was born. Then, lo and behold, from the surface of the Earth, where intelligent life developed, life able to perceive, measure, consider, meditate on, and appreciate what it sees, these two Randomly formed masses, the Sun and the Moon, just happen to be almost precisely the same size.

How marvelously rich. What a fantastic coincidence. In fact, what a joke—but who exactly is the joke on?

It must be on me and others like me, for this coincidence does not leave me laughing, it leaves me doubting the lovely new-old gods of my world, the ancient gods all dressed up and presented to us as fresh, new ones by Science. If Chance is in charge and brings everything into being through his consort Randomly—no, my mind rebels and simply can't accept this. The Sun and the Moon share a common disc size in our sky. Surely Randomly, no matter how great her power, could *not* have accomplished this. Yet if we let Design creep in, even into a tiny little patch of the overall picture—no, it is too frightening. Once let Design in, she might forge ahead like a cancer, wildly determined, with no inhibitions, to overwhelm the entire Chancy edifice so carefully constructed by Modern Science. Yet not to let her in—

Sun and Moon are the same size in our sky. That remains a stubborn fact and my mind stubbornly insists upon seeing at least the possibility of Design in it. I can't rest easy in a world where I doubt the gods, so there would seem to be only one thing to do, as frightening as it may seem: Open the door an inch and face Design, who stands on the threshold waiting.

If, in the identical disc size of Sun and Moon, we *do* spy the hand of Design, what purpose could possibly have lurked in Her mind when this identity of size was foisted on us?

Could there possibly be a reason for it?

Throwing caution to the winds, let's ruminate and speculate. At this point in our history, Design may be a scary, formidable foe, but nothing ventured, nothing gained. Let's not invite Her in—no reason to be that foolhardy about this—but just for kicks let's venture forth to face Her. Why not?

2
LAW VERSUS CUSTOM
The Law Is The Law Is The Law—Or Is It Merely Custom?

> Custom doth make dotards of us all.
> Thomas Carlyle (1795-1881)

Do we really live in the universe that those Learned Ones of our time, the Scientists, tell us we live in?

The Learned Ones of earlier epochs have not always been right. Their theories and "truths" have not always stood up under the test of more sophisticated observation.

From earliest times Man has needed some practical acquaintance with the universe he lived in in order to conduct his life intelligently. In primitive societies, hunting, fishing, sowing, reaping were governed by the natural rhythms of Earth, Sun and Moon. All early peoples, among them the Chinese, Egyptians, Summerians, Babylonians, Celts and Mayans, observed the skies and drew logical conclusions from what they observed. In the sixth and fifth centuries B.C. the Greeks began systematizing observational fact into theory.

Thales of Miletus (c640-c546 BC), who successfully predicted a solar eclipse, held that the Earth was a flat disk floating in water and the heavens were a hemisphere moving around the floating Earth.

Anaximander (c611-c547 BC), a pupil of Thales, believed that the Earth was a cylinder, its depth one third of its breadth. It was suspended freely in the center of the universe, with man living on one of the flat cylindrical faces.

Pythagoras of Samos (c582-c500 BC), a giant of classical astronomy, taught that all celestial bodies, including the Earth, are spheres. The Earth was at rest, occupying the central spot in the universe. The star embedded celestial sphere rotated from east to west on an axis which passed through the poles of the Earth while the planets moved independently from west to east.

Aristarchus of Samos (c320-c250 BC), another giant of classical astronomy, was the first Learned One known to promulgate the theory of a heliocentric universe: the fixed stars and the Sun were unmoving while the Earth, spinning daily on its axis, revolved about the Sun in a circle. This heliocentric theory was rejected in its day, running counter as it did to common sense. The work in which Aristarchus proposed it has been lost, but the theory was described by another giant intellect of the ancient world, Archimedes (287?-212 BC), only to be dismissed with disapproval.

Hipparchus (c190-c125 BC) was another early astronomer with unchallenged preeminence. Working at Rhodes between 140-120BC, he established astronomy on a sound geometrical basis. He initiated trigonometry, discovered the precession of the equinoxes, compiled a catalog of stars in which he divided them into classes of brightness, or magnitudes, and is generally considered to have initiated the system of epicycles later perfected by Ptolemy. He held firm to the geocentric theory of the universe, a theory no longer held to be valid by our present day Learned Ones.

Ptolemy (c127-c151 AD) was another distinguished superstar of the ancient world. He revised the star catalog of Hipparchus, collected material on eclipses, and proposed a sophisticated system of epicycles—circles rolling on circles—which satisfactorily explained the observed motions of the Sun and the five then known planets around the Earth. The Ptolemaic system was so beautifully worked out, in fact, and harmonized so well with the observed movement of heavenly bodies, that it held undisputed sway in the western world for well over a thousand years. (Admittedly, however, most of the Learned Ones of that millenium plus were Christian churchmen with a vested interest in keeping the Earth firmly placed at the center of the world.) Not until fourteen hundred years after Ptolemy's death was his system seriously and successfully challenged.

In 1473 Nicolaus Copernicus was born. In 1543, the year of his death, this learned Pole published a treatise, *De Revolutionibus Orbium Coelestium* ("On the Revolutions of the Celestrial Spheres"), in which work he put forth a heliocentric universe. The Sun was a stationary object at the center of the Solar System. The Earth rotated around the Sun in a circle, with uniform motion. In addition, the Earth rotated on its own axis, that axis being directed at the celestial pole, which allowed the fixed stars to stop revolving around the Earth diurnally and remain fixed.

The heliocentric view of the universe set forth by Copernicus found little favor with any branch of the Christian Church. It was considered opposed to Holy Scripture and therefore false. Toward the end of the 16th Century, the Copernican theory was rigorously espoused by a spirited Italian churchman, Giordano Bruno (1548-1600), who was imprisoned by the Roman Inquisition, defrocked, excommunicated, tortured, and, when he still refused to recant, burned alive at the stake.

In 1546 Tycho Brahe was born. As a boy of fourteen, this Danish nobleman became interested in astronomy. He worked to construct astronomical instruments, built the first observatory in modern Europe, and spent years of his life patiently compiling tables of observed planetary motion. He knew of the heliocentric theory of Copernicus but did not accept it. Not only was he, as a good Christian, reluctant to take a stand against his church, he also argued that the heliocentric view simply did not fit the observed facts. If the Earth moved around the Sun, the stars should show an annual shift, which they did not show. (Actually, according to our modern Learned Ones, this shift exists but is extremely small due to the great distance of the stars; being extremely small, it was not detectable by the instruments available in the 16th Century). Also, if the Sun is at the center of the

System with the Earth in revolution about it, Mercury and Venus should have phases similar to the phases of the Moon; Brahe could detect no such phases. (Astronomers today say that such phases *do* occur, but could not be detected then.) In addition, Brahe argued, if the Earth is in motion, objects falling should fall at an angle, not straight down. (This shift from the vertical *does* occur, we are told by modern Scientists, but again is so small as to be almost imperceptible, and not detectable by 16th Century instruments.)

Johann Kepler (1571-1630 AD) began working with Brahe in 1599, two years before the latter's death. After a decade spent studying and analyzing Brahe's observations of the movement of Mars, Kepler in 1609 published *Astronomia Nova... De Motibus Stellae Martis* (The New Astronomy... On the Movement of Mars), in which work he announced two laws of planetary motion. Ten years later he published *De Harmonice Mundi* (Harmony of the World), adding a third Law. These three Laws of Kepler are a watershed mark in astronomy. The Laws are:

1. The planets move in ellipses, with the Sun at one focus.

    This buried, possibly forever, geocentrism: The Earth is *not* a stationary object at the center of the universe with the Sun and all other heavenly bodies revolving around it.

    It also knocked out the cherished notion, rooted in the teaching of Aristotle, that in a properly constructed and properly run universe, motion would be in that perfect figure, the circle. Orbits were, according to Kepler, based upon the meticulous observations of Tycho Brahe, elliptical, not circular.

2. The radium vector sweeps out equal areas in equal times.

    This dispensed with another cherished notion, that of uniform motion. The planets orbit not at uniform motion but at varying speed in order to sweep out equal areas in equal times, slowing down when farther from the Sun, speeding up when closer in.

3. The square of the time of revolution is proportional to the cube of the mean distance.

This sets up a fixed relation between the *size* of the orbit and the *period* of revolution.

These three Laws of Kepler have been completely verified and remain to this day the basis for study of orbital motion, not only motion within our Solar System but also motion out among the distant stars and stellar systems.

In 1564 Galileo Galilei was born. After empirical study of the motion of falling bodies, he formulated three Laws pertaining to such motion. He inaugurated the modern practice of telescopic observation by turning a newly discovered instrument, the telescope, to the skies. He studied the surface of the Moon, observed the four brightest moons of Jupiter in orbital motion around that planet, and was the first to observe the phases of Venus. His work corroborated the banned Copernican theory and helped to bury the geocentric.

In 1642, the year in which Galileo died, Isaac Newton, a giant even among giants, was born.

> Nature and nature's law lay hid in night.
> God said, Let Newton be, and all was light.
> Alexander Pope (1688-1744)

In his masterwork, *Principia Mathematica,* Newton took the well known force, terrestrial gravity, and extended it out into the heavens to show that this same force governed the movement of planets and satellites. He formulated the Law of Gravitation—all bodies in the universe attract each other in inverse ratio to the square of the distance between them—and applied this Law to explain with great success the observed phenomena of the Solar System. In so doing, he gave us the Great World Machine. This model of the world, though subjected to spectacular modification by Albert Einstein early in this century, is still accepted as a generally valid first approximation to reality.

Scientific knowledge expanded so rapidly following the glorious Newtonian integration that by the late 19th Century the Learned Ones happily believed they were on the verge of complete understanding of the universe and all its workings.

Little more than a mopping up operation to clarify a few murky points was left to accomplish. Minor questions still remained, of course—questions like, "What is light and how does it manage to travel through space?" and, "What precisely is gravity and how does it work?"—but these questions would surely be answered soon and everyone could rest content with a job well done, contemplating the fully comprehended universe.

In the biological Sciences, Charles Darwin (1809-1882) had expounded the brilliant theory of Natural Selection, which by the late 19th Century was embraced by almost all of the Learned. Man in all his complexity had evolved from the simplest imaginable form of life in a perfectly logical and understandable manner, so in this field of study too there was little left to discover, just a few minor questions still to be answered, questions such as, "What is life and how did it ever manage to get started?" But these few nagging questions would surely be answered soon for Newton had proved beyond doubt that we live in a comprehensible universe, a universe subject to Natural Law. With close observation and the application of rational thought, Man would soon have all the answers, be a complete and perfect know-it-all.

Newton's Great World Machine, while mind boggling in its beauty and simplicity, did fail to resolve a question or two, so by the late 19th Century Scientists were working hard to pin down the final answers and wrap up the job.

Newton had shown that gravitation worked to explain the Solar System, with only a minor problem here and there, but he had not given any explanation as to what gravitation is. Newtonian gravitation called for action at a distance, which was faintly distasteful and perplexing. How was such action at a distance accomplished? Another problem: light was perceived as a wave and waves need some medium through which to travel. Solution: All of space is permeated by an unmoving substance, the ether.

The Earth in its journeys around the Sun would of necessity be traveling through this ether, so a German-born American physicist, Albert Michelson (1852-1931), later joined by another American physicist, Edward Morley (1838-1923), set up ingenious experiments to detect the velocity of the Earth through the ether. They devised an apparatus so sensitive that it would have recorded a velocity through the ether of only one kilometer per second. The results of their experiments: the Earth had absolutely no detectable velocity through the surrounding ether.

This experimental result was startling and upsetting. At first glance it would seem that either there was no ether or the Earth wasn't moving. The latter explanation resurrected the discarded geocentric theory and put the Earth right smack back in the center of the universe, unmoving while all heavenly bodies revolved around it. This was clearly unthinkable. The Earth *had* to move—far too much depended on this—therefore the ether must not exist. But without the ether how did light waves travel to us? How did gravitation work? We *needed* the ether—surely could discard the concept only at our peril—so rather than toss it out, why not come up with some explanation as to why it could not be detected?

Presto, an explanation was soon forthcoming, in 1893 by Irish physicist George Fitzgerald (1851-1901), and in 1895, independently, by Hendrik Lorentz (1853-1928). The reason no velocity through the ether could be detected was not due to either of the simple explanations that come immediately to mind: the Earth isn't moving or there is no ether. Rather, it is due to a devious joke that the Laws of Nature are conspiring to play on us, a joke that makes it impossible for us ever to measure our true motion in space. And why can't we? Because matter contracts in the direction of its motion just enough to offset the motion, thus making such motion forever undetectable. With this made-to-order explanation, the ether was saved, light waves could continue to travel to us through space, and the Great Machine could go spinning happily on its way.

This salvage job on the ether did not last long, however. Two giant intellects put the torch to it early in this century, postulating theories that did away with the need for ether. Once ether was no longer needed, it was quickly and joyfully swept out of existence, or more accurately out of non existence. No need, no ether.

The great Albert Einstein (1879-1955) did away with the need for ether as a carrier of gravitational forces. He elevated our inability to detect our motion through space into a hypothesized Law of Nature: the universe is constructed in such a way that it is impossible to determine absolute motion by any experiment whatsoever.

To phrase this Law in another way: the phenomena of nature will be the same to two observers who move with any uniform velocity whatever relative to one another.

Stated this way, few of the Learned would quarrel with it. Newton wouldn't have. But as this Theory of Relativity was subjected to exhaustive study and interpretation, it became apparent that Einstein had placed before us a not quite imaginable universe in which time becomes the fourth dimension, mass and energy are convertible one to the other, and the curvature of space, not force acting at a distance, accounts for gravitational effects.

In 1921 Einstein was awarded the Nobel prize for physics, not for his Special Theory of Relativity published in 1905 or his General Theory of Relativity published in 1915, but for his work on the photoelectric effect having to do with the properties and behavior of light.

What is light? Is it a wave? Or a particle? This controversy is considerably older than any living Scientist. It raged back in Newton's time. Newton favored the corpuscular (particle) theory. Particles can theoretically travel through empty space. Christian Huygens (1629-1695) a Dutch mathematician, physicist and astronomer, a contemporary of Newton, favored the wave theory. For a time Newton's corpuscular theory was in the ascendent, but then experiments established the wave theory of light and the particle theory was abandoned.

In time, predictably enough, problems arose with the wave theory, one of them being the photoelectric effect. When ultraviolet light falls on a metal surface, electrical changes occur. Electrons are emitted. The velocity of these ejected electrons, however, is not dependent on the intensity of the light but depends on the wave-length of the light. This didn't make sense in terms of waves. A more powerful light wave should transfer greater energy to the surface of the metal, sending the emitted electrons off at a higher speed, but observation showed this didn't happen.

Einstein offered a solution. He suggested that as light radiated from its source, it did not travel evenly but remained localized in little bundles. Upon striking the metal, each little bundle transferred its energy to an electron. The velocity of the electrons upon emission would, in this theory, be independent of the intensity of the light, which had already been observationally established as occurring. If light was thought of not as a wave striking against the metal, but as discrete little packets of energy, quanta of energy, the photoelectric effect was explained.

A German physicist, Max Planck (1858-1947), had already formulated the quantum theory in which he suggested that energy, or light, did not flow continuously, as had always been assumed, but instead was composed of pieces, energy atoms or *quanta* (Latin for "How much?"). The theory was so revolutionary that few could or would accept it, including Planck himself, until Einstein made use of quanta to explain the photoelectric effect. Suddenly light was in some respects a particle again, though it had already been proven to be, through the interference patterns it caused, a wave.

As a particle, light could presumably travel through empty space so the makeshift salvage job on the ether could be forgotten and the concept of the ether relegated to the trashbin.

So which is light, a particle or a wave? Today the Learned Ones of Science have decided it is both. The wave nature of light has been well established. The particle nature of light has also been established. Experiments show that light behaves at times like a wave, at other times like a particle. So who can say what it's ultimate nature, if it has one, is?

This uncertainty about such a common phenomenon might have little importance except for one thing: almost all of our knowledge of the Solar System and absolutely *all* of our knowledge about anything outside the Solar System is based upon the radiation which reaches Earth. We have within the last few decades had personal, direct contact with our neighbor, the Moon. We have sent spacecraft on spy missions to several nearby planets and had the craft relay information back to us. Apart from this, we remain entirely Earthbound in our attempts to gather information and explain the universe. We have never visited a single star nor had an authenticated visitor from one. When it comes to the stars and the galaxies they form, we have only one source of information: the electromagnetic radiation which reaches us. This does not seem to trouble our Learned Ones nor give them pause. Despite their inability to verify their conclusions through some other, independent source, they forge ahead, undeterred. They have now built for their own delight a fantastic model of the universe, have, they say, pushed back the foundations of knowledge to within 10^{-43} seconds (.0000000000000000000000000000000000000000001 seconds) of the start of the whole thing, all of this based upon the radiation which reaches us. Yet they can't really say what radiation is or satisfactorily explain its behavior.

Surely if you set about building an entire universe on one informational source, you ought to be absolutely sure that you understand that source, its properties, behavior under any and all conditions, and every possibly vagary. Otherwise, without this solid foundation, no matter how carefully you build, you may find you have built your elaborate structure on shifting sand. If the foundation is the least bit askew, the most logical, carefully constructed structure built upon it will lean perilously and in the end, soaring high enough, will topple.

The structure built upon the one informational source the Cosmologists have—the electromagnetic radiation which reaches Earth—rests on several unproven assumptions:

1. That the speed of light as measured on the surface of the Earth holds true throughout the universe.

2. That spectrum analysis which has proven to be valid on Earth remains valid for light sources radiating upon the Earth.

3. That light traveling to us through space is bound by the same rules that govern wave motion on Earth. Because the Doppler effect exists on Earth (waves from an approaching source are shortened, from a receding source are lengthened), it is assumed to exist throughout the universe. Therefore the red shift (a shift toward a longer wave length) in the spectra of stars has only one explanation: the stars are rushing away from us. Hence we live in an expanding universe.

4. That Einstein's explosive equation, $E = MC^2$ (Energy = Mass Times the Speed of Light Squared), expresses a valid exchange rate throughout the universe, from the beginning of the Creation. The equation proved out spectacularly here on Earth (tragically for the inhabitants of Hiroshima and Nagasaki, to the sorrow of millions of thinking people worldwide, placing in mankind's hands the most fearful murder/suicide weapon ever devised). Because the equation proved out in the atomic laboratories here on the surface of our planet, the Scientists assume that it also holds true in the interior of stars, explaining their radiation, and that it has been an established Law throughout the universe from the beginning.

On such unproved and untested assumptions as those listed above, the Learned Ones of our time have constructed a fantastic universe and believe themselves to be on the verge of pushing knowledge right back to the instant of Creation. This is as far back as knowledge can ever go, they say, for once the Primeval Egg exploded, it obliterated all that went before. As no evidence survived, there is no way to trace the universe's origin or structure prior to the Big Bang.

How *real* is the universe constructed by our Scientists?

Is it really written in the stars that, because light has been clocked by some on Earth at a certain speed, it *must* travel at that same speed through the vast reaches of empty space (if such vast reaches exist), out where no one has ever clocked it?

Here on the surface of the Earth, the instrument known as the spectroscope reveals that the spectral pattern of light varies for different light sources. Can this "truth" be projected onto the universe just because it holds true on Earth?

Is there really only *one* possible explanation for the ruddy shift found in the spectra of stars?

Must the Sun's lifegiving radiation come from an explosive destruction of matter as expressed in Einstein's equation $E = MC^2$?

Yes, say the Scientists; yes, and again yes, to each of the above questions. For the universe to be comprehensible, the Laws that apply on Earth must apply everywhere. There can't be one set of physical Laws for Earth, another for the Sun, another for distant stars. Such a discriminatory system would be patently unjust. Worse, it would render the universe unintelligible. If light could adjust its speed to suit itself, not in accordance with immutable Law; if an element could give off one spectrum if it is of Earthly origin and not give off the same spectrum if the light from it has traveled to us through space; if wave motion waves in some erratic fashion unbeknownst to us; if, in the interior of the Sun, radiant energy is released by some process not in accordance with the Law we have found to be valid here on Earth, then the Creator or the Creative Force, Whoever made up this game, has played a dirty trick on us, and God, if Such a One exists, does indeed play dice with us despite Einstein's disapproval.

The above would seem to be valid thinking. Either there are rules to the game—either Laws discovered here on Earth apply throughout the universe—or Science might as well grab its bat and ball, declare a forfeit and go home, at least until such time as we are able to travel to the Sun or outward through the galaxy to learn what the rules are *out there,* if they differ form our Earthbound rules. Assumptions such as the Scientists make *have* to be made or there is no Science. And only with the aid of Science can we hope someday to leave our planet home, rush around the Solar System, then around our galaxy, then possibly out beyond our galaxy, to check on our assumptions to prove or disprove them. So, please, Science, don't go away, we need you.

But the fact that we need Science—the inquiring spirit, the curiosity-driven mind—does not mean that we have to accept without closer inspection the particular rules Science has decided it needs at the moment in order to render the great game playable.

Certain physical Laws pertain here on Earth. We all know that. Gravity is a force over every square inch of our planet's surface. Everywhere on Earth ordinary water is H_2O, two parts hydrogen to one part oxygen, and everywhere rain falls it is wet. No matter where it is clocked, the speed of light follows the rules, and the well established Laws of Motion reign. With such uniformity all over our planet home, it is no wonder that our Learned Ones assume that it is valid to project these same "Laws" out upon the universe, especially as it is so manifestly in their interest to do so. Applying home town rules without compromise makes any game easier—for the home team.

But the fact that this is done with such unquestioning ease should perhaps make us a bit uneasy. Certain well established physical Laws have been proven to operate everywhere on Earth, but what about other types of Law? Behavior that is a heinous crime in one country may be a far lesser crime or no crime at all in another. It is illegal for an unclothed adult to walk down the streets of Beverly Hills, California, yet in other parts of the world such a state of undress is acceptable. As we shade from Law into Custom, the variation from one part of the world to another becomes enormous. English is commonly spoken in the United States of America, less commonly in Afghanistan. Portuguese is commonly spoken in Brazil but less commonly in Canada. Not only does language differ from place to place but so does dress, mode of shelter, courtship patterns, birth and burial practices. Physical Laws remain unchanged around the world but Custom, as all of us know, varies widely.

Custom not only varies with place, it has varied widely over time.

Back in prehistoric times, an unrecorded Scientist may have lived somewhere, a member of a small tribe. Driven by curiosity, imbued with spirit, our Scientist decides that she is going to formulate the Laws which govern human life. She will study first her own tribe and then, at great danger to herself, all other tribes known to exist. In earliest youth she sets out on her perilous journey of discovery, to return home only in old age to report on all she has learned.

Human life, she informs her eager listeners, is subject to the following Laws:

1. All people speak the one and only language of Gruntese.
2. All people live in caves.
3. All people subsist on berries and wild animal flesh.
4. All people have olive skins and dark eyes.
5. All people have curly or wavy dark hair.
6. All people wear animal furs as a cover against the cold.
7. The bride-price for human brides is two wild boar.

"These are the Laws which govern human life on Earth," she declares with understandable pride and certainty.

Our early Scientist formulated her Laws in the best scientific tradition, based on meticulous observation. We can't fault her technique. For the time and place her Laws were true and accurate, yet in a wider application they fail, for this reason: she made the unfortunate mistake of equating local Custom with universal Law.

Our 20th Century Scientists may be making precisely the same mistake.

Physical Laws which pertain on Earth may be simply local Custom, Laws which cannot with any validity be projected outward upon the Cosmos. The entire structure the Scientists have erected would topple at once if by any chance they have made a basic error in mistaking local Custom for Law.

"Nonsense!" I'm sure the Scientists would argue. "Law is law, custom custom, and any discriminating intellect can distinguish between the two. Physical laws as established on earth *must* be valid throughout the universe or the universe will be forever incomprehensible to us, a fate worse than death, a fate we instantly and categorically reject!"

One is tempted to agree, but—wait just a minute. Some universal Laws *have* to be established or the universe won't be comprehensible. That would seem self evident. But because *some* Laws are required—or possibly only *one*

Law—is no proof that the particular Laws the Scientists have focused on are the valid Laws in question.

On Earth the *physical* aspects of life—dress, dietary staples, mode of shelter—are most often subject to *Custom,* not Law.

Laws are more apt to pertain to the *moral* aspects of life, ie, it is almost universally against the Law to take the life of another (unless the killing is sanctioned by the group behavior of war; as long as everyone's in on the slaughter, it's okay), also to steal, bear false witness, etc.

The Scientists have taken local *physical* Law and elevated it to universal Law.

What if this is a mistaken approach and what we ought to do is take local *moral* Law and elevate *that* to universal Law?

If we look at the matter dispassionately, we will have to admit this possibility: that discovered Laws of physics as they apply on Earth need not be valid elsewhere in the universe while we can still live in a universe that is intelligible. If Earth's physical rules are simply local Custom, all we need do is discover *other* universal Law or Laws to render the universe intelligible.

For the sake of further discussion, let's sweep aside all currently held scientific assumptions about the nature of the universe, and see if we can produce a new set of assumptions upon which a better, more real, more valid theory of the universe can be built.

This is a tall order to be sure, but let's give it a try. Possibly we can not only achieve it, but in achieving it can render the universe not only intelligible, but infinitely more intelligible than the Exploding Egg-Big Bang universe the Scientists have put before us.

Throughout the centuries of Mankind's existence on Earth, one thing has occurred with unvarying regularity: the expert knowledge of one century has been re-edited, re-defined, or has suffered outright rejection in later hands. What the Learned Ones of one century teach will almost surely be corrected, added to, subtracted from, or thrown out by succeeding generations. All of history teaches us that while our Learned Ones of today may have stumbled upon a kernel or two of truth, of objective fact, most of what is believed today will be swept aside in time and relegated to the trashbin, from whence it may in time be dragged out again to add to the vast store of mankind's amusing myths.

For all their sophisticated equipment, esoteric mathematical proofs, and excited sureness, it remains a possibility that today's Scientists have completely lost all grasp of reality. While becoming carefully educated and knowledgeable, loading their brains with multitudinous detail, they may at the same time have lost their street smarts. For almost all of unrecorded and recorded history, Man has instinctively known that he *mattered,* that the Creation existed for him, he did not exist for the Creation, nor did he exist as an accident or afterthought. He found himself existing and sought to know *why.* Science has dedicated itself to an exciting scamper after the *What,* the *How,* the *When,* the *Where,* but has little apparent interest in the philosophical *Why.* Science rarely to never asks, "Does the universe have a purpose? If so, what is the purpose?" Such questions are not viewed as within its province. But in losing sight of these questions, in deliberately cutting itself off from such questions, Science may be cutting itself off from any hope of finding and describing a valid and viable universe.

The universe exists. We exist in it. *Why?* What is the point of it all, if it has a point? Purpose may have to be taken as our starting point before we can discern the true foundation and outlines of the structure. Once we have these, we can fill in details, rendering the universe ever more comprehensible.

The Sun and the Moon appear as the same size disc in our sky. Why? Is their Design in this? If there is, what lies behind the Design? Let's take this tiny hint of Design, follow its thread, and see where it leads.

3

RESTORATION COMEDY

If Man Is An Accidental Nothing, How Can We Pretend He's Something?

> Nothing tis but thinking makes it so.
> "Shake-speare"
> Edward DeVere,
> 17th Earl of Oxford (1550-1604)

Science in our century claims that we are living in a vast, old universe in which life happened onto the scene by accident.

The Scientists base their universe on the premise—they could not possibly construct their universe without it—that physical Laws which are discovered to be valid on Earth are valid throughout the universe.

As Carl Sagan states it in his marvelous book *Cosmos:* "The laws of nature are the same throughout the Cosmos."

Mr. Sagan does not identify this statement as an article of faith, not a proven fact, but that is clearly all it is. No one has ever gone out into the Cosmos to verify this statement experimentally, to test its truth. Scientists accept it on faith and we are asked to do so too. However, as discourteous as it may seem, we deline to do so.

Instead we toss out the basic premise of Science—the above stated article of faith—and start with a different premise, a different article of faith.

Our premise, upon which we intend to construct a universe, is, as we have previously stated, this:

Man has significance, or, the Creation was created for Man, or, the Creation exists because Man exists.

We will now attempt to arrive at a rational explanation for the universe, and for all currently known facts about the universe, built upon this premise.

To start, let's shrink the universe back to manageable size. Forget those billions and billions of stars in billions and billions of galaxies out in those vast reaches of black, all but empty space. Next put the Sun, the Earth and Man right back at the center of things.

Unthinkable!

Of course it's unthinkable, but let's steel ourselves and think it anyway.

Not so long ago, at the turn of this century, we—the species *Homo sapiens*—lived in a much younger and smaller universe, not as small a world as primitive Man lived in but nevertheless appreciably smaller than the fantastically vast and ten to twenty billion year old universe the Scientists have us living in today.

Until the beginning of this century, astronomy was largely concerned with our own private Solar System. All that was known of the stars other than our Sun was their color and brightness. There was only one galaxy, it was believed—our very own Milky Way—and we were at the heart of it. Earth was no longer at the center of Creation, but our Sun was. It was strategically enthroned at the center of the one and only galaxy. This obviously allowed us notable significance. But then along came an American astronomer, Harlow Shapley (1885-1972), who in 1915 coldly and audaciously booted the Sun out of this favored position at the core. It has now been decided that our Sun with its brood of planets is situated on the fringe of a spiral arm some 30,000 light years away from the galactic center, and that our beloved Milky Way is only one rather undistinguished spiral galaxy in a universe boasting billions of galaxies of various sizes and descriptions.

No human observer has ever journeyed out of our Solar System and deeper into the Milky Way to verify the location to which we've been assigned, or at least if one has she has failed to report back to us. No Cosmologist has ever flown clear of our galaxy to get a closer look at the rival galaxies which are said to exist. No one can say with any certainty exactly how our Earth, our Solar System, our galaxy fit into the great scheme of Cosmic Creation, if there is such a scheme. But Science currently gives us extremely little about which to boast.

There are a few very minor things, however, that even in the scientific scheme of things set us a bit apart. Our Milky Way is undistinguished, we are told, our location in the galaxy nothing to write home about, our Sun, a yellow dwarf, a very mediocre star, but still our Sun *does* have one small distinction: as far as is known, it is not part of a binary system or a multiple star system. The majority of stars, in nearby neighborhoods at least, seem to have paired up with at least one other star while many are members of multiple star systems. In contrast, our Sun is a loner, unpaired. This is possibly not too much of a distinction, but is a distinction nonetheless.

Even this small distinction may not hold up, however. According to a recent newspaper report (*Los Angeles Times,* February 21, 1984), Scientists now suggest that our Sun may have a partner, after all: a small, cool dwarf star whizzing around in an elliptical orbit that takes it as far as 2.4 light years from our Sun. This as yet merely hypothesized partner star would be the closest celestial object to our System. It has not yet been sighted, or if sighted not yet identified, but is currently being sought, and the expectation is that it won't be too hard to find, that it may, in fact, already be listed in star catalogs.

This exciting new star has been dubbed the "Killer Star" for this reason:

Some 65 million years ago the dinosaurs that roamed and ruled the Earth were mysteriously wiped out in a mass extinction. The Killer Star has come into hypothetical existence as the one who done it. Some 2.4 light years away, a comet cloud containing 100 billion comets is said to exist. The Killer Star, it is suggested, orbits through this cloud, picking up comets. It then drags these comets along with it and, as it orbits closer to us, flings these comets into the Solar System. Some of the comets naturally enough strike the Earth. If a large enough chunk of comet, or asteroid, struck the Earth, it could kick up a cloud of dust which might hang in the atmosphere for months, blocking out sunlight, preventing photosynthesis, killing off Earthly inhabitants in a mass extinction as they succumb to cold and hunger.

The Killer Star, if it exists, rampages by us every 28 million years, it is said, causing mass extinction of Earthly life. We can look forward to another visit, with the attendant barrage of lethal comets, in about 14 million years.

There is another minor distinction in which we on Earth can perhaps take pride. While our own private satellite, the Moon, is not the largest satellite in the Solar System, it is the second largest satellite in the System in relation to its parent planet. Until very recently, the Moon was considered to be the largest in relative size, but that honor has now been snatched away to be conferred on Charon, the moon of Pluto. Given a mythical visitor from *out there*, we could show her the Moon and brag about that. As viewed from a distance, the Earth-Moon system would suggest a pair of planets, as would the Pluto-Charon duo, the only two such pairs in the Solar System.

To sum up:

In the universe at large, most stars openly pair, but our star, the Sun, is either a loner or is paired with a mysterious absentee killer.

In the Solar System, planets are loners, but with our satellite the Moon we come close to forming a planetary pair.

These may be distinctions without significance, but they are distinctions nonetheless.

The Earth has other distinctions too. For one, it has the highest density of any body in the Solar System, though tiny Mercury, the planet closest in to the Sun, a relatively unevolved object similar to our Moon, is now believed to have a comparable density.

Among the smaller planets, known as the Terrestial Planets—Mercury, Venus, Earth, Mars—it was long believed that only the Earth has a magnetic field, but Mariner 10 flybys of Mercury, an almost completely unknown object until the Mariner probes of 1974-1975, revealed, to the surprise of Astronomers, that Mercury too has a significant magnetic field, one that apparently has the same north-south nature as the Earth's. It is now believed that the interior of Mercury resembles the interior of the Earth, while its surface bears a strong resemblance to our Moon.

In effect, though it is a great deal larger and possesses an atmosphere and a moon, Earth shares the weightiness and the magnetism of the next door neighbor to the life-giving, life-sustaining Sun.

Another distinction: Earth alone, as far as we know, has brought forth life.

But life came forth as an accident, Science claims, By Chance out of Random happenings, so with a sigh and a becoming blush we should perhaps refrain from mentioning our existence as any kind of important distinction.

While our existence may not be an important distinction, the purpose of this book, as previously stated, is to go down the road abandoned by Science; to start from the unproved assumption that Man has significance, that we did not come into existence by accident but rather that the Creation exists for us; and attempt to arrive at a rational explanation for the universe, and for all currently known facts about the universe, built upon this premise.

The first step to take, now that we have steeled ourselves for it, is to forget those billions and billions of stars in those billions and billions of galaxies, and shrink the universe back to manageable size.

But how can we, how do we dare, sweep aside the universe so painstakingly described, even more than that, lovingly *photographed* for us? Surely everyone by now has seen the magnificent plates taken at various observatories around the world showing the stupendous galaxies way *out there*. Are we not to believe the evidence we see, through these magnificent photographs, with our very own eyes?

Possibly we should believe what we see with our own eyes, most of the time anyway, but look again at those plates, and ask yourself exactly what you see. When I look at them, this is what I see: points or smears of light against a dark background. Many of us can close our eyes, relax, and watch very similar points or smears of light jump around on our mind's eye. Does that mean we have galaxies embedded in our closed lids? Possibly we do. *Are they the same kind of galaxies photographed by our Scientists?*

As we gaze at the photographs put before us by the Scientists, assuming we should believe what we see with our own eyes, does this help us much? Numerous studies have shown that if the same scene is watched by a dozen witnesses, a dozen accounts of the scene will be forthcoming. The same with photographs, or ink blots. Different people see different things, or interpret what they see differently. Our interpretation of what we see will be very subjective, therefore very different. Let's assume for the moment that the Scientists in viewing the photographs they take are only human, and being only human they are also interpreting what they see very subjectively.

Light falls on their photographic plates and after a certain time exposure an image results. Does that really tell us what is *out there?* Obviously it does not tell each and every viewer, for I can look at one photograph after another and have not the least idea what I am looking at, other than that I am looking at pinpoints or splashes of light against a dark background. I have to read the accompanying text to know what I am viewing, to know which specks of light come from nearer light sources, which come from more distant light sources, etc. In other words, to make any sense of the

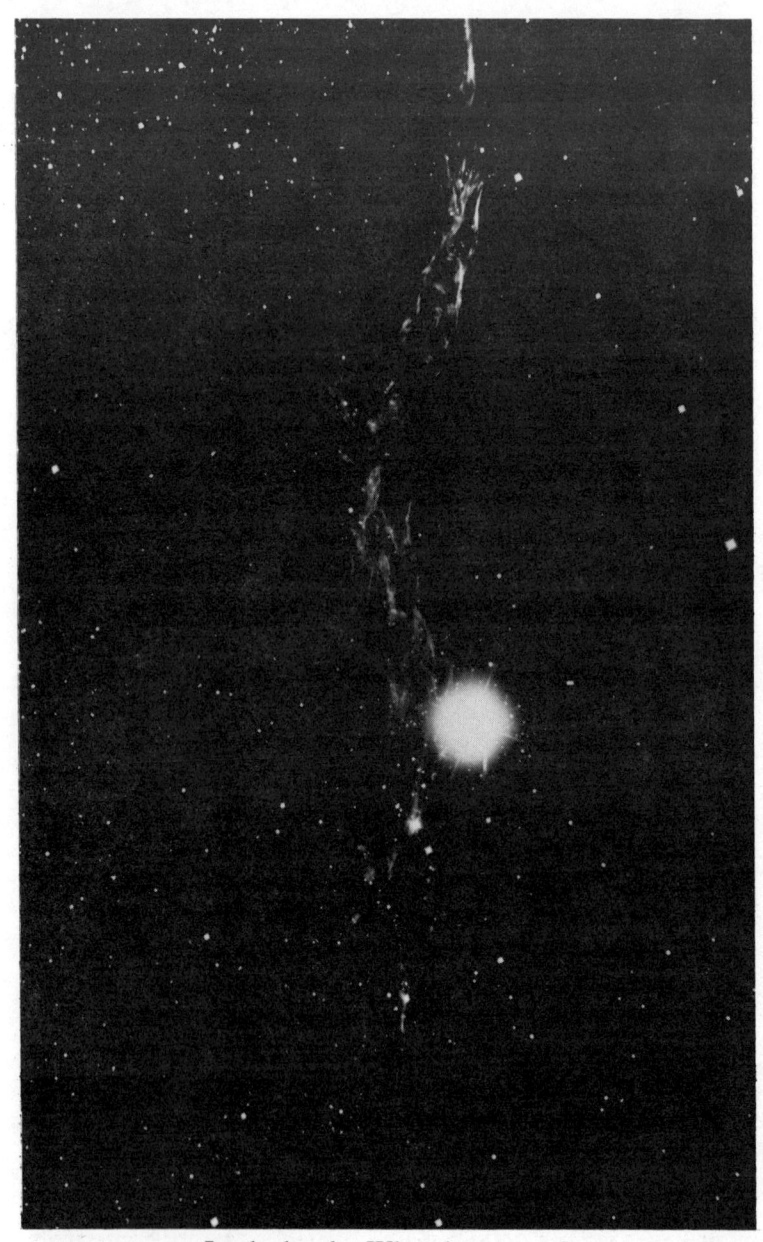

Look closely. What do you *see?*

Courtesy of Mount Wilson and Las Campanas
Observatories, Carnegie Institution of Washington.

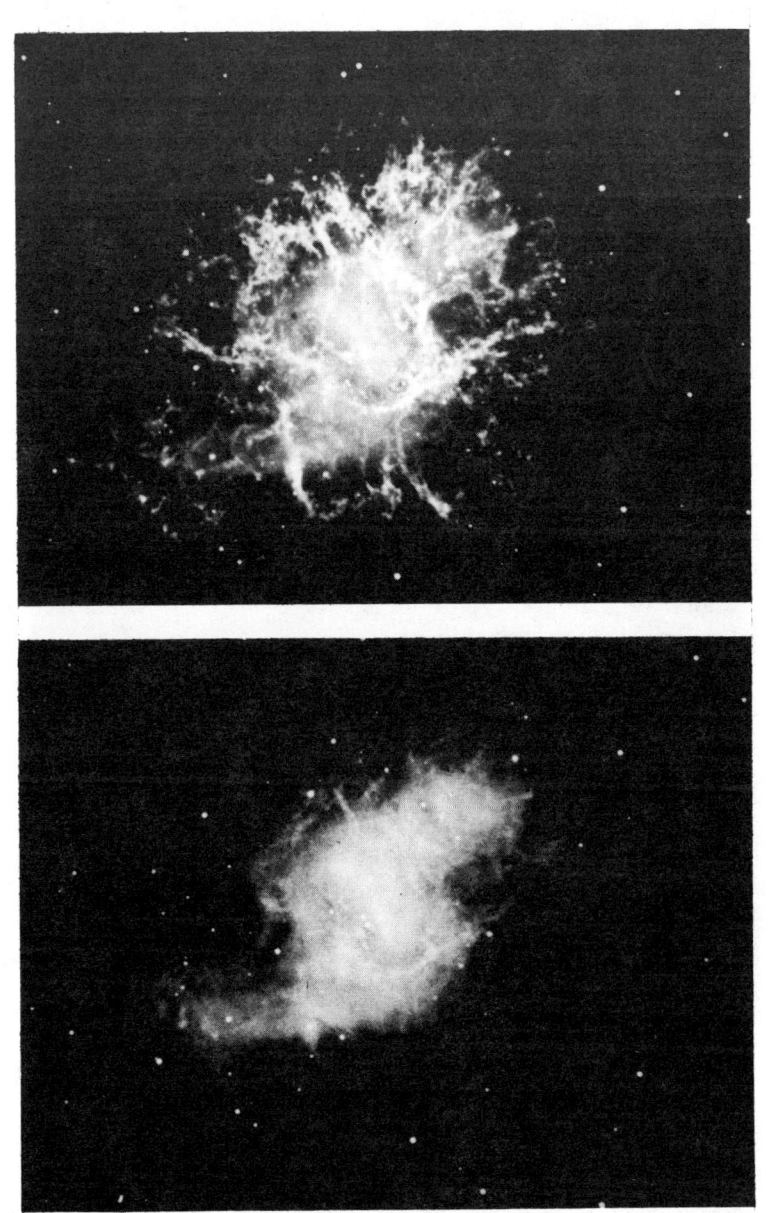

If you didn't "know" what this was,
what would you *think* it was?

Courtesy of Mount Wilson and Las Campanas
Observatories, Carnegie Institution of Washington.

photographs, I have to be given additional information, ie, the interpretation put upon the photographs by the Scientists.

Isn't this true of all photographic evidence?

Not entirely. I can go for a sitting and when I see proofs, the photographer does not have to tell me that the photographs are of me. I already possess independent knowledge that allows me to make this judgment. I can be shown a photograph of someone else and if I know that someone, I don't need to be told the source of the image. I can glance through a magazine and remain unbaffled by photograph after photograph. I have a working knowledge, just as most people do, of any number of marvelous things, natural objects, man-made objects, and a wide assortment of living creatures. Photographs of any of these objects or creatures will register on my mind without any need for an interpretative text. Generally I know a monkey from a chair and a man from a woman. All I need do is refer to my own stored knowledge to sort everything out.

But when it comes to the skies, I leave familiar ground behind, just as most of us do. I have seen the Sun and the Moon often enough to recognize their reproduced images in photographs, also possibly a star group or two, such as the Big and Little Dippers. Beyond that I am lost and have to depend on the experts, The Learned Ones, to tell me what I view when I look at their photographs. But as we have already stated, we are going to part from the Learned Ones, no longer listen to them or accept their interpretations, and go down the road they have abandoned.

As we have rejected the foundation upon which the Scientists built their universe, we naturally must sweep away their entire edifice. This does *not* include the ever growing assortment of celestial photographs, but does include the interpretation placed upon those photographs. Any interpretation offered by the Scientists if not actually based upon their underlying premise is at the least tainted by it, so we have no choice but to toss any and all interpretation out and start afresh.

How to begin?

The obvious place to begin would seem to be with the hint of Design we have already stumbled upon: the identity of size of the Sun and the Moon as discs in our sky.

If there is Design in this, what possible purpose could it serve?

Rather than attempt a straightforward answer to this, let's circle around and creep up on it.

If we view the universe from the perspective of Man's existence and judge solely on this basis, there are only three astronomical bodies of any significance: the Earth, the Sun, and the Moon. We live on the one, the Sun provides our light and our warmth, and the Moon dwarfs every other object in the sky except for the Sun. These are the Big Three, known to Man since the beginning of time.

Two of these bodies, the Earth and the Sun, are absolutely essential to Man's existence, and the third, the Moon, has its uses. If every other material object in the universe melted away into nothingness, if we ignore the possible gravitational wrenches involved, this reduction to nothingness would not materially affect Man's continued existence. We might feel a bit lonely with Earth as the only planet circling our Sun, with no bright morning or evening star to enchant us, and we would certainly miss the sparkling display of night stars, not only for its beauty and the awe it inspires in us, but more practically for the great navigational aid it has always been. But aside from the loss of guidance, as long as the Earth, Sun and Moon continued on their customary paths, with the stipulated lack of gravitational dislocation, Man's life would be little affected.

In effect, from Mankind's perspective we live in the world of the Big Three. Only the Big Three have crucial significance.

A further stripping away is possible. The Moon, while a delight to have around and influential when it comes to tides, could also be allowed to melt into nothingness without significant loss to Man if gravitational dislocation is again ruled out. As long as the Earth and the Sun continue to exist, with the Earth revolving around the Sun in its accustomed orbit, Man could adjust to the loss of the Moon and life would continue much as before. So, in a sense we don't live in the world of the Big Three, after all, but in the world of the Essential Two: the parent Sun and the dependent planet Earth.

If a visitor were to arrive on our planet from somewhere *out there,* someone from a world so bathed with light she had not the least familiarity with the absence of light, how would an Earthling go about explaining what a shadow is?
What is a shadow?
According to my desk dictionary (Random House Collegiate, revised edition, 1982), a *shadow* is: "1. a dark figure or image cast on a surface by a body intercepting light. 2. shade or comparative darkness, as in an area."
Take our imaginary visitor for a walk and show her her shadow cast on the sidewalk. "But that can't be my shadow," she exclaims in bewilderment. "I am four feet tall and if I am intercepting light, as you say, then surely my shadow would also be four feet. As you can see, it's much longer than that. How can a four foot body intercept more than four feet of light?"
"Because of the position of the Sun and the angle at which sunlight is reaching us," you explain, "our shadows are lengthened. But those are still our shadows."
The visitor is a bright creature and soon catches on. In no time at all she grows accustomed to shadows, and even when a given shadow is elongated or foreshortened she has no problem pinpointing the body casting it. She walks around saying to herself in delight, "Ah, yes, that's the shadow cast by the tree, that's the shadow cast by the structure, that's the shadow cast by me."

In most fun houses there are mirrors in which we can view ourselves in comically distorted form, ridiculously elongated or broadened. The intention is to amuse us, not deceive us. As distorted as our images are, no matter how tall or short or fat or thin our reflections appear, we recognize ourselves.
How distorted would the image have to be before we failed to recognize ourselves?

Imagine a trick mirror which could do more than distort the form. Imagine one that could throw open your shirt and implant your facial features in your chest, rip off a leg and engraft it upward from one shoulder, take an arm and attach it so that it dangles from the empty hip socket. This trick mirror also reflects the back of your head as you stand facing it, and in general throws back at you an image that is all you but is you in an arrangement of bodily parts such as you have never experienced at any moment in your life. Would you recognize yourself? How soon would this recognition strike? How long before the horrified confusion lifted enough for you to be able to know, with certainty, "That's me! That's a weird and distorted reflection of me!"

How good are we at recognizing the shadows we cast and our own reflections?

If the universe happens to be—in a very real sense—a reflection of Man, would we recognize it as such? How long would it take for this recognition to strike? If the notion struck and we intuitively *knew* it was so, how would we go about gathering and presenting proof?

We live in a world extremely familiar with translation. *Translation:* "1. the rendering of something into another language. 2. a version in a different language . . . 3. change or conversion to another form, appearance, etc.; transformation . . ."

Literary works are translated from one language to another, also from one art form to another, book into play or movie, play into film, etc. Translation from one language to another often requires modification, ie, some distortion. A word in one language may not be exactly translatable into another language. Even more change or modification is often required when a literary work is translated from one art form to another. What reads beautifully on the printed page may not be dramatic enough for direct translation to a visual medium such as the movies. A stage play when filmed is often opened up, taken to scenic backgrounds impossible on stage, to avoid a static or claustrophic feel. Musicians and poets work to express places, ideas or emotions in musical or rhythmic form. On an even more basic level, we translate thought into action daily. Through electrical impulses and chemical transformations, we move and think and have our being.

Translations,

Imagine for a moment that we, you and I, have been given a fantastic opportunity: we have the limitless power to create a world. It's a game, one we have all eternity to play. After a little thought, we realize that what we'd most enjoy is re-creating ourselves, that is, fashioning a world in which a godlike creature will emerge, a creature with free will and the power to create *her* own world.

As we envisage this, it occurs to us that there's an obvious problem. If our offspring is endowed with free will, as she must be to be godlike, she will be free *not* to listen to us, her creators, if she prefers not to, so how to communicate with our child once we've created her?

In a flash of genius we realize there's an easy solution to this problem, and one that will be great fun. While direct communication will be iffy—kids can be so stubborn!—we can create a world in which we communicate *indirectly,* a world of symbols, a world with cue cards on every side.

That's it, the perfect solution. The world surrounding our godlike creature will be a *reflection* of her, the physical/non physical truth of her being translated into the material world that surrounds her. The truths of her being will be translated into the physical Laws which govern the universe she lives in. The day that she sees this truth, the day she realizes that the world she lives in is nothing more nor less than a mirror reflecting herself back to herself, she will know the truth of her being, will know herself to be the god-creature she is. Marvelous!

As we proceed, let's keep clearly in mind what we, as the creators, have resolved to do: we are going to take the human physical/non physical condition and translate it onto a material cosmic background. Create a world that is a gigantic fun house mirror. A world with cue cards on every side. A symbolic world which reflects back to the human race what human life is all about.

So let's take a shot at it, this fantastic challenge, and see what kind of an imaginary world we can dream up.

In our world life will of course emerge. Once this emergent life becomes sophisticated enough, it will reproduce itself through union, the union of sexual opposites. Human life—the life in which we are most interested—is sparked, in the natural order of things, through sexual intercourse, with the male and female joining. The male experiences orgasm, ejaculating seed. The seed penetrates the female egg and the explosion into life begins.

How can we best translate this into the beginning of the universe?

Easy. We can start with a Cosmic Egg. There's the Big Bang of ejaculation, the Cosmic Egg is fertilized, and the universe begins.

At the time of this writing, as we dream up this imaginary universe, the instant of conception, the instant during which life begins, will for most human creatures be lost in the mist. While there are those living beings who claim lingering memory of life in the womb, and those who have experienced vivid dreams of this uterine life, and while there is mounting evidence at this point in time of the sensate life in the womb, few human creatures at the time of this writing, during the final decades of the 20th Century, are able to push conscious awareness back to the actual instant of conception. The Big Bang of ejaculation which preceded the conception is even harder to recall; for almost everyone it remains an event that is long ago and far away. Therefore the Big Bang that started the universe on its way will also seem, during this time slot—the final decades of the 20th Century—long ago and far away.

As an aside, it is perhaps relevant to remind ourselves that the most common explanation among primitive peoples for the existence of the material universe is that it came into being through the sexual activity of gods. For example, in an ancient Egyptian creation story, the god Atum started things off by masturbating. His seed created a god and goddess whose union produced Earth and Sky. With most primitive peoples, once wasn't enough. Renewal occurred each spring because Father Sky coupled again with Mother Earth. Until the end of the 19th Century in parts of Europe, farmers copulated with their wives in the fields after sowing to ensure a good crop.

Following the ascendency of the Christian Church, with its ingrained anti-sex bias, the creation story was sanitized. As it comes down to us in the Bible, God created the heavens and Earth by unspecified means, with no implication that the means were sexual. It wasn't until after World War I and the mini-sexual revolution of the twenties, which swept out much of the lingering Victorian repression, that the modern day Big Bang creation story was formulated. After World War II and the highly successful sexual revolution that followed, the Big Bang theory became entrenched. I sometimes wonder whether Cosmologists today can present their theory with straight faces—or do their eyes twinkle merrily?—as they revert to the most primitive kind of sexual creation myth: the Cosmic Egg expanded to create the universe after a Banging.

But to return to the task at hand and get on with our imaginary creation:

After the Big Bang conception, followed by gestation, when the new life finally comes to birth, she emerges into the world as a member of a triangle: father, mother, infant. Therefore, in our imaginary universe, we will make the home planet of human life part of a similar triangle. Because the new life is dependent on the parents, we will have the body representing the child revolve around two parental bodies, in an elliptical orbit, with one parent body at one focus, the second parent body at the other focus. Perfect.

But—wait a minute. Is that perfect, or even very logical? Does it really express the human condition? New life is dependent on two parents, yes, *before* conception. Yet once conception has occurred, only two members of the triangle become essential: mother and child. The father can fade out of existence immediately after supplying the seed and the new life, the new universe exploding within the egg, will continue merrily on its way, unaffected.

Obviously we should create not a three body configuration, but a two body system. Once the Big Bang has occurred, sparking fertilization, the new life is dependent on only one source: the mother. As long as the mother remains, a source of food, warmth, comfort and enlightenment, no other body is essential. Therefore our home planet should revolve around the parent body in a perfect circle with the parent body at the center.

Now we've got it!

Or have we?

Such a configuration is almost a mirror reflection but somehow not quite. The problem is it ignores the role of the father completely. If there is only the Mother and the Offspring, what body supplies the seed to ignite the explosion? We've got to change the orbit back to an ellipse and put a parent body at each focus.

But we've already tried that and it doesn't fit either. Once conception has been achieved, the very instant after conception, the supplier of the seed can vanish into nothingness without materially affecting the course of the developing life.

All right, a compromise. And this *should* work. The dependent body revolves around the parent body in a *nearly* perfect circle, but *not* a perfect circle. The parent body occupies one focus in the resultant ellipse and the second focus is *unoccupied,* an ever present remainder of the essential/non-essential male parent.

Good enough. To make it all crystal clear, we'll create a universe around our crucial bodies in which visible stars clearly pair, clearly belong in couples or clusters. Our parent body will *seem* to be alone, will *seem* to be different, but in actual fact will have a partner too, an absentee partner off roaming in space, possibly gathering ammunition with which to chastise his Offspring upon his return, much as Earthly fathers go out back to cut off a switch when their children become too obstreperous.

Our godlike little human beings, once they grow up enough to read the story so magnificently spread before them in the heavens, will surely enjoy the humor and appropriateness of the translation into material form we've just decided upon.

But—wait a minute again. We're not through yet. So far we have translated into a material system only the *physical* aspects of the human condition. Our godlike Offspring will not only have physical life, she will also have *consciousness*. This too must be cued into our material system if we would accurately reflect in our imaginary world the human condition.

But consciousness has already been cued in! We've stipulated that the parent body will provide not only food and warmth but comfort and enlightenment, ie, *consciousness*. That's what the entire creation is all about, the creation of this consciousness. It could hardly be cued in more directly.

Yes, but our creation still doesn't reflect the *child's* consciousness, the reactive consciousness. The parent body, as agreed, pours light—visibility, awareness, consciousness—onto the child, but each child responds in her own unique fashion, with her own mental/emotional patterns and yearnings, with her own particular ebb and flow of thought/feeling. So far this has *not* been translated into our imaginary world.

All right, here's an idea. We'll introduce a third major body. This third body will represent the child's bit of consciousness, her reactive mental/emotional patterns. This material body will be the closest material body to the child body, the home planet, and will seem almost a twin of the home planet to express the close relationship between physical life and consciousness. This third body will revolve around the child body, waxing and waning much as thoughts/emotions roll over and through the child.

Fine.

How about relative sizes?

Well, the parent is obviously such a vital source to the dependent child that we'll express this by making the parent body vastly larger than the body representing the child. The third body we've introduced will be even smaller than the child body, a great deal smaller than the parent body, for the child's reactive consciousness is a shrinking or funneling of consciousness. This third body will have no light of its own but will shine solely from the reflected light of the parent body, expressing its reactive nature.

Now have we got it all worked out, translating the underlying truth of the human condition into our imaginary world?

Possibly.

To recap what we've decided on:

We will have a small body, the home planet for life which we will call Earth. To emphasize the importance of this body we will give it great weight: *it will have the highest density of any body in the system,* an easy clue to its great importance that will surely not be overlooked for long.

The planet Earth will revolve around a much larger body, as a child's life revolves around her parent's, and this much larger though less dense body will radiate light and warmth, and we will call this body the Sun. The Earth will revolve around the Sun in an ellipse with the Sun at one focus, the second focus remaining unoccupied in honor of the essential/non essential, absentee, roaming partner.

A third body, smaller than the Earth, very close in, will revolve around the home planet Earth. This body we will call the Moon. It will shine only with reflected light, representing the child's consciousness, a reactive consciousness. As the Moon bobs around the Earth, it will wax and wane to reflect human mental/emotional response, and it will exert primary influence over the ebbing and flowing of the planet Earth's watery surface. Earth will be solid to represent physical life, but covered by a great deal of water to represent emotional life, with an additional covering of air, or atmosphere, to represent mental life. As our godlike child stands upon the surface of her solid yet water-plentiful Earth, the cue cards will be there in her sky, also under her feet, all around her, waiting for the day she learns to read.

Good enough. Have we got it all now?

Almost but not quite. While the triangle, father-mother-child, is basic, or the stripped down duo, mother-child, in actual fact other bodies will abound. To represent the human condition, we need to recognize this and scatter a few other material bodies into our system.

Right you are. No sooner said than accomplished, in our imaginary world. We'll toss in several other bodies to revolve around the Sun, the Source. But where should we put our planet of greatest interest, the Earth, in relation to these other orbiting bodies?

How about closest in to the Sun, as a clue to the Earth's supreme importance?

Fine. On second thought, hold it a minute. Such a positioning presents certain problems. Again we have to take a closer look at the human condition. Loving parents are essential to normal development, or one loving parent, but if the loving parent holds too closely to the child, not allowing the child to explore and experiment, to try on roles for herself, to become her own person, normal development will be thwarted. For optimum development the child must be loved, surrounded with warmth and light, but not held too tightly, too close in. If normal development is thwarted by too rigid a bond, anger can result, inflammation, a heating up. Therefore any material body revolving too closely around the parental Sun should have a surface temperature too hot to support the proper development of life.

All right then, shall we have the Earth the body farthest from the Sun to signify its primary significance?

Unfortunately, that won't work well either. A loving parent is not too distant. In many cases distance does not lend enchantment, it activates a sense of alienation. To feel isolated and alone is to feel cold and bereft. Material bodies too far distant from the Sun should have surface temperatures too cold to support Earth-like life.

Then we have no choice but to put Earth in orbit at a respectable but not too great distance from the parent Sun?

It would seem so. How else can we translate the proper parental role in the life-giving and life-sustaining process?

But don't we risk that this neither-first-nor-last Earth orbit may conceal the Earth's overriding importance?

For a time, possibly, but surely not for long. Two clues are too blatantly obvious for us to fear eternal concealment.

One, as we have already noted, a clear clue as to the importance of Earth will be given in its weight: it will have greater density than any other body in the System. To give weight to something is to give it importance, so anyone who can't read that clue isn't trying. To make it even more crystal clear, we will underline the clue in this fashion: we will give the tiny body closest in to the Sun a comparable density, which will link the two bodies in a way that can't be overlooked. We will also give these two bodies a similar magnetic field, so that Earth will be twin-like in these two respects to the body in the innermost orbit. In effect, Earth will enjoy the same physical properties it would have were it tucked in right next to the radiant Sun.

Our second clue will be even more blatant. Conscious life will spring up on Earth and nowhere else in the System, and conscious life will instinctively know its own importance, regardless of where its orbital home is. So I don't think we need worry, especially as in time our bright Offspring will surely figure out why Earth's orbit was placed where it is.

But even so—

All right, we'll toss in another clue, one so obvious that even the most stubborn and closed minded child will not be able to blind herself to it: *we'll have the Sun and the Moon appear in the Earth sky as identical size discs.*

So brazen a clue can't possibly be overlooked. The odds against such an identity of size occurring accidentally must be astronomical. And this dual disc size can serve as a symbol for more than one aspect of reality, as a good symbol should.

First, two large, identical size discs in the sky will be a constant reminder to our Offspring of her origin, that in the physical world she has not one but *two* parents, while the waxing and waning of the one will serve to remind her of the essential/non essential role of one as compared to the other.

Secondly, it will be a fine representation of our Offspring's emotional life. As she identifies with one parent and that parent becomes her Sun, the source of her being, she will feel sexually/emotionally drawn to the other, who will be her Moon, the primary force ruling the tides of her watery/

emotional self. The parent with whom she identifies may well shift over time, of course, that is, the parent who is the Sun of her childhood may become the Moon of her adolescence, and vice versa. But regardless of such shifts, as she identifies with one parent—internalizes the influence of one parent—she will be drawn emotionally to the other.

Last but not least, this identity of disc size will serve to express the most profound truth of the human condition, which is that human consciousness sees duality in every direction: male and female, light and dark, good and evil, hot and cold, self and non self. This duality that our godlike child sees all around her, in every direction, will also appear in her sky: Sun and Moon as identical size discs. But she will soon learn how deceptive this seeming duality in her heavens is. The Sun and the Moon are not really the twin bodies they appear to be, rather they differ mightily in size, distance and substance, the waxing and waning Moon being visible only through the grace of the light-radiating Sun.

Through the deceptive duality she sees in the sky, our godlike Offspring will surely realize in time the deceptive nature of all her perceived dualities. At this point, if she ponders on what she sees, she may begin to understand the truth of her being and the underlying truth of the universe.

When that happens, we will have successfully met the challenge we gave ourselves: to create a godlike creature with free will with whom we can nevertheless communicate. It may take time, all of eternity possibly, to get her to pay attention, to listen, but in imaginary games of this kind there is all the time in the world, in fact all of eternity.

All of eternity, you say. But what of the interruption known as death?

Good point.

Shouldn't we toss into our creation a clue as to the nature of death?

Right you are. How's this? The Sun pouring out warmth and light symbolizes the gift of life. This life develops on Earth. To symbolize physical death, we need great distance from the Sun, an area of darkness and cold. Here we will place an oddball planet as a clue to death. It will be the least dense permanent body in the System, also the smallest, to signify that death is lightweight and of little importance. We'll also give our tiny death planet an orbit tilted in rakish fashion from the plane of the other planetary orbits to show that death is in reality simply movement onto another plane.

Marvelous. I've got another idea to underline the clue. As tiny as it is, let's give this stand-in for death planet—let's call it Pluto—a satellite that's the largest in the System in relation to its parent, a moon almost half its size. In the Earth-Moon system, we agreed that one of the uses of the Moon was to symbolize the reactive life, the emotional side of life, so we need a large satellite attached to our death planet Pluto to indicate the expanded emotional life which follows death.

Right. We'll make the satellite huge in relation to the planet, almost half its size. From a distance the pair will appear almost like a double planet system, in imitation of the pairing of stars, like near twins.

Just like the Earth, with its giant satellite the Moon.

From a proper distance, the Earth, the planet of life, will appear like a near twin.

From a proper distance, our tiny oddball planet, the planet of death, Pluto, will appear like a near twin.

With a proper perspective, life and death will not be viewed as antagonistic strangers to each other, but as near twins.

Translators differ in method, in both style and approach, but the above is one way that the human condition could be translated, with a reasonable degree of accuracy, into a different medium: a material background. In general outline, in this translation, we know what the local neighborhood— the Sun-Earth-Moon-Planet-System—would be like were the Creation tailor-made to reflect the human condition.

But what about out beyond the local neighborhood? What of the distant stars and the stupendous galaxies they are said to form?

4

LIGHT: THE CORPUSCULAR WAVE

Star Light, Star Bright, You've Traveled
How Far To Get Here?

> And God said, Let there be light;
> and there was light.
> Genesis 1:3
> Christian Bible

In a universe constructed for Man, why stars?
What Earthly good are they?
Why in the world do they exist?
From an Earthbound, Man-as-godlike-creature point of view, we can easily assign purpose to the existence of stars. From the surface of our planet home, they provide a startling night view. They are fun to look at. They are also of pivotal importance in navigation. Man in his travels on Earth has been guided primarily by the stars. In a universe constructed for Man, in which Man has the ultimate significance, there is no problem assigning a purpose to stars. *Stars exist as a helpful guide to Man.*

But for travel purposes a few hundred fixed stars, certainly the few thousand visible to the naked eye, would be enough. Millions are superfluous. The billions of stars that are said to exist constitute a disconcerting oversupply.

If in fact billions and billions of stars do exist in the billions and billions of galaxies they are said to form, this would tend to undermine any theory that Man is the last or latest word in significance. Such an excess of riches would be almost impossible to explain. If Man is the key figure in the Creation, a premise we are endeavoring to defend, why would the Creator humiliate him so badly, make him appear as small as he *must* appear if the universe as described by the Scientists is real? That Man has an Earthly need for a few thousand stars is easily claimed, but how can he possibly have any Earthly need for billions and billions of them formed into billions and billions of galaxies?

This overabundance of stars and galaxies is such an obvious embarrassment that let's take the easy way out and deny its existence, or, if such stars and galaxies do exist, let's deny that we are getting from the Scientists just the facts, Ma'am, about their existence. Let's set out to show that much of what we are told about stars and galaxies may be nothing more nor less than a figment of the scientific imagination. Science has attacked the importance and grandeur of Man. Let's fight back by attacking the reasoning and interpretative power of Science.

Within the last few years, Astronomers have found something new in the sky: gravitational lenses. Faint dots of light near to each other in space but far distant from us have been found to be identical in chemical composition and in their computed distance from Earth. This led to the suspicion that such twin dots were more than identical twins, that we were in fact seeing double, were seeing two images of the same vastly distant object. In time it was decided that this was indeed what was happening: we were picking up two distinct images of more than one distant light source.

This effect is explained as follows:

According to Albert Einstein's Relativity Theory, light rays travel in a curved path through the distortions of space caused by concentrations of mass-energy. Distant concentrations of mass-energy in the form of galaxies are acting as gravitational lenses, curving the light radiating to us in such a way that we receive multiple images.

For such an effect to occur, we are told, the source of the light, the galaxy or galaxies acting as a lens or lenses, and the

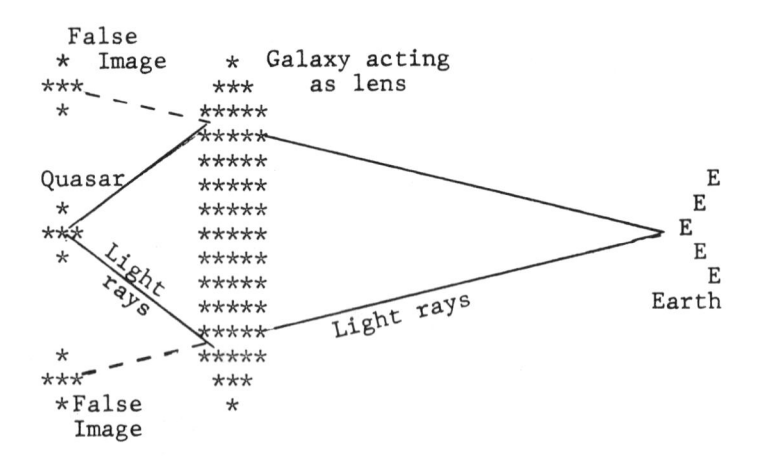

```
        False
      *  Image        *  Galaxy acting
    ***_ _ _ _       ***    as lens
     *            *****
                 Z*****
                  *****
  Quasar         *****                          E
    *            *****                           E
   **☆           *****                            E
    *   L        *****                             E
         i       *****                              E
         gh      *****                               Earth
          t      *****              ra ys
           ra    *****         ht
            ys  *****      Lig
                Z*****
    *       _ _ *****
   ***_ _ _     *****
    *False       ***
     Image       *
```

With the bending of light rays by a galaxy acting as a lens, we on Earth perceive two images for one quasar. (Quasar: a quasi-stellar radio source, a celestial object from four to ten billion light-years distant which is a powerful source of radio energy.)

Earth have to be in alignment, and distances have to range over billions of light-years. These criteria have been met in five instances so far, and five multiple images have been identified: four are double, one a triple. More are expected to be found now that Science is excitedly searching for them.

This discovery of gravitational lenses may be the first clear tip-off to Science—one that has not yet been generally recognized as the fantastic clue it is—that we live in a reflecting universe, that the incredible vastness of space that Cosmologists are so diligently mapping isn't really there, it's all an illusion, it's all done with mirrors.

Science would immediately reject any such notion, of course. We don't live in a Hall of Mirrors, they would contend; the universe *out there* is real and in earnest. Science claims not just to believe this but to *know* this, to have proved it beyond any shadow of doubt.

Scientists have unquestionably proved the existence of their vast universe to their own satisfaction, but as we read of their "proofs" and their new discoveries, let's keep firmly in mind that their one and only informational source is the electromagnetic radiation which reaches us. If Science isn't reading this radiation right, if Scientists have let their imaginations run wild with it, then they aren't constructing a valid universe, they are dreaming dreams and having visions.

All of us are familiar with the way a straight stick appears to bend if it is put in water. We soon learn that the stick doesn't really bend, it's a trick of the light. Light entering water bends for the simple reason that it travels at different speeds in different mediums. The denser the medium, the more slowly light travels through it. In round figures, light travels through crown glass at approximately 124,000 miles per second, through water at 139,000 miles per second, and across empty space, according to the Scientists, at about 186,000 miles per second.

This last figure, the speed of light through empty space, whatever that speed may be, has since Albert Einstein's day taken on almost mystical significance. In the world of Scientists, the speed of light is the outside limit. Nothing can travel faster than light. According to Einstein's predictions, if an object could reach the speed of light its length would be reduced to nothing and its mass, that is, its resistance to change of speed, would become infinite. Yet the photon, the quantum particle of electromagnetic radiation, traveling at the speed of light, far from having infinite mass is considered to have no mass at all, to be massless.

For centuries it was widely believed that light was propagated instantaneously, ie, that it traveled at infinite speed if it could truly be said to travel at all. In the 16th century the notion arose that possibly this was erroneous. Light, like sound waves and mechanical vibrations, might instead travel at a finite velocity. Galileo Galilei (1564-1642) was one of the first to consider the possibility that the velocity of light could be measured. Observers placed on two distant hills would be equipped with lamps and shutters. The first observer would open his shutter. When the second observer saw the light, he would open his shutter. The first observer would then note the time lapse between the opening of his shutter and the observed flash of light from the second lamp. The reasoning was sound, but the experiment failed as the velocity of light is far too great to measured in this fashion.

In the 17th century a Danish astronomer named Olaus Romer (1644-1710), working at the National Observatory in Paris, observed an irregularity in the travels of the first satellite of Jupiter. The intervals between eclipses were smaller when the Earth was approaching Jupiter and lagged behind as the Earth moved away. Romer interpreted this time differential as being due to the time it took for light to travel across the diameter of the Earth's orbit. In 1676, after comparing observations for the Jovian satellite eclipse during conjunctions of Earth and Jupiter and then at the opposition of these two planets, Romer announced a finite velocity for light. The value he gave of 214,000 km/sec. was of the correct order of magnitude though too small, the error being due largely to the uncertainty regarding the diameter of the Earth's orbit.

The discovery that light traveled with a finite velocity—at least as measured by an observer on Earth—was not universally accepted until after 1728, when James Bradley (1693-1762), an English astronomer working at Kew Observatory, discovered the aberration of stars. In observing the star Draconis, Bradley found that its position as observed from Earth changed during the course of a year in a way that could not be attributed solely to the Earth's orbital movement around the Sun. He deduced that this aberrational displacement was due to the finite velocity of the light streaming toward us, and computed a value for that velocity of 301,000 km/sec.

Bradley's work established the principle of a finite velocity for light, but it was over a hundred years before attempts were made to measure this finite velocity more precisely.

Methods for measuring light's velocity fall into two categories. In the first method, the passage of an electromagnetic wave over a known distance is timed. In the second method, the wavelength of a wave of known frequency is measured and the velocity is mathematically attained. In recent years, there has been a reassuring uniformity in result regardless of the method used. The currently accepted figure for the velocity of light *in vacuo* is: 299,792.5 plus or minus 0.4 kilometers per second, or 186,282.42 plus or minus 0.2 miles per second. Rounded off the figures are 300,000 kilometers or 186,000 miles per second, *in vacuo.*

These figures have been arrived at with the greatest precision and care known to modern Science, but let's not forget that all such measurements have been made here on Earth or, if made on a space craft of some sort, well within the Solar System. Even when the measurement involves nearby or distant heavenly bodies, the measurement is still made here. No one has gone outside our local neighborhood to see what kind of value would be obtained *out there,* or to see how that particle-wave phenomenon we know as light travels or behaves when out from under our Earthbound eye.

The accepted value for the velocity of light is given for velocity *in vacuo.* In vacuum. In my desk dictionary (The Random House College Dictionary, Revised Edition, Copyright 1982), *vacuum* is defined: "1. a space entirely devoid of matter. 2. An enclosed space from which matter, esp. air, has been partially removed . . . 3. the state or degree of exhaustion in such a space. 4. anything suggesting an exhausted place or void."

The first definition of vacuum, "a space entirely devoid of matter," is something that has yet to be achieved on Earth and such an absolute vacuum may not exist anywhere, even in the all but infinitely vast universe in which the Scientists claim we live. The Learned Ones of Science can now create fairly exhausted partial vacuums, however, that contain only a few million molecules per cubic inch (16 cubic centimeters).

How does this partial vacuum compare to the conditions said to exist in outer space?

If all matter were evenly distributed throughout space, we are told, there would be approximately *one atom of hydrogen per cubic meter of space.* Yet all matter is not uniformly distributed, according to the best available evidence. Matter, according to all available evidence, has gathered itself into large and small clumps: stars, planets, asteroids, etc. This leaves vast stretches of space between these clumps with less matter than one hydrogen atom per cubic meter to fill the emptiness.

On Earth: partial vacuums that contain only a few million *molecules* per cubic inch (16 cubic centimeters).

In "empty" space: less than one hydrogen *atom* per cubic *meter*.

A centimeter is one-hundredth of a meter. Atoms are smaller than, and combine to make, molecules.

As we can see, the vacuums achieved on Earth are millions multiplied by nearly a million less exhausted of matter than the vacuum postulated for empty space.

The above indicates clearly that the velocity of light has never been measured here on the surface of the Earth in any vacuum even approximating the conditions of outer space.

Adjustment is made of course for this inability to test experimentally, the adjustment being made on the basis of sound mathematical logic. However, what is clearly logical and logically sound mathematically does not always prove to correspond with the way Nature actually works. Aristotle (384-322 BC), the great philosopher, scientist, and logician of the ancient world, taught that heavy objects fall faster than lightweight ones. The logic of this was so self evident that no one bothered to test it experimentally for almost two thousand years. Aristotle also taught that the male, being obviously superior to the female, had more teeth in his head than she had in hers. This too was so logical that no one bothered to look inside the mouth of an adult female to find if this self evident logic squared with observational fact. The history of knowledge has been a constant revision of what seems logical by what is in fact the fact.

This is true even of those logical propositions supported by sophisticated mathematical "proof." Well over two thousand years ago Zeno of Ela (c490-c430 BC) "proved" all kinds of marvelously nonsensical things with logic and numbers.

First, motion is impossible. If anything were to move, it would have to reach the middle of its course before it reached the end. Before it could reach the middle point, it would have to reach the quarter point, before the quarter point the eighth point, before the eighth point the sixteenth point, and so on *indefinitely*. Into infinity. Therefore the motion can never begin, and no motion is possible.

Another proof by Zeno that motion is impossible: Take the smallest unit of time, the unit which cannot be further divided. Call this unit the "instant." In any given instant of time, an arrow is either at rest or is moving. If it is moving—if it travels during the instant of time—then the instant of time becomes divisible, which by definition it cannot be. The arrow *cannot* move during the smallest instant of time; therefore it cannot move in time at all and must always remain at rest.

In another clever use of logic and numbers, Zeno easily "proved" that half the time at times is equal to double the time. To this day, some mathematicians still struggle to prove the illogic of Zeno's logic, to get mathematical theory to square with experience.

The velocity of light under non vacuum and partial vacuum conditions is adjusted with mathematical logic, but until this velocity can be measured in a vacuum which begins to approximate the actual conditions in outer space, Science is basing its figure for that velocity on logical conjecture, not fact.

We have one and only one source of information about the universe beyond our Solar System: the electromagnetic radiation which pours in upon us. From this one and only source, the Scientists have constructed an incredibly vast, spectacular *out there*.

The heavenly object closest to us outside the Solar System is, we are told, the star Alpha Centauri, seen in the Southern Hemisphere. This star is 4.3 light years away, a light year being the distance light travels in a year traveling at the rate of 186,200 miles per second. (It has recently been suggested that our Sun may have an absentee partner out roaming in the wilds gathering ammunition to belt us with. If the Killer Star exists, it would be closer to us than Alpha Centauri. But so far its existence has not been proved.)

Stellar distances are determined, for the ten thousand stars close enough for this to work, by much the same surveying method used to determine the distance of inaccessible objects on the surface of the Earth. A baseline is established, angles measured at each end of the baseline, and distance calculated through trigonometric means. For stellar distances, a baseline larger than the Earth's surface is needed, so the diameter of the Earth's orbit is used. Measurement of a given star's position in relation to a background of fainter and presumably more distant stars can be taken at a certain point in the Earth's orbit, then taken again six months later when the Earth has moved 186,000,000 miles from its original position. With this orbital baseline (double the 93,000,000 mile distance from Earth to Sun) a displacement of the star's position relative to background stars can be determined, for those 10,000 stars close enough for displacement to be detected, and the star's distance calculated.

Measurement of such displacement—the parallax of stars—is now an important branch of astronomy. Numerous photographs are taken, measurements made, parallax determined, and a vast universe takes form, constructed out of points of light dancing in our skies much as a child creates a picture by connecting the dots.

The universe the Cosmologists have put before us has been based almost entirely on *visible* radiation, on light. When we look at stars, or photograph them, we assume we are getting an accurate fix on location, time delayed of course, the time it takes for the light to reach us. But what if light and Nature are in some fashion playing a trick on us?

This can't be, of course. We can't possibly live in a Halloween universe in which light plays tricks on us. Surely not. In recent years, however, light has done nothing but play one confusing trick after another on those investigators attempting to pin her down and gain more complete understanding of her baffling ways.

To illustrate:

As has already been mentioned, for centuries generations of Scientists less sophisticated than ourselves believed that light was either a particle or a wave. It either charged forth independently on its own, a particle, or it moved forward through some medium as a wave motion.

There are two forms of waves: longitudinal and transverse.

Water waves are transverse. The individual water molecules move up and down at right angles to the forward progression of the wave itself. Sound waves are longitudinal. The individual molecules move back and forth in the same direction that the sound wave is traveling.

If light is a wave, which type of wave is it?

Early researchers favored the longitudinal wave, but difficulties soon arose so there was a shift toward the transverse wave. For either or any type wave, it was believed that there had to be a substance through which the wave traveled, so the ether was postulated. For this ether to allow the passage of light as a transverse wave traveling at 186,200 miles per second, the ether had to be indistinguishable from a vacuum yet more rigid than steel. All well and good—or silly, fanciful and utterly preposterous on the face of it, depending on how one looked at it—until repeated experiments tended to prove that this miraculous ether did not exist.

This was indeed a puzzlement as experiments had already "proved" conclusively that light was a wave. An English physician, physicist and mathematician, Thomas Young (1773-1829), conducted a simple experiment which settled the question of what light was once and for all: light was a wave.

In 1803 Dr. Young placed a screen with two slits cut in it in front of a light source. Each slit could be easily covered. When one slit was covered and the light traveled only through the remaining open slit, the light diffracted onto the wall behind the screen. Bright light at the center shaded into darkness without a sharp boundary in a typical wave diffraction pattern. When both slits were open for the light to travel through, a different pattern was created on the wall: alternating bands of light and dark. The center band was the brightest, with bands of darkness on either side, then less bright bands of light, followed by darker bands of darkness.

How could this happen? Simple. It's an example of a well known wave phenomenon: interference. Waves can overlap, one crest joining another crest to reinforce the cresting, or a crest can meet with a trough so that each cancels the other out. In the double slit experiment light was clearly revealed for what it was: a wave.

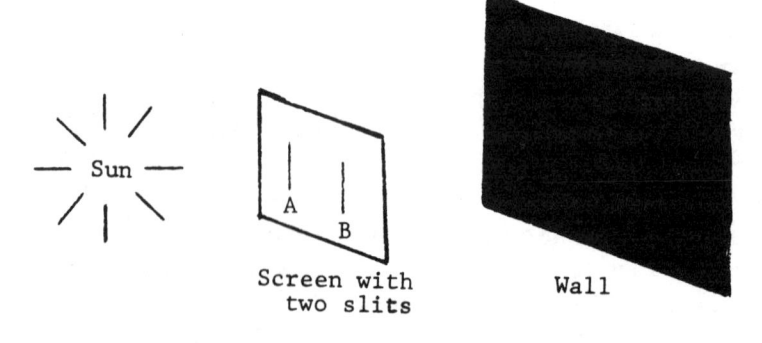

Screen with two slits   Wall

Dr. Young's Experiment.

Pattern thrown on wall if only one slit is open.

Pattern thrown on wall if both slits are open.

This meant the Scientists had to bestir themselves to prove the existence of the vacuum-like, more rigid than steel ether, for waves need a substance through which to travel. Unfortunately, the ether, if it exists, proved too subtle to be detected, and in time the ether concept was tossed into the bin of superannuated scientific creations.

With the wave nature of light firmly established, a German, later American, physicist named Albert Einstein (1879-1955) came along and in 1905 published a paper describing the quantum, or particle, nature of light. Light-as-wave was inconsistent with the photoelectric effect; therefore light had to travel in small packets of energy, a beam of light being similar to a stream of bullets, each bullet a photon. This pinned down the essential nature of light, or another aspect of the essential nature of light: light is a particle.

A Danish physicist, Niels Bohr (1885-1962), developed the concept of complementarity: wave-like characteristics and particle-like characteristics are *complementary,* mutually exclusive aspects of light. Wave-like behavior and particle-like behavior are not *properties* of light. We *invest* light with these properties through our interaction with it. We can set up an experiment to reveal light as a wave, or, if we'd rather, we can set up an experiment to reveal light as a particle. In each case, our interaction with the light causes the sought after behavior to manifest.

In 1923 an American physicist, Arthur Compton (1892-1962), set up an experiment in which he fired x-rays at electrons. The x-rays, which were well known to be waves, bounced off the electrons like billiard balls, losing energy consistent with the glancing or direct nature of the hit. This demonstrated the particle nature of the x-ray wave.

Scientists experimenting with light could now display its wave-like nature, its particle-like nature, or, in Compton's scattering effect, its wave-particle nature. Light was really being shed on the elusive subject of light. But how *real* was what was being revealed?

If we look back at the double slit experiment while keeping in mind all that has been learned of light since 1803, we will note something very tricky. If light approaches the double slits as a wave front, then it behaves exactly as it ought to, creating alternating bands of light and dark. But Albert Einstein, whose brilliant theories have been proved right time and again, said that light traveled in discrete packets of energy and suggested we think of a beam of light as a stream of bullets from a gun. So let's visualize these streams of bullets approaching the screen with the two slits in it. Surely each individual bullet-photon which penetrates the screen must go through one slit or the other, either Slit A or Slit B.

But—wait a minute. Different light patterns are thrown on the wall behind the screen depending on whether one slit is open in the screen or both slits are open. As the photon-bullets approach the screen, how do they know where to go as they splash light on the wall? If only one slit is open, they must illuminate the wall in a certain way. If both slits are open, they distribute themselves in an entirely different pattern. A stream of photon-bullets is presumed to go through Slit A. This stream behaves a certain way if Slit B is closed, a different way if Slit B is open. How do these photons know, as they stream through Slit A, whether Slit B is open or closed? Somehow they *do* know, for they never make a mistake. When both slits are open, an interference pattern *always* forms; when only one slit is open, it *never* forms. The experimenter may be thoroughly perplexed, but those speedy little massless photons, if they exist, always know what they're about.

It has been suggested that photons accomplish the ingenious single slit/double slit results because they are conscious and process information.

What kind of a universe do we live in if massless photons (the quanta of light) have consciousness, process information, and communicate with each other instantaneously or with lightning speed?

Photons may not be the only particles able to process information and communicate instantaneously or with lightning speed. In his charming and entertaining book, *The*

Dancing Wu Li Masters (William Morrow and Co., Inc., New York: 1979), author Gary Zukav describes another experiment, a thought experiment having to with electrons and a known property particles possess: their spin. In this thought experiment, instantaneous communication or communication at an illegal, superluminal (faster than light) speed would seem to occur between the electrons.

If such instant communication—interconnectedness—exists in the subatomic world, what lesson might this hold for us as we attempt to understand the underlying truth of the visible world?

While it was believed for centuries that a wave is a wave, a particle a particle, and never the twain shall twine, the tricky behavior of light forced a revision of this unsophisticated common sense belief. Light, a wave, acted at times strangely like a particle. While the Scientists were still struggling to make sense of this disturbing news, a young French physicist, Louis de Broglie (born 1892), proposed a startling corollary: not only do waves sometimes act like particles, particles have associated waves. This hypothesis was verified experimentally a scant two years later by an experimenter, Clinton Davisson (1881-1958), working with his assistant Lester Germen (1896-1971) at the Bell Telephone Laboratories. Electrons, which are particles or were believed to be particles, behave at times as only waves behave. Shoot a beam of electrons through tiny openings and the beam diffracts just as light diffracts, as waves diffract. (*Diffract:* "to break up or bend by diffraction." *Diffraction:* "Physics. 1. the phenomenon exhibited by wave fronts that, passing the edge of an opaque body, are modulated, thereby causing a redistribution of energy within the front; it is detectable in light waves by the presence of minute dark and light bands at the edge of a shadow. 2. the bending of waves, esp. sound and light waves around obstacles in their path.") Subsequently it was found that *all* subatomic particles, out of which all matter is made, have associated waves. Common sense departed the world of Science and quantum mechanics (*Quantum:* quantity. *Mechanics:* the science of motion) was developed to deal with this mind-boggling new world where nothing was what it should be and everything was what it shouldn't be.

Quantum mechanics, it is claimed by some, has reconciled the wave and particle concepts of light.

> Today, the theory of light has again reached a point at which all known terrestrial phenomena are included in one logical theory. The known unsolved problems concern the transmission of light over the vast distances of intergalactic space.
> Encyclopaedia Britannica
> 15th Edition (1979)
> Volume X, pg. 930.

The fact that there are known unsolved problems concerning the transmission of light over the vast distances of intergalactic space does not keep the present day Astronomers and Cosmologists from building a gigantic universe on top of these problems.

A universe built on top of unsolved problems may in time prove problematic.

As scientific techniques for observing, measuring and mathematizing the invisible world forged ahead by gigantic leaps, it was found that the world being observed—the subatomic physical world—like a stubborn, balky, hyperactive child, refused to sit still for its definitive portrait. Man as observer interfered with the observation he was trying to make. The experimenter could not—and according to the Uncertainty Principle of German physicist Werner Heisenberg (1901-1976), never will be able to—put himself outside the picture.

For the classical laws of motion to be applied to a moving object, initial location and momentum of the object must be known. (*Momentum: "Physics.* a quantity expressing the motion of a body or system, equal to the product of the mass of a body and its velocity." *Velocity: "Mech.* the time rate of change of position of a body in a specified direction.")

To learn the position and momentum of a subatomic particle, an electron for instance, illumination is required. To illuminate position, a radiation with a wavelength smaller than the electron must be used. (A longer wavelength will bend right around the tiny electron without illuminating it.) Unfortunately radiation with a very short wavelength has extremely high energy. This high energy, used to illuminate the electron's position, will collide with the electron and in so doing will change the electron's direction and speed, ie, its velocity, which changes its momentum.

To detect momentum, radiation of a longer wavelength/ lower energy may be used, but this longer wavelength will bend right around the electron and won't reveal its position. The experimenter can determine position *or* he can determine momentum, but he cannot determine both, now or ever, according to the Uncertainty Principle. Therefore there is no way to apply classical Laws of Motion, or the classical concept of causality, to the subatomic world.

The Uncertainty Principle.

Uncertainty seems a poor principle upon which to base a certain world.

Ah, but it is only in the world of the microscopic, the subatomic world, that uncertainty reigns. In the macroscopic world, the world of the visible, there is no such confusion. We will never know precisely, according to some of our Learned Ones, the world of the infinitely small, which is right under our instruments, but other Learned Ones have no such trouble understanding what happened long ago and far away, ten to twenty billion years ago when Man was not yet, so they tell us, even an accidental glimmer in the eye of whatever gods there might have been.

Light exhibits wave-like properties when we set up an experiment to have it do so. Light exhibits particle-like properties when we set up an experiment to have it do this. In each case, the observer and his method of observation are intimately involved in the results. In effect, what we are observing and measuring are not the properties of light, but *the effects of our interaction with light.*

The universe the Cosmologists currently have us living in has been based almost exclusively on *visible* radiation.

Below the red part of the visible spectrum, there is a band of long wavelength radiation called *infrared.* (*Infra:* from the Greek meaning *below.*) This radiation is invisible to human eyes; in addition, our Earthly atmosphere filters out most infrared signals. Therefore these invisible radiations played little role in the scientific construction of our universe. In 1983, however, a Dutch-British-U.S. spacecraft was launched into orbit high above the Earth's atmosphere equipped with infrared-sensitive eyes to scan the heavens. The universe revealed turned out to be a different one from the familiar universe revealed to us by visible light.

Any matter with a temperature above absolute zero radiates infrared light, or heat radiation. With its infrared sensitive eyes, the Infrared Astronomical Satellite (IRAS) could detect nonluminous material previously undetected by Earthly observers.

During its ten months of service in orbit, the IRAS found an unexpectedly untidy sky. Dust was everywhere. "In fact, the satellite uncovered so much dust and debris, the cumulative mess may force astronomers to recalibrate cosmological distance scales." ("The Cosmos Through Infrared Eyes," by Michael Gold, Science 84, March issue.) Estimated stellar distances are based in part on brightness: the dimmer the star source, the farther the distance was assumed to be. But if visible radiation is being markedly dimmed as it struggles to reach us through dirty space, heavenly bodies may be much closer to us than is currently believed.

In addition to all this heretofore unsuspected cosmic debris, there may well be other factors not yet taken into consideration affecting the visible radiation which reaches us.

Consider this:

If we were miles above the surface of a large bathtub into which someone had stuck a telephone pole, and, unaware of the refraction of light, we were calculating the true position of the pole in the water solely on the basis of what we could see, how accurate would our calculations be?

If the stellar light that reaches us is being deflected, refracted or otherwise toyed with in ways we are not yet aware of, all our astronomical calculations become meaningless and the vast universe *out there* dissolves away, to await the day we can build a more accurate one.

The universe grew to the gigantic proportions it is now said to have largely through detection and interpretation of the so-called "red shift."

For centuries it has been known that a prism disperses light. (*Prism:* "1. *Optics* a transparent solid body, used for dispersing light into a spectrum or for reflecting rays of light.")

The dispersive action of the prism has been put to use in an instrument known as the spectroscope. This instrument reveals that differing light sources give off light with varying spectral patterns. Sunlight, certain lamp filaments and molten metals all give off a *continuous* spectrum, ie, all colors in an unbroken array. Incandescent gases give off *bright-line* spectra, ie, only certain colors are present in fine lines.

Joseph von Fraunhofer (1787-1826), a German optician and physicist, observed that continuous spectra were crossed by numerous dark lines. He charted what he could not explain, over seven hundred of these dark lines, which today are called *Fraunhofer lines* in his honor.

Some fifty years later two men, Gustav Kirchhoff (1824-1887), a German physicist, and Robert Bunsen (1811-1899), a German chemist, explained the dark lines. First they found that certain vaporized substances gave off light with the expected bright-line spectra. But when the emitted light was passed through a cooler vapor of the same substance, the dark lines appeared. The cooler vapor had absorbed the characteristic light from the substance. Experiments showed this was always the case, and the spectral lines thus formed were called *dark-line* or *absorption spectra*.

Further experiments showed that a given element, heated to incandescence, always gives off light with the same spectral pattern, a bright line spectrum if the light comes directly from the incandescent element, a dark line spectrum if the light has been passed through a cooler vapor containing the same element. This made it possible to determine which elements were present in unknown substances, such as the Sun and the stars (on the unproved assumption that the same spectral Laws operate *out there*).

In the youthful years of our century, two American astronomers working at Mount Wilson Observatory in Southern California, Milton Humason (1891-1957) and Edwin Hubble (1889-1953), discovered a shift to the red in the spectral lines of distant galaxies. This red shift was interpreted as due to the Doppler effect, and the expanding universe was born.

(*Doppler effect:* "*Physics*. the apparent change in the frequency of a wave, as a light wave or sound wave, resulting from relative motion of the source and the receiver, named after Christian Doppler (1803-1853), Austrian physicist.")

A shift to the red is a shift toward lower frequency, which indicates that source and receiver are moving apart. (A shift to the blue would indicate a movement toward each other by source and receiver.)

Once the red shift had been detected, it was found everywhere, in every direction. Every observable body in the universe seemed to be rushing away from us at breakneck speed.

But why? Why flee *us?* Do we on Earth have such bad body odor that the entire universe is repulsed and can't wait to escape from us?

Of course not, say the Learned Ones of our time. Any such notion would place us rather too strategically, however negatively, in the center of things, and if there is one thing that the Learned Ones are determined *not* to do, it is to give Earth that kind of importance or human life any hint of exalted meaning. After all, they have before their eyes the example of centuries of wishful, wrongful thinking when men *did* believe that the Earth was the very center of the universe and human life the key to the entire Creation. Once burned, twice shy. They aren't about to fall into that pit of error again. The universe isn't truly rushing away from *us,* it is simply an expanding curved space where, as on the surface of a balloon being inflated, everything, no matter how insignificantly placed, is increasing its distance from everything else.

Once the expanding universe was born, like Topsy it jes growed and growed.

Some few Cosmologists have an uneasy feeling that possibly all is not quite as clear cut and sure as it is presumed to be, that maybe a trifle too much universe rests on unproved assumptions—there are red shifts in Nature *not* caused by the Doppler effect, for instance—but for the most part the Learned Ones, delighted to accept without challenge the overall picture, are rushing in, with their instruments and their obtuse mathematical proofs, to sketch in the final details, painting us into our tiny little meaningless corner in the grand and glorious scheme of things.

In the subatomic world there is no longer a sure and certain world of matter and force. Matter can't be pinned down and the concept of force is giving way to the concept of *interaction*. Everything interacts with everything else, the experimenters tell us. Man cannot put himself out of the picture. As observer he can't keep from interfering with what he is attempting to observe.

In the world most familiar to us, here on the surface of our Earth, the world of matter and energy in which we live and move and have our being, there is overwhelming evidence that we cannot interact with our world without changing it.

This holds true not only in the subatomic world. Walk outside in a pouring rain and the raindrops are deflected. Stand in the sunshine and you cast a shadow, intercepting the passage of light. Flash a powerful beam of light into a forest area and wild life scurries away. The cells of our body spend their lifetimes interacting with each other. Intellectually and emotionally we interact with one another. In our everyday world, as in the subatomic world, everything is interaction.

The same holds true for the Cosmos. Gravity—whatever gravity is—controls the entire structure, holding everything in place. Gravitational interaction governs the universe.

With interaction the rule in every direction, on every level of being, we are forced to accept the fact that we do not know—possibly cannot ever know—the truth about objective reality. What we experience—the only thing we can study and know—is our *interaction* with whatever reality there is.

Yet the Cosmologists, the Scientists who put before us an incredibly vast universe billions and billions of years old, seem to forget this basic law of interaction. They seem to accept the odd notion that we can interact with this universe, with whatever exists *out there,* without in any way appreciably changing it. When it comes to the great *out there,* subatomic law breaks down, everyday Earth law breaks down, even Cosmic law breaks down, and as we co-exist, observing, we do not cause change. Suddenly we have become objective, have successfully put ourselves all but completely out of the picture—we remain only as accidental mites in one very tiny, uninteresting and undistinguished corner of a spectacular Creation—and external reality dances unaffected before our eyes, ready to be stripped bare and revealed.

Their confidence in this scenario does not seem in the least shaken by the fact that their entire structure is based solely on interpretation of the electromagnetic radiation streaming down on us.

Is their confidence justified?

To erect their edifice they have to *project* Earthly Law out into the great *out there,* and *ignore* the Law of interaction which seems to rule everywhere. This seems highly arbitrary and selective of them. Is such selectivity justified?

Consider these possibilities:

1. That in interacting with cosmic radiation, we on Earth *cause* a red shift in the spectral patterns, that this red shift is *not* caused by our motion or the motion of the light source, but is produced by us in an entirely different fashion.

2. That when we set up experiments to measure the speed of light, we are not determining any objectively valid speed for light. No matter how precise and careful we are, or become, we will never determine any objectively valid speed for light. All we do—all we are able to do—all we will ever be able to do—*is measure our ability to interact with light.*

Sweeping aside the unproved assumptions upon which the Scientists have built their universe, and substituting these two possibilities as a base, which kind of universe can we construct?

5

INTERACTION

Does Consciousness Warp Space-Time?

> *Cogito, ergo sum.*
> I think, therefore I am.
>   Rene Descartes (1596-1650)

    Primitive man gazed up at the night sky and used his common sense to arrive at an intelligent explanation of what he saw. The sky was a great revolving vault bedecked with tiny flecks of fire. These tiny flecks of fire, the visible stars, remained sensibly fixed in place as the vault revolved daily around the Earth except for the five rebellious ones, named Planets (Wanderers) by the Greeks in recognition of their wandering ways.

    This model of the universe has of course fallen into total disrepute in the civilized, western world. There is overwhelming evidence that the Earth along with the other Planets revolves around the Sun and that the fixed stars are external to this Sun-Planet system.

    There is also rather convincing evidence that on the third wanderer out from the Sun, on the Planet Earth, there is life which has consciousness, life which *thinks*.

    According to Einstein's relativity theory, mass warps space-time.

    What about consciousness? How does it interact with space-time? Does it also cause warpage?

There is a widespread notion abroad in the land that if one person stares intently at the back of another, in time the staree will respond by glancing around at the starer.

Is this superstition or fact?

Many of us have had the experience often enough that, even if we're not sure it's immutable fact, we tend to think it has some substance to it.

In the book *The Original Sin, A Self-Portrait,* Anthony Quinn's absorbing autobiography (Little, Brown and Company, Boston, Toronto: 1972), Quinn writes of one important encounter, "...I felt someone's eyes on my neck." Few reading this will quibble or scoff, as most of us at one time or another have "felt" someone's eyes on us.

With which of our senses do we accomplish this *feeling?*

How do we know we are being gazed at? Is it through thought transference—telepathy—however that may work? If it is the transference of thought, if we are picking up interest in the mind of the one staring at us, does this transferred thought travel through the air as sound waves do? Do thought waves disturb the peace of the air around us and in this way gain our attention? Or does thought cause a subtle temperature change in the air as it passes through, raising it or lowering it?

Possibly this starer-staree interaction, if/when it occurs, involves something other than thought transference or subtle disturbance of the air. Does the eye in observing an object send out a ray of some kind which connects it with the object under observation, a la the evil eye of cartoon fame? If it does, how exactly does this connecting ray affect the person or object under scrutiny? What precisely is the interaction, if any, between observer and observed?

Years ago when I was in college my friends and I learned a psychic parlor trick. We took ten ordinary playing cards and placed them in a row, face down, on any suitable surface. Then one of us left the room. Those remaining, without disturbing the lay of the cards or even touching them, picked one of the cards. The one who had left returned. She stood before the row of cards, running her hand slowly over them, first one way, then the other, a few inches above them, while the rest of us mentally concentrated on the card we had picked. Our mental concentration was supposed to cause the hand moving slowly above the cards to dip preceptibly over the card upon which we were concentrating. The dip inevitably resulted, alerting the one moving her hand as to which card was the chosen one. The trick worked to perfection every time we attempted it.

How did our thoughts accomplish this, getting a hand to dip precisely where we wanted it to dip?

Until we know with greater certainty how thought works, and the precise interaction between observer and observed, surely no valid external universe can be erected on the basis of what Earth observers observe.

In our study of how thought works, we must take into consideration the transference of thought, for incidents of telepathy *do* occur. Let any Scientist who doubts this gather together one hundred people selected at random and initiate a conversation on the psychic. The chances are overwhelming that at least one member of the group will relate some experience not explicable on the basis of the five universally accepted senses. Reduce the number of participants from a hundred to a dozen randomly selected people and the chances remain good that incidents of telepathy, clairvoyance, accurate psychic prognostication, or out of the body experiences will be elicited. Paranormal phenomena occur and in recent years have even gained a modicum of academic respectability as reputable Scientists turn their attention to investigation of them.

The majority of Scientists, however, still withhold their Scientific Seal of Approval on the paranormal, often on the basis that such events are not reproducible at will in the laboratory, therefore remain unproven. This is a specious argument. Many phenomena accepted by Science are not reproducible at will in laboratories or observatories, solar and lunar eclipses, for example, or the return of known comets. Scientists cannot bring these occurrences about but must wait for them to happen; they occur only when circumstances are right for them. They *are* predictable, though not reproducible at will. In the same way, psychic events, though not repeatable at will, are nevertheless reasonably predictable. When circumstances are right—usually stress conditions of great pain, fear, danger or death—the phenomena occur, as thousands of people will attest. Laymen as a rule are courteous where Science is concerned and will accept the word of Scientists as to many workings in the universe. Many Scientists, sadly enough, do not return the courtesy. Because they themselves, for one reason or another, are often cut off from such experiences, they take a hard line and refuse to believe they occur at all. For myself, I have to accept on faith many claims put forth by Science as I have no way of testing experimentally for myself. I do not have to take on faith the occurrence of psychic phenomena, for I have personally experienced such phenomena, as have thousands to millions of others.

Unfortunately, Scientists tend to discount the word of laymen in a fashion that laymen do not discount the word of Scientists, which may be injurious in both directions. The world might conceivably be far better off if laymen believed less of what Science claims, and Scientists paid more attention to what laymen affirm.

For centuries the Christian Church was the primary power in the western world. When the first scientific stirrings threatened its position, it fought back by closing its eyes, its ears, and its mind, damning out of hand anything which failed to agree with dogma.

For the past three centuries, Science has been the religion of choice for many in the western world, and now that new rumblings are running counter to some of its teachings, many of its adherents are reacting, naturally enough, as entrenched power often does: by closing eyes, ears and minds and damning out of hand anything which fails to agree with its dogmatic assertions. As new winds sweep across the land, as more and more interest is expressed in the paranormal, as psychic phenomena become every day more a shared experience, the power structure of Science ridicules, denounces and does its best to excommunicate those who are straying from the strict religious canon laid down by the Learned Ones.

> ... 'tis true, 'tis pity.
> And pity 'tis 'tis true.
> Hamlet

Telepathy is defined in my dictionary as "communication between minds by some means other than sensory perception." This communication has been shown to occur, under strict laboratory conditions, by more than one scientific investigator. Out in the wide world, under non laboratory conditions, it seems to occur unhampered by scientific incredulity, distance or weather conditions. A common type of telepathetic communication occurs between two people emotionally bound together but spatially separated. One is gravely injured or killed and at a moment roughly approximate in time the other suddenly knows of the injury or death, on occasion even waking abruptly out of a sound sleep aware of the distant disaster. This type of experience has been reported so often that only die-hards with closed minds who refuse to review the evidence deny that it happens.

When this type of thing happens, how close in time are the two spatially separated events, the sending of the message and its reception? In the relativistic universe the Scientists say we live in, nothing travels faster than the speed of light. What of the speed of thought? Not the speed of electric impulses as they occur within a given brain, where mental activity is tied to the physical in some as yet little understood way, but the transmission of thought through the air from one mind to another? Is there such a thing as instantaneous knowledge of distant events? The people involved seem to feel that telepathetic knowledge was gained simultaneously with the happening—timepieces tend to bear this out—but the transmission may seem instantaneous simply because thought travels at an incredibly high speed, in the same way that it was assumed for centuries that the speed of light was infinite because no way to clock its speed had yet been developed.

If thought does travel—if this is how telepathy occurs—at what speed does it travel? Slower than the speed of light? Faster than the speed of light? Or at the same speed as light?

Surely these questions should be resolved before any attempt is made to build a valid external universe. In the universe currently set before us by the Cosmologists, the fastest speed possible is the speed of light, and, according to relativistic calculations, any particle which reaches this speed will have no length but infinite mass. If thought travels, is it subject to these rules? If it reaches the speed of light, does it have no length yet infinite mass? If so, what does this mean? The photon, the quantum of light, traveling at the speed of light is massless. Is thought massless too? If thought and light are both massless and both travel at the speed of light—characteristics which are not common in our material universe—what other characteristics do they share?

Our current scientific universe is built upon the electromagnetic radiations which reach us from *out there,* primarily on visible light. If thought and light share unique characteristics, or uniquely share characteristics not shared with other known phenomena, possibly we should try constructing a universe on thought rather than on light and see what we come up with.

Possibly the two universes would be identical, for conceivably the universe we now think we live in has been constructed more on thought than on light.

If telepathetic communication is not achieved through the traveling of thought, then we have a truly unique phenomenon. If a given thought can just pop up in the appropriate mind at the appropriate time without having traveled from a sending mind, what does this say aobut the universe we live in? For over two centuries after Isaac Newton promulgated the Law of Universal Gravitation, it was begrudgingly accepted that gravitation was a force acting at a distance, as distasteful as this concept was, but at least this force acting at a distance did so without discrimination. All bodies attracted all other bodies, without known exception. But mental telepathy doesn't seem to work that way. Thoughts either travel to, or spontaneously combust in, *receptive* minds only, not to or in every mind in the neighborhood. Emotional bonds often seem to be the crucial element in receptivity. A mother suddenly wakes from sleep and *knows* her son has been captured in battle; it later turns out that her sleep was disrupted with this disheartening awareness at almost the exact time the capture occurred. Other residents on the street continued to sleep unaffected. How did the telepathetic communication know into which mind it should pop?

Whether thought travels from one mind to another or simply exists everywhere, ready to be picked up by those sufficiently interested, it remains a pretty unique phenomenon.

Through human thought Scientists have constructed a universe, yet until we know the rules that thought itself obeys, how can we possibly hope to build a valid external world? If we don't know the whys and wherefores of our primary instrument—thought—how can we begin to know the tricks it may play on us as we build? At the very least, a cautious, open minded approach would seem to be in order. Otherwise we may find ourselves caught under a toppling universe.

Prior to the beginning of the 20th Century, Scientists had formulated two laws of conservation, which they then proved to their own satisfaction: the Law of the Conservation of Energy, and the Law of the Conservation of Matter. Energy could change form in numerous ways, but throughout the changes the amount of energy remained unchanged. The same with matter. Regardless of what chemical or other changes were wrought on matter, the amount of matter remained unchanged. Neither energy nor matter could be created or destroyed. Both operated under the immutable Law of Conservation.

In our century Einstein theorized that mass and energy were convertible and gave us his famous equation, $E = MC^2$ (Energy equals Mass times the Speed of Light Squared), which has since proved out to the satisfaction of nuclear physicists and to the current sorrow of mankind. With convertibility proved, the two conservation laws were wedded into one: the Law of Conservation of Mass-Energy. Mass can be converted into energy and energy into mass, but the sum total of mass-energy in any system, while it can undergo all kinds of changes, can't be created or destroyed and is always conserved.

What about consciousness? What about thought? Isn't it time now to turn our attention to postulating a Law regarding the Conservation of Thought?

Consciousness exists. Thought exists. Man *thinks*. In fact, consciousness is so basic to our existence that in current medical practice one primary test for whether we are alive or dead has to with how our brain is doing. If we are brain dead, we are really and truly dead, according to the medical and legal criteria of our age.

Throughout our lives consciousness churns out thought. Awake we think, asleep we dream. If these thoughts are created out of nothing and dissolve away into nothing, then thought has got to be the most powerful, the most unique phenomenon on the face of this Earth. All that we know of in Nature is subject to Laws of conservation, and if man's consciousness isn't, if thoughts can rise and fall from nothing into nothing, that is truly unnatural and miraculous. If that's the story of thought, it makes miracle workers and gods of us all.

But, the objection will surely follow, thoughts *don't* arise out of nothing. Stimulus, internal or external, causes thought. It is all a natural physiological process, one that is increasingly understood. Chemical and electrical happenings in the brain trigger images, memories, musings, feelings, and all the other stuff of consciousness. Thought does not arise out of nothing, it arises from the natural working of a non-dead brain.

All right. But what happens to thought once it is thought? Telepathic communication would indicate that some thoughts at least have what appears to be an independent existence. Such thoughts either travel to receptive minds or permeate the air in such a way that properly motivated brains can snatch them therefrom. In laboratory studies the thoughts communicated aren't even of a high order of importance, are rarely weighted emotionally. Yet even these thoughts appear to have a life of their own, in the sense they seem capable of leaving one mind and traveling to, or in some other fashion occurring to, another.

If we deny independent life to thought, we will find ourselves up against a perplexing situation. We would then have to postulate that Brain B, the receptive brain, has somehow, across a distance, managed to merge in such a way with Brain A that the stimulus causing thought in A also causes it in B. While this may be what happens, it is so blatantly in opposition to all current understanding of matter and space that it's perhaps better to allow thought a bit of independent life.

If thought has an independent life, how long a life does it have? Possibly the life is only for the 10^{-31} seconds of existence attributed to some subatomic particles, but some extension in time must be granted unless we allow tremendous extension in space, for it takes one or the other to explain how Brain B gets hold of it.

If we decide to grant the time extension, what happens once the 10^{-31} seconds is over? Does thought then dissolve into nothingness in a miraculous victory over conservation? If all mass-energy has to obey the Law of Conservation, and thought alone is exempt, what a miraculous thing is thought. It would almost seem easier to allow the thought continued life.

If we grant thought an independent reality—loose it from the physical brain which gave it birth—what if anything can we say about it? What is thought? Is it a subtle form of energy? A fine form of matter? A so far invisible form of mass-energy? Shouldn't it—doesn't it—have a Law of Conservation like everything else?

If thought travels, does it, like light, travel in all directions? Does it travel at different speeds through different mediums? Is it capable of escaping from the atmosphere of the Earth? The atmosphere itself is capable of escaping—hydrogen atoms escape—and when the atoms of the atmosphere escape, do they take thought with them?

If thought doesn't travel but simply has sufficient extension in space to be plucked out of the air by those interested in plucking, in what way does this permeation of our atmosphere by thought affect our instruments? our measurements? the universe we mentally construct?

Man has lived with consciousness all his long life on Earth, yet we still don't know what thought is, whether it is a particular form of mass-energy, or the rules under which it operates if it is. We know thought exists. In fact we have far greater evidence for the existence of thought than for the existence of the stars or subatomic particles. Interaction seems to be the basic law of the universe. So how does thought—how does consciousness—interact with everything about it?

Does consciousness—like other forms of mass-energy—warp space-time?

Many of us have had some experience with the confusing power mind exhibits on occasion over external objects or with regard to distant events. Even more of us have probably experienced the occasional irritating impotence of intent thought directed at the mind itself.

Surely this is a common happening: we are traveling merrily along on a certain train of thought, then, for some exasperating reason, we become derailed. A familiar name or number refuses to rise into consciousness. We have blanked out on it. No matter how we struggle, ordering our mind to disgorge the information we seek, we can't remember. The harder we concentrate, the more abject our failure. Finally, in defeat, we drop the effort, and some time later, after our mind has relaxed sufficiently, has wandered off into fresh, green pastures, lo, the name or number we had earlier sought in vain suddenly pops up.

In all fields of creative endeavor, whether artistic or scientific, people of renown have reported much this same kind of experience. After the consciousness has been seeded by days, months or years of intensive study, with little advance achieved, suddenly when the mind is at rest or freshly awake from sleep, there will be a gigantic leap forward, an exciting, intuitive insight—the light will break through.

On other occasions the breakthrough seems to occur while the conscious mind is asleep.

This story is told about Elias Howe (1819-1867), American inventor of the sewing machine:

For years Howe had tried to perfect a machine that would sew, without success. Then one night he had this dream: he had been captured by a primitive tribe. The tribe would spear him to death within twenty-four hours if he didn't come up with a machine that would sew. In the dream he struggled desperately for a solution, but none came. All too soon his time was up and the warriors surrounded him with upraised spears, ready to carry through their sentence and spear him to death. At this point Howe woke up, leaped out of bed and hurried to his laboratory. In his dream the spears of the warriors had had eye-shaped holes at their points. This was the answer he had sought for so long in vain: the hole in his needle had to be at the tip, not at the top or middle. With this kind of needle, his machine would sew.

My older son had this experience. When he was a freshman in college he and his roommate became ardent devotees of bridge. A problem was put before them. The cards were distributed into four designated hands. There was a way, they were told, that the hand winning the bid could take all thirteen tricks without the opposition hands committing any error. How was it done? The two young men set up the hands and for two to three hours struggled to find the answer, without success. Eventually they gave up, went to bed, and fell asleep. Around five my son woke suddenly, thinking excitedly, "I've got it!" He bounded out of bed, returned to the card table, set up the problem and proved to himself he had solved it. The answer that he couldn't find while awake was achieved with apparent ease while he slept.

This type of experience is not uncommon. Few of us doubt the wisdom of the advice: sleep on it. A problem may seem insoluble as we grapple with it in daylight and into the evening, then off to bed we go, fall into sleep, and when we wake in the morning the solution is there. The problem has solved itself in our sleep. It is almost as though, at times, we must push thought aside, fall into sleep or lull our minds into a semi-drowsy state for the light to break through.

To rephrase this centuries long experience of Man: the stream of conscious thought seems, at times, to block out or slow down the breakthrough of awareness, the coming in of the light.

Current scientific estimates place the age of our Sun and the rest of the Solar System at about five billion years. Life began sometime after that, with the emergence of Man placed at something like a million years ago. When in time consciousness arrived would depend on some as yet undetermined factors, such as whether consciousness can only exist in some form of life, and if so, at what point in the evolution of life consciousness can first be said to appear. In any case, once *Homo* arrived, thought was here. This means that, according to the time table of the Scientists, thought has been generated on our planet for around, or at least, one million years.

What has happened to all this thought?

Is the first thought ever thought still circulating somewhere, in accordance with an as yet undiscovered, not yet formulated Law of the Conservation of Thought? Or do thoughts, like radium, disintegrate with time? Disintegrating into what? Do thoughts, like many subatomic particles, decay in split-split fractions of seconds? If so, what do such thoughts decay into? Does one thought decay into another thought in a never ending chain? Is that how the Law of the Conservation of Thought works?

Human memory indicates that the brain acts not only as a generator of new thought but as a storage bin for used thoughts. Does the brain store every thought we've ever had, no matter how trivial? Experiments with hypnotized subjects indicate that the brain retains a great deal of information in storage areas not easily accessible to ordinary memory. Are these stored up, forgotten thoughts so securely tied to the physical brain which warehouses them that they can never go aroving? Or can they too, like fresh new thought, travel out into the world to be picked up by receptive minds? If old thoughts, like new ones, have independent life and can travel, when does this process end? With the death of the physical brain which stores the used thought? Or, possibly, does the death of the physical brain release upon the world all its stored up thoughts, as crumblng prison walls might release a flood of prisoners? Trend setting ideas are frequently said to be "in the air" during periods of social change. Is this literally true? If so, does the flooding of the air come from thoughts released at death or does it come from live brains? When certain thoughts are "in the air," how does this affect us, the living? How does it affect the non living environment? Does the effect travel outward to affect the rest of the Solar System?

How are we to know how thought interacts with the rest of the Creation until we become more knowledgeable as to how thought itself works?

According to the scientific script, our home planet, the Earth, has been revolving around our Mother Sun for about five billion years. During the last one million years of that time, if not for far longer, consciousness has existed, in *Homo* if nowhere else. This means that with each revolution around the Sun, not only has our hard little rock of a planet—the densest matter in the Solar System—made the journey, so has an uncounted amount of mysteriously behaving thought. Do we travel through space leaving trails of thought behind us? Does thought, escaping from the brain which gave birth to it, travel out in waves, wave after wave after wave, so that we are in effect seeding the entire inner and outer Solar System with consciousness?

Is the Solar System unique in that it alone is with life?

Here in the United States during the second half of the 20th Century, most of us have had some experience with, or have heard of, either from friends or in some entertainment work, the flyspeck-town-as-speed-trap. A motorist rolls smoothly down the highway at top legal speed, fails to note the posted sign that tells her she is now entering the outskirts of Nowheresville, and the first thing she knows she hears a siren, a police officer pulls her over, and she is ticketed for exceeding the twenty-five mile per hour limit allowed on the main street of Nowheresville. Either our motorist pungles up a goodly sum of cash or she spends the rest of the day and that night in the Nowheresville slammer.

Whether or not this is more legend than fact, the notion that it could and does happen is abroad in our land. According to popular belief, speed traps *do* exist.

A possibility that we of this century should consider:

That the Solar System, heavy with life, permeated with thought, with consciousness, is similar in nature to a speed trap in that once radiation enters the perimeters of our System, local Law forces an immediate slowdown.

In individual experience, intent thought often blocks out awareness: we can't remember something known to us, no matter how hard we concentrate. Drop the attempt to remember, however, and awareness will often break through.

In somewhat similar fashion, we can, while asleep, often solve problems which baffle us while we're awake, as though conscious thought blocks out or slows down the coming in of the light.

What if this ability to block out or slow down awareness or light is an innate property of thought?

We have been spewing thought out into our System for a million years or more. If by any chance this huge build up of accumulated thought slows light down as it enters our System, the Learned Ones of our time will have to go back to the drawing board to construct a whole new universe.

HYPOTHESIS:

Out there beyond our System—if any such *out there* truly exists—light does not travel at the speeds at which it has been clocked on Earth. Rather, *out there* light does not travel at all; it simply *is*, everywhere—and nowhere—at once. The star light we seem to see is simply glimpses we get of this all encompassing light surrounding us through rents or tears in the thick, almost impenetrable cloud of accumulated thought in which we live.

Apart from our Sun, stars as such don't truly exist, nor do galaxies. Tears in the thought-cloud do, however, offering guidance to us, reminding us that there is a region which is composed of pure light.

The red shift in spectra is caused by heavy, thick, angry-red thoughts overabundantly generated throughout the centuries. If and when consciousness rises to a higher energy level, to where most thoughts are lighter and finer, there will be a corresponding shift away from the red.

****

Light, we are told, travels at the approximate speed of 186,200 miles per second.

For this statement to have any meaning, miles have to exist, and seconds have to exist, for speed measures motion through space in a given time. Do away with either space or time, and the notion of speed dissolves away.

There is little in this to cause concern, for we all live in space and time and know that they exist. Space surrounds us, time runs through us. Only if our thoughts deceive us can there be any question about the reality of space and time.

But apparently we are deceived, at least a little, by our minds, for Einstein tells us—and Scientists claim that both mathematically and observationally he has been proved right—that we don't live in three dimensions of space and one dimension of time, as our perceptions tell us; rather we live in a four dimensional space-time. However, we'd have to go whizzing through space at close to the speed of light for this to matter. As we plod away our lives here on the surface of the Earth, we needn't be troubled by the sophistication of the space-time continuum we are said truly to live in.

Time is still considered to be unidirectional, for all practical purposes, certainly as it manifests itself in the macroscopic world, the world of the visible. Ever since time began, it has moved forward, never backward—The Arrow of Time, as the distinguished English astronomer and physicist Arthur Eddington (1882-1944) phrased it. Unidimensional. Moving in one direction only.

Currently, in the subatomic world, in the world of quantum mechanics, things are getting rather hectic, in some experiments it is impossible to tell whether some particle is coming into being or is decaying into something else, is being born or is dying, but up on the gross level of the macroscopic world where most of us live, we know perfectly well that time moves in one direction only: forward. The past is behind us, the present is now, the future is on its way to us.

But what of prophetic dreams which have been occurring at least since the dawn of recorded history?

J. W. Dunne in his book *An Experiment with Time* (The Macmillan Company, New York: 1927) relates various dreams he has had which seem to be stimulated by, and to deal with, events of which he becomes aware subsequent to the dream. To test whether this could possibly be a natural aspect of dreaming, Dunne enlisted volunteers who wrote down their dreams each morning upon awakening. These dreams were then compared with the day to day life of the subjects, and it was found that people do indeed weave very ordinary dreams around external stimuli which they have not yet experienced but will experience in a time that is in the future when the dream is dreamed. The younger the subjects, the more they tended to weave their dreams about stimuli not yet encountered rather than around the dead stimuli of their yesterdays.

How does this fit in with our common experience of the unidimensional flow of time, from past to present to future? How do we manage, in our dream state, to react to what has not yet happened to us in our waking state? Is time quite the stiff, unbending, swiftly flying in one direction Arrow we ordinarily accept it as being?

There are not only prophetic dreams, there are psychic predictions, too may of which have proved to be accurate for the phenomenon to be dismissed. If I can know on a Monday what is going to happen on a Wednesday, I am not quite helplessly strapped onto the Arrow of Time, unable to move except as it moves. If I can know that a sudden, unexpected death is going to occur very soon, and it does occur, I am doing something more than swimming along in the Now instant of time.

Prophetic dreams and psychic premonitions, which are the common stuff of experience, both indicate that at least some aspect of our consciousness, on occasion at least, is free of the ordinary restrictions of time.

What does this say of the mind and of time?

Clairvoyance as a phenomenon has also been well established. Some people can perceive objects and actions taking place in a distant space, through some means other than by relying on the so-called normal sensory apparatus. For such people, some aspect of their consciousness is apparently free of the ordinary restrictions of spatial positioning.

What does this say of the mind and of space?

Until we can explain how the mind, under any and all circumstances, interacts with space and with time, how can we say with any certainty what space and time are?

In the 18th Century a German philosopher Immanuel Kant, (1724-1804), after analyzing the process by which stimuli flooding the mind pass into knowledge, postulated that time and space are not external realities but are forms of perception, *a priori* intuitions of the mind existing prior to and independent of experience. In order to make sense out of sensation, Kant wrote, the mind imposes order upon experience through a sense of space and a sense of time. Time and space, devoid of external reality, are simply organizational aspects of mind, filing cabinets used to sort out the flood of incoming material so that the mind can get a knowledgeable grip on things. Without an organizing system of some kind, the mind would drown in a chaotic ocean of sensation, making no sense out of anything.

As most of us have heard though some of us may not wish to deal with it, some minds escape the limitations imposed by time. Some minds escape the limitations imposed by space. These escapees lend credence to Kant's contention that time and space are not external realities but *a priori* intuitions of mind, for if time were what it seems to be, an inexorable march forward in which we are caught and held in an ever renewed present, how do some minds break out of lockstep to soar into the future? If space is an external reality in which we have position, how do some escape this position to go roaming? If time and space aren't external reality at all but are instead organizational aspects of mind, limitations adopted for the benefit of mind, it seems reasonable that on occasion some minds can and do throw off these self imposed limitations to roam at will.

Presented with a magnificent painting, we must back off from it in order to view it whole, to get the overall effect. If we move in close, we must perforce view it in tiny sections, a bit at a time. Conscious life may be a process of moving in for inspection, space and time the necessary limitations we accept in order to get in close, to savor detail while sacrificing perception of the whole.

If time and space are by any chance simply organizational aspects of mind, the concept of speed becomes meaningless. Cast doubt on the accepted value for the speed of light—on the behavior of light through space and in time—and the entire universe of the Cosmologists begins to wobble. To build on uncertainty is to build on Jello, but that is what most of the Learned Ones have done. Psychic phenemona do not fit into their preconceived framework so they exclude them. Mind is elusive and little understood, so why deal with that either? Take what's easy, and easily measured—like the speed of light—and build a fantasy world.

Constructing a universe without taking consciousness into account is like fashioning a human being and deciding that, since mind is a puzzlement, don't struggle to incorporate it, just toss it aside. But how complete is Man without mind?

Two, five or ten centuries from now it may be said of us that while we were acute in many of our observations and excelled in our mathematical analysis, we had not yet solved the puzzle of consciousness, therefore failed to include in our calculations new and used thought in all its manifestations, which unfortunately rendered our calculations meaningless. While we were extremely bright—it may be said of us—we were at the same time too naive, and too outwardly directed to understand the power of thought to create its own world.

Let's put mind back into Man, consciousness, with all her baffling, wanton ways, back into the Creation, and take a closer look at the universe we live in.

6

FUN HOUSE MIRROR

*Do We Quake in Fear or Bow Down in Awe
Before Our Own Shadow?*

> Science does not know its debt to
> imagination.
> Ralph Waldo Emerson
> (1803-1882)

If thought is a form of mass-energy—and if it isn't that, what is it?—then consciousness, as a form of mass-energy, like any other form of mass-energy must warp space-time.
In what way does consciousness warp space-time?

A physical body in motion casting a shadow could be said to warp the shadow. As the body moves, altering the way in which it intercepts light, the shadow changes, is bent or twisted out of its original shape, ie, is warped.
If space and time, as Kant postulated, have no objective reality but are simply human modes of perception, then the material universe may be nothing more than a projection of consciousness, undergoing changes as human awareness changes.
Consider this:
Until a century ago the universe placed before us by the Learned Ones was a relatively small one. The gigantic explosion of the universe began right as Man, after the birth of modern spiritualism and the teachings of Freud, Jung and

others, became aware of the vastness of his untapped consciousness.

The universe within us, the universe around us: our growing awareness of one coincided with our growing awareness of the other.

Beware of coincidences, the Scientists warn us.

Is there any way this coincidence can be abolished, exposed as natural and necessary rather than as an unlikely chance happening?

"... there is a resonance between the way we think and the way the world works..." Carl Sagan reminds us in *Cosmos*.

Is there any way to prove that this resonance is not a curious happenstance but is the fundamental truth underlying all Creation?

Possibly.

We might start from this premise:

HYPOTHESIS:

The material universe exists as a reflection—a projection—a shadow—an echo—of consciousness.

****

Formulating such an hypothesis is easy enough, but is there any way to go about proving or substantiating it?

The *out there* and the deep *in here* remain, at this pont in our history, relatively beyond our grasp. We cannot yet travel to the great *out there,* if it exists, to check our theories, and as we attempt to travel to the deep *in here*, we are frustrated by size: we and our instruments are simply too big for the subatomic world. At best we can only peer at tracks left in clouds or bubbles and from this postulate a quantum world, much as the ancient Romans studied the entrails of dead chickens to discover the truth of their world. Operating under such limitations, it is difficult to prove anything about the great *out there* or the incredibly small, deep *in here.*

For this reason, let us ignore for now the unexplored depths—in both directions—and turn our attention to natural

Laws right under our noses, and from these natural Laws attempt to detect the shadowy nature of Nature. If the natural Laws operating here on Earth speak to the human condition, are translations of the physical/emotional Laws of human nature, are a fun house mirror version of what human life is all about, then educated guesses can be made about the great *out there* and the deep *in here*. If the Nature we can observe and pin down into natural Law turns out to be of a shadowy turn of mind, we can perhaps stipulate that the Nature we can only guess at partakes of this nature.

". . . there is a resonance . . ."

Let's clear away the worst debris between our ears and see if we can tune in to this resonance.

Where to start?

Life as we know it is a cooperative affair, both within a given body and between different bodies.

Cooperative: "1. working or acting together willingly for a common purpose."

Life on Earth began, we are told, as simple molecules combined into ever more complex forms. Plants developed tiny factories for photosynthesis, ie, the conversion of sunlight, oxygen and carbon dioxide into carbohydrates and oxygen, and in this way, working cooperatively, changed the environment of the Earth to where tiny animal organisms could survive.

As life grew ever more complex, cooperation remained the key element for survival. In human life, egg and sperm unite in cooperative activity to spark the new life. The mother's body cooperates in the growth of the fetus. Within the growing organism, cooperation must occur or growth and life cease. If the blood vessels don't cooperate with the heart, if the lungs don't cooperate with the nose and trachea, if the stomach, liver and intestines don't cooperate, disaster is certain. For a healthy body to remain healthy, all systems must work together for the common good. United they stand, divided they fall.

Early man survived where numerous other species fell by the wayside because man's increasingly complex brain gave him this advantage: he could communicate with his fellows in such a way that he became a master at cooperative activity. Where one lone hunter stood little chance against wild game, a band of hunters could outwit animals that were fiercer or fleeter. Settlements were established, based on farming, and cooperative activity became more than ever the way of life. As communities became ever more complex, specialization set in, and with the rise of specialization the need for cooperation became ever more imperative.

In our western society of the late 20th century, specialization is well established. Many of us who regularly eat three square meals a day have never planted a vegetable seed nor watered growing plants, pruned fruit trees or milked a cow, gathered eggs, wrung a chicken's neck, gone deep sea fishing, fattened a steer for market, or slaughtered a pig. We stay healthy and fit by the grace of those who do these things. In our highly specialized society, cooperative activity has been honed to a high state of art.

As far as we know, those forms of matter which we think of as inanimate do not cooperate in lifelike fashion. Two stones of different sex do not cooperate to produce little stones, which they then nurture until the day that Papa Stone can take Daughter off to fish while Mama Stone and Son stay home to straighten up and sweep out their immediate environment. Not only between pieces of inanimate matter but also within any given bit of inanimate matter, lifelike cooperation seems to be absent. From our admittedly biased and limited viewpoint, cooperation seems to be the way of life, and not the way of materialized non-life.

A primary distinction between life and non life: cooperative activity.

This cooperative activity has not been seen as an active force on life's evolutionary path, it must be conceded. It does not at all figure in in the Darwinian scheme of things.

Evolution as an idea had been kicking around for centuries before the advent of Charles Darwin, in fact almost since the dawn of history. (*Evolution: "Biol.* the continuous genetic adaptation of organisms or species to the environment by the integrating agencies of selection, hybridization, inbreeding and mutation.") Philosophers explained the great variety of plant and animal life by offering natural ways they could have developed: environmental conditions caused life forms to change. A French naturalist, George Louis Le-clerc, Comte de Buffon (1707-1788), published a thirty-six volume *Natural History* in which he wrote that modern animals had evolved from earlier ones, this process going clear back to the beginning. French naturalist Jean Baptiste de Monet de Lamarck (1744-1829) theorized that life forms progressed from simpler to more complex forms due to an inborn tendency to do so. Environment played a part in modifying this progression, as did habit, the habitual use or disuse of parts; and adaptations to the environment could be inherited.

English naturalist Charles Darwin (1809-1882) was acquainted with the various attempts to explain evolution. His own grandfather, Erasmus Darwin (1731-1802), had written several books on the subject. Young Charles felt that these various naturalists had theorized too much without backing up their theories with facts. On December 27, 1831, he sailed from England as an unpaid naturalist on the exploring ship *Beagle,* and for the next five years, as the *Beagle* sailed down the southern coast of South America, making numerous side trips on land, Darwin studied geologic formations, collected fossils, and took careful note of the animal and plant life before him. After his return to England, he continued to collect facts and to study them. In 1859, over twenty years after his historic trip on the *Beagle,* he published his monumental work, *On the Origin of Species by Means of Natural Selection,* and Darwinism was born.

Darwinism: "the Darwinian theory that the origin of species is derived by descent, with variation, from parent forms, through the natural selection of those best adapted to survive in the struggle for existence."

In Darwinism there is a great deal of competitive struggle, with the fittest edging out the less fit, and precious little cooperation.

Origin of Species, establishing evolution on a sound factual basis, swept through the scientific world, winning the minds of almost everyone.

Today the establishment theory is neo-Darwinism, a synthesis of Darwinian theory with genetic theory which occurred during the first half of this century. (*Neo-Darwinisim: "Biol.* the theory of evolution as expounded by later students of Charles Darwin, who hold that natural selection accounts for evolution and deny the inheritance of acquired characters.")

In neo-Darwinism there is still plenty of struggle with little cooperation. All creatures compete, and those that are fittest win the competition and survive. Reproduction by these fit ones passes along winning characteristics, as evolution takes life ever upward into greater and greater adaptabiilty. Man now stands at the apex, the most adaptable of creatures, ruler of land, sea and sky, having evolved not along a cooperative pathway but along a fiercely competitive one.

So much for life as a cooperative activity, insofar as life's past history goes.

While neo-Darwinism still holds sway among the majority of biologists, in recent years leaks have appeared in the evolutionary vessel. Fossil evidence does not support the notion of gradual evolution. Species appear and then die out, with little observable change between first appearance and eventual disappearance. Links between species are missing. Some species seem to appear suddenly, popping into existence. The fossil evidence suggests that our species, *Homo sapiens,* popped into existence amid several other man-like creatures, with no gradual sequence. Other hominids (*hominid: "Anthropol.* a member of the *Hominidae,* the family of man and his ancestors.") seem to have been parallel evolutions, not ancestral lines. There are indications that evolution takes place with discontinuous jumps, and the idea that the changes which survive increase adaptability doesn't always hold true. Harvard biologist Stephen Jay Gould and his collaborator, paleontologist Niles Eldredge, have formulated a theory which takes into account these sudden, unexplained jumps from one species into another. They call their theory "punctuated equilibrium," the word *equilibrium* used in an effort to explain how species apparently remain unchanged over eons. The Gould-Eldredge theory, however, retains the basic Darwinian belief in intense competition, with no reliance on cooperation.

A more fundamental challenge to neo-Darwinism has been mounted by a versatile, Vienna born scientist with wide ranging interests. Erich Jantsch began his professional career as an astrophysicist, but his interests included music, theater, engineering, business, English poetry. He acted as consultant to a number of national governments, forecasting technological developments.

In the theory he proposed, which he called co-evolution, Jantsch accepts the Darwinian tenet that evolutionary adaptation occurs and agrees that individuals have often had to struggle for survival as Darwin claims, but he denies that this adaptation to competition was the primary driving force on the evolutionary pathway.

In his book *The Self-Organizing Universe: Scientific and Human Implications of the Emerging Paradigm of Evolution* (Oxford: Pergamon Press, 1980), Jantsch wrote:

"The earliest life forms were by far the best adapted. If the meaning of evolution was in adaptation and increasing the chances for survival, as is so often claimed, the development of more complex organisms would have been meaningless or even a mistake."

Bacteria are better adapted for survival than Man, with his great complexity, is.

The evolutionary drive was not fueled by ever greater adaptation to increase chances for survival, Jantsch claims. Rather it was fueled by a drive toward ever greater openness, toward a greater intensification of life, and *the underlying mechanism was not competitive struggle but cooperation.*

Early living and not-quite-living structures cooperated, according to Jantsch, and after the emergence of life, the living cooperated with each other. Bacteria developed into forms capable of photosynthesis, and photosynthetic bacteria then spent two thousand million years transforming the

Earth's atmosphere, pouring into it the free oxygen necessary for the creation of multicellular organisms. The bacteria did not need this free atmospheric oxygen for their own survival; they were already well adapted to an oxygenless environment. But for life to become more open, more complex, more intense, multicellular organisms had to be created and these organisms needed the free oxygen the bacteria were producing. All along the evolutionary pathway, Jantsch claims, all of life is connected through complex feedback mechanisms, cooperation is the key, and the myriad life forms with their individual characteristics which we see all around us did not evolve in response to survival needs but arose spontaneously in the creative, flowing play of the universe.

Jantsch's theory of co-evolution is a new one, a theory which has not yet pushed the established theory of neo-Darwinism off center stage, and the possibility exists that it never will do so. But regardless of whether or not cooperation was an active force along the evolutionary path helping us to arrive where we are today, cooperative activity within our bodies has always been a must and without social cooperation, civilization as we know it would be impossible. On the most basic level, if human bodies of the female persuasion stopped cooperating in the production of new beings, it would be the end not only of civilization but of human life itself.

As living beings we are dependent on cooperative activity.

Cooperative activity leads to specialization, with a distribution of responsibilities. Each specialist then gets his cut of production, ie, shares in results. If a given specialist failed to get his share of production, he would soon rebel, starve to death, or in some fashion fall out of the system. Sharing of results *has* to follow for the specialists to continue specializing.

Both within the human body and within human society, cooperation is a must and leads of necessity to sharing.

To sum up:

Life = cooperative activity.

Cooperative activity = the ability and willingness to share.

Life = the ability and willingness to share.

Chemistry is "the science that deals with or investigates the composition, properties, and transformations of substances and various elementary forms of matter."

There are two major branches of chemistry: organic and inorganic.

Organic chemistry: "the branch of chemistry dealing with the compounds of carbon."

Inorganic chemistry: "the branch of chemistry dealing with inorganic substances."

Inorganic: "1. not having the structure or organization characteristic of living bodies. 2. not characterized by vital processes. 3. *Chem.* noting or pertaining to compounds that are not hydrocarbons or their derivatives."

Carbon: "1. *Chem.* an element that forms organic compounds in combination with hydrogen, oxygen, etc., and that occurs in a pure state as the diamond and as graphite, and in an impure state as charcoal."

Life on the planet Earth is carbon and water based.

Without the element carbon, if life existed at all on Earth it would not be the life we know.

Carbon is found in all living things. Plant and animal tissues are composed of elements grouped around rings or chains of carbon atoms. Carbon is also the source material of all our common fuels: coal, coke, oil, and natural gas.

Carbon (Symbol C, atomic weight 12.011, atomic number 6) has the unique ability to combine into marvelously complex molecules with itself. It combines in forms so different that it has been called the "Dr. Jekyll and Mr. Hyde" of elements. Carbon not only combines with itself, it combines readily with most metals to form compounds known as carbides, with oxygen to form oxides (carbon monoxide, carbon dioxide, and carbon suboxide), and with hydrogen to form a class of compounds known as hydrocarbons. Although carbon accounts for only 0.09 percent by mass of the total of all elements in, on or above the Earth, it has such a uniquely high ability to form bonds with other carbons to build chains, and with other elements, *that it forms more compounds than all other elements combined.*

When elements get together to form compounds, there are two fundamental types of chemical bonding: 1) electrovalent or ionic; 2) covalent.

In electrovalent or ionic bonding, one atom loses electrons to become negatively ionized, while the atom it is bonding with gains electrons to become positively ionized. (*Electrovalent bond, ionic bond:* "the bond formed between two ions through the transfer of electrons." *Ion:* "*Physics, Chem.* an electrically charged atom or group of atoms . . .") The elements with only a few outer energy level electrons (nearly all of the metals) tend to lose them, while elements with a high number of outer energy level electrons (many of the non metals) tend to gain them.

For example, when the element sodium, a metallic element, gets together with chlorine, a nonmetallic, poisonous gas, to form sodium chloride (NaCl), which is ordinary table salt, this is what happens:

Sodium (Symbol Na, atomic weight 22.9898, atomic number 11) has, as the atomic number indicates, 11 protons (positively charged particles) within the nucleus and 11 electrons (negatively charged particles) attached to the nucleus. Two electrons occupy the innermost energy level and eight the second, leaving one lone electron left over in the third energy level.

Chlorine (Symbol Cl, atomic weight 35.453, atomic number 17) has, as the atomic number indicates, 17 protons in its nucleus and 17 electrons roaming around outside. Two of these 17 occupy the innermost energy level, eight the second level, seven the third energy level.

As the third energy level fills at eight electrons, chlorine is minus one electron for completion of this energy level.

Sodium has one electron and only one on this energy level.

When the two elements combine, a shift occurs. Sodium gives up its loner to complete chlorine's unfilled outer energy level. Both become ionized. Sodium still has its 11 protons but now has only ten electrons, leaving it with a plus one charge. Chlorine still has its 17 protons but now has 18

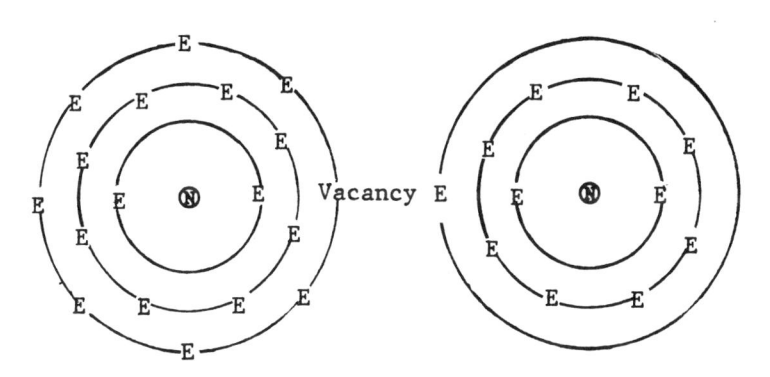

The chlorine atom:
17 protons,
17 electrons;
2 electrons fill the innermost energy level,
8 the second;
7 remain for the third energy level, which fills at 8, leaving 1 vacancy.

The sodium atom:
11 protons,
11 electrons;
2 electrons fill the innermost energy level,
8 the second, leaving 1 over. Sodium gives up 1 electron, ionizing both atoms, forming an ionic bond.

negatively charged electrons, giving it a charge of minus one.

In the electrical world, opposites attract. The positively charged sodium forms an ionic bond—a bond between two ions with opposite charges—with the negatively charged chlorine. A pronounced chemical change occurs. Both sodium and chlorine as non ionized atoms are extremely toxic and dangerously unfit for human consumption, but put them together and they become salt, something we sprinkle on our food and in fact need at least a trace of to keep our bodies functioning properly.

In covalent bonding, the second fundamental type of chemical bonding, electrons are *shared* rather than gained or lost.

For example, when the element hydrogen, a gas, gets together with the element oxygen, also a gas, to form water

(H_2O, two hydrogen atoms, plus one oxygen atom), this is what happens:

Hydrogen, the lightest known element, believed to be the most abundant element in the universe (Symbol H, atomic weight 1.00797, atomic number 1), has, as its atomic number indicates, one positively charged proton in its nucleus and one negatively charged electron attached thereto. The innermost energy level takes two electrons for completion, so hydrogen is one electron short.

Oxygen, a colorless, odorless gas (Symbol O, atomic weight 15.9994, atomic number 8), has, as its number indicates, eight positively charged protons in its nucleus and eight negatively charged electrons swarming around. Two electrons fill the innermost energy level, leaving six for the second energy level—a minus two situation, as it takes eight to fill this level.

When hydrogen and oxygen get together, they do not ionize each other. Neither gains at the expense of the other or gives up anything. Instead they share. Two hydrogen atoms bring one electron each to the bonding, and these two electrons complete oxygen's outer energy level. Meanwhile, each hydrogen atom completes its innermost energy level by sharing an electron brought to the bonding by oxygen. In this manner, two gases form a *covalent* bond to become a liquid essential to life.

Carbon, atomic number six, needs two of its electrons to complete its innermost energy level, but this leaves four electrons over with which to combine with other elements.

With these four valence electrons (*valence: "Chem.* 1. the quality that determines the number of atoms or groups with which any single atom or group will unite chemically. 2. the relative combining capacity of an atom or group compared with the standard hydrogen atom"), carbon forms covalent bonds. It *shares.* In fact, carbon is the greatest little sharer in the world, and the most versatile. It shares itself, combining to form rings or long chains. It combines with both metals and nonmetals, sharing itself. It forms many compounds that exist as *isomers,* molecules that have the same number and kinds of atoms but in different arrangements with different properties. Carbon is so busy sharing itself, in fact, that approximately one million carbon compounds are known, *accounting for about 95 percent of the total number of known compounds.* If carbon weren't the unique and prodigious little sharer that it is, our world wouldn't be recognizable and life as we know it would not exist.

Scientists often use thought experiments—experiments performed mentally using only pencil and paper, logic and math—to prove to their own satisfaction something about how the world works.
Here's a thought problem or challenge:
Mentally construct a life-as-we-know-it-existing-on-a-planet-within-a-Sun-system in which the physical is a reflection, a shadow image of the consciousness existing in the life forms.
Create a physical element fundamental to life which reflects the truths regarding consciousness-in-life.
Understood?
All right, here we go:
For starters, life in its complexity is fundamentally a cooperative affair, with specialization and a distribution of product, ie, sharing.
> To reflect this, the fundamental element upon which life depends will have to be an element which shares.

Consciousness expresses itself in myriad life forms, from ermines to eagles to elephants, from minnows to mice to Man.
> To reflect this, the fundamental element upon which life is based will have to appear in many and diverse forms.

Although life forms abound, in the Solar System as a whole non living material far exceeds in bulk living matter.
> To reflect this, the fundamental element upon which life is based will have to be a relatively rare element quantitatively.

From the viewpoint of Man, life can be lived on numerous moral levels, from the pure brilliance of a saint to the black soot of a Hitler.

        To reflect this, the fundamental element upon which life is based will have to be a master magician, able to disguise itself in startling and confounding ways.

Last but not least, life has vigor; it is energized.

        To reflect this, the fundamental element upon which life is based will have to be an energy source.

Mentally create such an element, base life upon it, and you will have translated into elementary terms what life on the imagined planet is all about. Such an element will be a mirror image of the fundamental truths of consciousness.

After we mentally create this element, to exact specifications, if we compare our creation with known elements, we will find that we have created an element that is already known, one that fits every requirement.

Congratulations to us: we have just created carbon.

Life is a sharing process, both within a given organism and among organisms; carbon shares both with itself and with numerous other elements.

Life appears in myriad forms; carbon forms more compounds than all other elements combined and is known to exist in approximately one million compounds.

Living cells are vastly outnumbered by non living atoms and molecules in our Solar System; carbon accounts for only 0.09 percent by mass of the elements in our immediate Earthly neighborhood.

Moral life can be lived with the hard brilliance of a saint or the black sootiness of a Hitler; carbon in pure crystalline form makes itself into a diamond, in another form it is the black greasy mineral graphite; carbon with impurities gives us the soot and smoke that clogs our cities.

Life has vigor, is energized; carbon is the source material of all our fuels: coal, coke, oil and natural gas.

The facts of life, the facts of carbon: mirror twins.

It might be argued that since life began with carbon's unique ability to share with itself to form rich complex molecules that it *had* to evolve in the manner it did, wholly dependent on the ability to share. How else could it have developed? But such an argument is after the fact, and limiting to that limitless faculty, imagination. Sweep away all preconceived notions and this leaves ample room for speculation as to alternate ways life could have evolved.

Electrovalent or ionic bonding occurs naturally in our world. Atoms are bonded as they gain or lose electrons. This is not a fair atomic give and take, where each gives and each takes. Rather one takes without giving, the other gives without taking. In human society we see this type of behavior all the time: the pillagers and their victims. But life does *not* depend on this type of activity; in fact, few would consider such behavior life enhancing. But life *could* have developed from this type of non-share bonding.

Carbon, or whatever element we substitute for it, could conceivably have been an active little pillager rather than a sharer. Each carbon atom has four valence electrons in its outermost energy level, a level which remains incomplete with fewer than eight. Carbon could have bonded in every direction in ionic fashion, grabbing onto electrons, building itself into complex forms with never a thought of sharing. Stronger carbon atoms could have grabbed electrons away from weaker carbon atoms, bonding in ionic fasion as they built themselves into complex forms. In time one such complex molecule could have stumbled accidentally onto the secret of reproducing itself—in the same manner in which life is believed to have sprung out of the primeval soup—and lo and behold, carbon based life totally divorced from any history of sharing. *But life, once it happened, in order to grow and thrive, would still be dependent on the ability to specialize and the willingness to share.*

In this script, carbon would pillage.

Life, though carbon based, would still have to share.

In their natural workings, *carbon and life would not be mirror twins.*

Another possible script:
Size, strength, endurance, complexity could all conceivably have been acquired through neither pillaging nor sharing but through accretion. (*Accretion:* "an increase by natural growth or by gradual external addition.")

The galaxies, stars, planets and planetary satellites all came into existence, we are told, through accretion. Random motion brought about fluctuations in gas density, atoms moving randomly toward each other until a small cloud formed. If the cloud of matter grew large enough, gravity took over, dispersion was no longer possible, and a galaxy, star, planet or satellite was born.

Life could possibly have formed this way on the surface of the planet Earth, in imitation of the birth process of planets, stars and galaxies. Through random motion, atoms could have accumulated to where gravitational pull held them together. Bouncing along in the primeval soup, this clump of matter would have been subjected to repeated shock waves, ie, ripples in the soup. All manner of elements could have been swept up and held within the gravitational field, then rippling shock waves through the clump could have caused compression, extension, distortion, leading to a "gradually increasing complexity, until one day, quite by accident, a molecule arose that was able to make crude copies of itself, using as building blocks other molecules in the soup." (Carl Sagan, *Cosmos.*) *Voila,* a life form, ready to begin the long trek toward ever greater complexity.

Once life began, however, complexity could be achieved only through cooperative activity, as far as we know or I can imagine. Biological processes demand specialization and specialization requires sharing.

Life conceived in accretion would still grow to maturity through sharing. No mirror reflection here.

With carbon, sharing leads to sharing. Sharing reflects sharing. Mirror twins.

If Nature in its deepest nature is only a shadow—a contention I am expounding and defending on these pages—there have to be a dozen other ways to track down and expose this shadowy nature.

Please fasten your seat belt and grab onto the handrail for the bumpy, unpaved road and hairpin turns ahead.

7

WATER, WATER EVERYWHERE

*Why Are We The Only Ones In The System
With Plenty to Drink?*

> Alone, alone, all, all alone.
> Alone on a wide wide sea!
> "The Rime of the Ancient Mariner"
> Samuel Taylor Coleridge
> (1771-1834)

Life on the planet Earth is water based as well as carbon based.

As we all know from our earliest years, water is essential to life and to health. Indications are that life on Earth began in water. On the average about 65 percent of the human body is water. Every cell in the body contains water. Blood is over 80 percent water, muscle is over 75 percent water, bone is 22 percent water. (Figures taken from the easy-to-read, entertaining text, *Understanding Chemistry: From Atoms To Attitudes,* by T. R. Dickson, John Wiley and Sons, New York: 1974.) We lose water continually from our bodies and to maintain good health must replenish it daily. We do this not only through drinking water straight but through the intake of other liquids which have a high water content and through the intake of solid food, which also contains water. Some simple forms of Earth life can exist without oxygen. None survive without water.

On Earth we have an almost embarrassing abundance of this life giving and life sustaining fluid. How much liquid water is there elsewhere in our System?

Over 99 percent of the mass of the entire Solar System resides in one imposing radiant body: our Sun. The rest of the mass—less than one percent of the total—is divided between the nine planets, numerous satellites (32 are known), about 20,000 asteroids (the number counted by the infrared eyes of the IRAS, which is about four times the number previously known), and some 1,000 known comets, with new ones sighted every year (in 1983 the IRAS found five previously unknown ones).

Of the less than one percent of the mass which doesn't reside in the Sun, one large planet—Jupiter—has the lion's share. Jupiter posessses two and one half times more mass than all the other planets and smaller bodies added together.

The radiant Sun, possessor of almost all the mass in the System, has a surface temperature, according to scientific calculations, of $5,800°$ K ($10,000°$ F). The internal temperature is believed to reach about $15,000,000°$ K ($26,000,000°$ F). No liquid water at these temperatures.

The Sun's brood of planets is commonly divided into two family groups. The four small planets close in to the Sun—Mercury, Venus, Earth and Mars—are the Terrestrial Planets, so named due to their similarity in physical and chemical makeup to the Earth. These four are the rocky planets. The four larger, outer planets—Jupiter, Saturn, Uranus and Neptune—are the Jovian Planets. These four are all gaseous in their outer layers. Between these two groups are the stony asteroids, and out in the hinterlands the tiny, oddball planet Pluto roams. Pluto is ordinarily the outermost planet in the system, but if its drunkenly tilted orbit is projected onto the plane of the other planets, its orbit now falls within the orbit of its neighbor, Neptune. It moved inside Neptune's orbit in 1979 and will remain within it until the end of this century. On none of these material bodies, as far as is known, is there carbon and water based life except on our home planet Earth.

The difference between the four inner rocky planets and the larger outer gaseous group is explained in this way:

Eons ago, when the Solar System was forming, there was a wide diversity in conditions depending on nearness to the central mass which eventually contracted to become our Sun. Close in to the protosun, the gas density was much greater than it was farther out. This greater density led to more frequent collisions, which meant higher temperatures. Close in to the protosun, the temperature is believed to have been several thousand degrees Celsius (centigrade scale). This cooled to several hundred degrees out in the vicinity of the large outer planets.

The behavior of hot gases depends on temperature. Out in the region of the Jovian Planets, where temperatures were two hundred degrees Celsius or less, the heavier elements, oxygen, carbon and nitrogen, combined with hydrogen, the lighest and most abundant of all elements, to form water, ammonia, and methane ice crystals. In the inner regions, where temperatures were close to a thousand degrees hotter, ices couldn't survive, so the heavier elements combined in a way that produced the rocky planets.

Mercury, in orbit only about 36 million miles from the Sun, is believed to have a surface temperature of around 370° C (700° F), hot enough to melt lead. No liquid water here. With a diameter of only a little over 3,000 miles, and a mass of only 0.05 that of the Earth's, Mercury is not massive enough to have retained any atmosphere other than a very tenuous one.

Venus, the Earth's "sister planet," is a twin in size, although somewhat smaller, with only a little over 80 percent of the mass of the Earth. In orbit some 67 million miles from the Sun, it has a surface temperature of nearly 460° C (860° F), hotter than the surface of Mercury. Although there are traces of water vapor in the Venetian atmosphere, there is no liquid water.

Next comes our home planet, Earth, in orbit about 93 million miles from the Sun, with an average surface temperature of 20° C (68° F), and an abundant supply of water in liquid form.

Our heavenly neighbor on our other side is Mars, in orbit some 142 million miles from the Sun. Mars, which appears reddish in our skies, has been the object of the most intense speculation in Man's search for extraterrestrial life. We have all heard of the little green people from Mars. An American astronomer, Percival Lowell (1855-1916), popularized the idea that the fine, straight lines visible on the surface of Mars were canals constructed by some form of intelligent life to distribute scarce water over a generally arid planet. Current belief is that Lowell's canals were optical illusions. Nevertheless there is some evidence that at one time Mars *did* have a supply of running water. This is puzzling as scientific thought insists that liquid water would quickly vaporize in the rarefied Martian atmosphere.

In recent years the Viking probes have shown that the polar caps on Mars are primarily water ice. Ice *can* melt, so this possible source of liquid water on Mars has encouraged speculation that some form of Earth-like life may or might exist there. Mars has a surface temperature of approximately $-15°$ C ($5°$ F), with great daily and seasonal variation. The surface temperature at night at the equator can drop to -80 to $-100°$ C, and can drop even lower at the poles. Nevertheless there are certain life forms, such as lichens, which might possibly survive if transplanted to our heavenly neighbor. As for life native to the red planet, with all our probing we have yet to turn up any evidence that such exists. So far the little green people have eluded our search.

As we leave the small rocky planets behind, we venture into colder climes.

Jupiter, the giant of the planets, with a diameter of almost 89,000 miles and a mass over three hundred times the mass of the Earth, is so large that it just misses being a star. Its core temperature is believed to be around $30,000°$ C ($54,000°$ F), not quite hot enough to ignite thermonuclear reactions which would boost it into stardom. This roaring internal temperature drops to $-120°$ C ($-184°$ F) at the top of Jupiter's cloud cover. Nowhere on this gassy giant, in orbit almost 484 million miles from the Sun, are temperatures right for liquid water, although there are traces of water ices in its atmosphere.

Saturn, in orbit over 890 million miles from the Sun, has a surface temperature appreciably colder than Jupiter's, far too cold for liquid water. The same is true for Uranus and Neptune. Only recently has much of anything been known about our System's oddball little planet, Pluto, revolving in an eccentric orbit over three and a half billion miles from the Sun. It is now believed to be 2,500 miles in diameter, making it the smallest planet in the System, hardly larger than our Moon. Its density is believed to be 35 pounds per cubic foot, which means it is the lightest permanent body in our System. (For comparison, the Terrestrial Planets have average densities close to 300 pounds per cubic foot, the Jovian planets densities of 60 to 70 pounds per cubic foot.) Pluto's atmosphere, appropriately enough, is considered bizarre. At least part of its surface, it is now believed, is composed of frozen methane. Methane is a compound of carbon and hydrogen which freezes a few degrees above absolute zero, a temperature so low that here on Earth frozen methane is almost impossible to make. In addition, Pluto may have a certain amount of water ice and rock. Its surface temperature is far too cold to allow for running water and there is no indication it possesses Earth-like life.

The asteroids and the comets are all we have left, and there is little to indicate either of these types of bodies has freely running water.

All indications are that Earth alone, our rocky little home in its unspectacular orbit around the massive Sun, managed to evolve in such a way that on its surface liquid water not only exists but is plentiful.

How did Earth alone manage this nifty trick?

By being in the right place at the right time, according to the Scientists. In the early protosystem, place—distance from the protosun—determined temperature. The elements that combine to make water (hydrogen and oxygen) were present in the dust grains in the original swirling cloud. There was a narrow band—a band about 74 million miles in width, only about two percent of the radius of the Solar System—where the temperature was such that water molecules could exist in all three forms of matter: solid, liquid and gaseous. The protoearth gathered itself together within this narrow band, which meant that the hydrogen and oxygen present could combine into liquid water. After the Earth formed and began to cool, water was trapped inside rocks in the Earth's crust. Gradually this trapped water trickled out, and this trickle did it for us: liquid water formed the oceans, seas, rivers and lakes of our world.

The Earth not only has an abundant supply of liquid water, water on Earth is everywhere, the most common substance there is. In liquid or solid form, water covers close to three quarters of the Earth's surface. It is also in the air around us, in the ground under our feet, and in every living thing. In fact, all life forms are composed primarily of water.

Only about three percent of the liquid water that covers our Earth is fresh water, and some three-quarters of this fresh water is frozen in glaciers and icecaps. But the available one quarter of three percent of the whole is a sufficient supply of fresh water to support a mind-boggling array of life forms.

Once Earth came by its original water, it set up a marvelously efficient recycling system to keep the supply ample. Water, changing form as it goes, is constantly on the move. The heat of the Sun warms liquid water to where it evaporates. About 85 percent of the water vapor in the air comes from the oceans. The rest comes from other open bodies of water such as rivers and lakes, from damp ground surfaces, and from plants, which give up moisture through their leaves. An acre of corn, for example, will give off about 4,000 gallons of water per day while a birch tree will give off about 70 gallons. These plants draw water from the ground through their roots—water that has gotten into the ground through rainfall—then pass it back to the air through their leaves as part of Nature's endless recycling system.

Once water is vaporized from these various sources, it rises as a gas into the atmosphere. The air, a portion of which is water vapor, moves across the face of the Earth. As moisture-filled air is forced up either by colder air or by mountains, atmospheric pressure is lessened, the air expands and cools. If the temperature drops low enough, the water vapor condenses into droplets of water or ice. Close to Earth, these droplets form fog, higher up clouds.

A cloud is a mass of water droplets or ice crystals floating in the atmosphere. Clouds form at various heights, come in various shapes and sizes, and range in color from white through gray to black. The modern day study of clouds is considered to have begun in 1803 when an English chemist, Luke Howard, gave Latin names to the three most common forms of clouds: *cumulus* (Latin for *heap*), *cirrus (curl), stratus (layer).*

Today the classification system most widely in use by Meteorologists is based upon distance from the Earth's surface (sea level). Clouds are divided into *low*, clouds with a base below 7,500 feet, *medium,* between 7,500 and 21,000 feet, and *high,* above 21,000 feet.

High clouds are designated by the *cirro-* prefix *(cirrus, cirrostratus,* and *cirrocumulus)* and are composed almost entirely of ice crystals. Thin and silky cirrus clouds sometimes form higher than 35,000 feet.

Medium level clouds are *altostratus, altocumulus* and *nimbostratus.*

Low clouds are either *stratus* or *stratocumulus.* Stratus clouds, usually no higher than 6,500 feet, are wide and low hanging. Cumulus clouds, round and fleecy, form at about 1600 feet and can hold a maximum of water vapor. When the Sun's rays are such as to cause strong updrafts, cumulus clouds build upward and may turn into *cumulonimbus* clouds, the most spectacular of all clouds. A cumulonimbus cloud may reach a height as great as 60,000 feet above its base. When a cumulonimbus cloud turns dark, watch out. A thunderstorm may be about to strike.

Rain from heaven doesn't always fall as gently as mercy does. The estimate is that between three and four thousand thunderstorms are occurring around the world at any given moment, many of them ungentle. Our ancestors understood the heavenly brightness and sound accompanying storms: angry gods were hurling noisy bolts of light to express their displeasure. More recently, Scientists have explained lightning and thunder in other ways.

As large clouds form, some drops of water within the cloud become positively charged. Ice crystals within the same cloud become negatively charged. The positively charged water rises to form a positive-charge center and the heavier ice crystals move downward to form a negatively charged center. On Earth, positively charged forces gather below the cloud, drawn by the cloud's low negative center.

Air is a poor conductor of electricity, so the charges on either side build up until a critical point is reached, at which time air resistance is overcome and electric current travels from cloud to Earth, unseen, then from Earth to cloud in the brilliant flash we do see. Lightning also strikes between clouds and in some cases between charge centers in the same cloud.

The lightning flashes ionize the air in their paths, producing great heat. Suddenly heated up, the gases expand violently, creating compression waves, which we on Earth hear as thunder.

Lightning does more than frighten us, reminding us of how vulnerable we are. It also produces beneficial chemical changes in the atmosphere. The heat which is generated by lightning causes nitrogen and oxygen in the air to combine into nitrates and other compounds which fall to Earth with the rain, replenishing our soil. Nature seems to have thought it all out and does her very best for us.

On Earth water is common in the sense that it is plentiful. It is most decidedly *not* common in the sense of being run-of-the-mill ordinary.

Water is the only known compound which occurs naturally on Earth in all three states of matter: solid, liquid and gaseous.

This is only one of water's many extraordinary properties.

No other earthly substance is quite as extraordinary as water. None other can do all that water can do.

Water is liquid at the temperatures prevailing on most of the Earth's surface. *It is the only common substance which is liquid at these temperatures.* Other substances with structures similar to water are not liquid in this temperature range; they are gases. If water were an ordinary mixture of gases and behaved as its nearest relatives behave it would be liquid between $-100°$ C and $-90°$ C ($-148°$ F to $-130°$ F), in which case there would be no naturally occurring liquid water on Earth as the surface temperature of the Earth is substantially higher than $-90°$ C. Water-based Earth life exists only because H_2O is a marvelous maverick.

Water is unique in so many ways it seems to set its own rules, ignoring the natural rules that govern other substances. Nowhere is water's behavior more freakish than when it freezes into its solid form, ice. Nature's rule is that everything expands as it heats, contracts as it cools. If water followed this rule, ice would be heavier than water and would not float. Oceans, rivers and lakes would freeze from the bottom up, and soon life as we know it on Earth would cease, for there wouldn't be sufficient liquid water available to sustain it. Frozen water would be locked into icy beds too deep for the Sun's warmth to reach and melt it.

Water vapor—water in its gaseous form—follows the ordinary rules of expansion. Water as a liquid also follows the rules of expansion-contraction, shrinking as its temperature drops almost all the way down the temperature range, but not quite all the way. At a few degrees above freezing, something happens. Water declares its independence and stops conforming. Instead of contracting further, it begins to expand. As cooling continues, water expands even more and gets lighter. By the time it has reached the temperature at which it freezes (0° C, 32° F at sea level), it has gained about nine percent in volume. Because of this outlandish behavior, behavior which defies the ordinary rules, ice is lighter than liquid water and floats. Ice floating atop bodies of water acts as an insulating skin protecting the liquid water beneath. With the return of warmer weather in spring, the Sun's rays melt the floating ice, the recycling of water is uninterrupted, and water-based life on Earth goes merrily on its way.

Heat capacity is the ability of a substance to store heat. Water's ability to absorb heat, to store it as latent heat, is unusually high. To bring cold water to a boil takes an enormous amount of energy. Yet it takes *five times* more heat to convert boiling water into steam than it takes to bring freezing water to a boil, which means that steam holds a tremendous quantity of latent heat energy. This energy can be and is used to run machines. Another result of water's remarkable capacity to store heat is that every molecule of water vapor in the atmosphere and every droplet of water in each cloud contains heat energy. The climate of our world is tempered by the extraordinary ability of water to absorb the Sun's heat, then slowly release it again.

Water has other unique and exceptional qualities.

For one thing, it has an extremely high surface tension, which is the ability of a substance to pull itself together and stick to itself. Because of this high surface tension, it can support great weight, allowing heavy objects to float in it.

For another: In defiance of gravity, water climbs the walls of containers, pulling itself up molecule after molecule. This capacity, known as capillary action, is crucial to the flow of nutrients to plants and trees, and also to the circulation of blood in human and all other animal bodies.

Last but far from least, water is close to being the universal chemical solvent. Given time, it will dissolve almost any inorganic substance. Its ability to dissolve compounds is astounding, an ability upon which all living organisms depend. Plants and animals alike need to have their food dissolved before they can make use of it. Water is our solvent.

With all these amazing virtues, one would suppose water is totally benign, but such is not the case. While life as we know it on Earth could not exist without water, and without all the truly staggering qualities water displays, water, whether dripping, flowing or roaring, given enough time destroys everything in its path. It can disintegrate the toughest metal, or drown the life it ordinarily sustains. Through the movement of water vapor in the atmosphere, it creates our overall climate as well as local weather, and working slowly over countless millennia it has shaped the Earth to suit itself.

Water, colorless, odorless, tasteless, exerts enormous power in our world. It has a restless nature that is seemingly never still. Yet underlying this restlessness is a profound stability. The water molecule is so stable, in fact, that until late in the 18th Century it was considered an element. Water molecules remain intact when frozen or when heated whereas most chemical compounds disintegrate.

The two gaseous components of water, hydrogen and oxygen, have such a strong affinity for each other that they join forces at every opportunity, forming water and releasing energy. Once together, they don't part easily. The tremendously tight bonding of the water molecule is the underlying explanation for all the extraordinary qualities water has.

The most common water molecule, as everyone knows, is composed of two atoms of hydrogen, one of oxygen.

Hydrogen (Symbol H, atomic weight 1.0097, atomic number 1), a colorless, orderless, flammable gas, is the simplest and lightest of all the elements: one proton in the nucleus, one electron in orbit. The innermost orbit of any atom has room for two electrons, which means that hydrogen needs a second electron to fill this innermost shell.

Oxygen (Symbol O, atomic weight 15.9994, atomic number 8), another colorless, odorless gas, has two electrons in its innermost shell, six in its outer shell. This outer shell fills at eight electrons, so oxygen lacks two electrons.

Two atoms of hydrogen and one of oxygen come together to *share* electrons, forming a *covalent* bond. The molecule they form is an oddly shaped one, with the hydrogen atoms bulging out on either side of the oxygen atom at an angle of 105° to each other, like rabbit ears. This misshapen structure causes an unequal distribution of electric charge. On the hydrogen side of the atom there is a positive charge, on the oxygen side a negative charge. The molecule is therefore a *dipole,* a microscopic bar magnet. Opposite charges attract, so one water molecule binds electrically with another as the negative, oxygen side of one molecule is drawn to the positive, hydrogen side of another molecule, forming what is called a *hydrogen bond.* All the molecules link together in this way, positive to negative, to further stabilize water.

Hydrogen Atom   Hydrogen Atom

— Vacancies —

Oxygen Atom

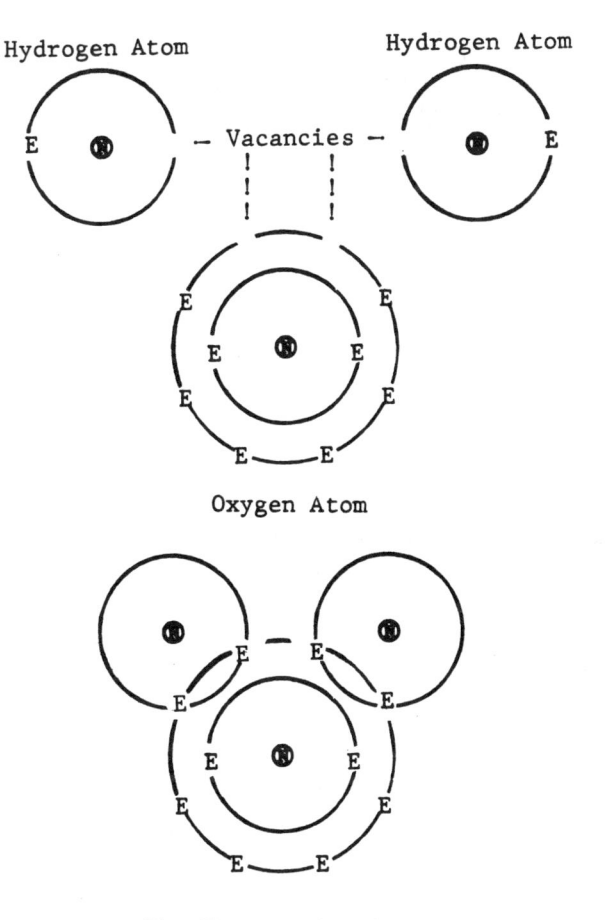

The Water Molecule

The atoms, sharing electrons, are bound together by co-valent bonds.

The covalent bonding *plus* the hydrogen bonding explains in chemical terms all the sturdy water molecule's wondrous powers.

Water.
Water is unique among Earthly substances not only in its abundance but in the way it grandly ignores seemingly

natural behavior and sets its own rules. If water didn't go its own way, if it suddenly decided to behave as its molecular makeup suggests that it should behave, hello disaster. The blood in our veins would boil, plants and trees would starve to death, our lovely home planet Earth would no longer resemble itself. But water molecules are bound together in ways unlike any other compounds, and this unique binding allows them to flout Nature's Laws and surround us with life, beauty and grace.

If the world is a reflection of Man, as is being argued herein, then water must be a prime reflector.

That water *does* reflect we know from experience. Possibly we've never had the chance to see our face reflected in a clear, placid pool, but we've certainly seen the calm surface of a lake reflect the magnificent mountains surrounding it, on a scenic calendar if not otherwise. But this reflection, we know, is only a trick of tricky light interacting with the master trickster, water.

HYPOTHESIS:

The watery nature of our world reflects the emotional aspect of consciousness: water is the translation into the material world of feeling.

****

To zero in on this mirror-like nature of water, we'll start at the most basic level.

Water is composed of two gases, hydrogen and oxygen. The air which surrounds us, the air we breathe, upon which our lives are dependent, is composed of gases. When the philosopher Rene Descartes (1596-1650) attempted to strip knowledge back to basics so it could be built up again on a firm foundation, he rested all certainty on the famous, "I think, therefore I am." The air we breathe is basic to human life; thinking is basic to human consciousness.

But man is more than a thinking animal. He is also a *feeling* animal. And our language shows that we tend to view thought unmixed with feeling as somehow not quite life affirming, as rather too light and meaningless.

Consider these definitions and slang phrases: *Airily:* "1. in a gay or breezy manner; jauntily." When something is done airily, it is done without much thought, or without heavy thought. *Breezy:* "1. abounding in breezes; windy." This adjective derives, of course, from the word *breeze:* "1. a light wind or current of air. 2. *Informal.* an easy task. 3. *Bat* or *shoot the breeze, Slang.* a. to converse aimlessly. b. to talk nonsense or exaggerate."

When someone expresses thought in which listeners find too little of substance, it is said of the speaker that he is full of *hot air.* Hot air rises, of course, flowing airily off on the breeze.

When one person rejects another, the person rejected has been *given the air.* The one who gives someone else the air is rejecting and unfeeling.

As thought and speech become more meaningful, they become weightier, less airy. To add weight is to add meaning, and to dip down into meaning is to begin to involve more than airy thought, to do more than bat the breeze, to spout hot air. As thought becomes meaningful, *feeling creeps in.*

Add one gas, hydrogen, to another gas, oxygen, and a substance is formed which is heavier than either one—liquid water.

Add weight to thought and feeling is formed.

We all know with our heads that the heart is simply a tough muscular organ that keeps the blood flowing. The first dictionary definition of the word confirms this. *Heart:* "1. a hollow, muscular organ that by rhythmic contractions and relaxations keeps the blood in circulation throughout the body." Yet the dictionary also confirms, in its second definition, the great weightiness we attribute to our hearts: "2. the center of the total personality, esp. with reference to intuition, feeling or emotion . . ."

The center. Especially with reference to feeling or emotion. Feeling originated in the heart, the ancients believed. Today we no longer believe this is literally true. The Scientists of today tell us that the mind, which somehow arises in and is connected to the brain, not the heart, is the source of all feeling just as it is the source of all thought. Nevertheless in common usage we continue to honor the heart as the centerpiece of our emotional being.

You broke my heart. I gave him my heart. She won his heart. She is wonderfully big hearted. He is generous and warm hearted. Have a heart. On and on we go, using the word *heart* in this sense with no sound physiological basis underlying the usage yet with near perfect communication.

Or perhaps there *is* a sound basis for this usage despite the fact that feeling is now believed to originate in the brain-related mind and not in that hollow muscular organ known as the heart.

The heart presides over the flow of blood, a liquid. Blood is over 80 percent water. In effect, the heart presides over the flow of water with additives. This fluid—water with its additives—is seen as partaking in feeling just as the muscle which oversees its flow, the heart, is viewed as the source of feeling. People are said to be warm blooded or cold blooded with reference not to the actual temperature of their blood but to their *emotional* temperament. Terror can make one's blood run cold, while anger or resentment can make one's blood boil.

Physiological changes which occur in the body when the mind is gripped with a strong emotion tend to reinforce our belief that the heart and the blood are somehow involved in feeling. If we feel angry or frightened, the heart speeds up, our blood begins to pound. If we're in the grip of excitement, our pulses race, or skip, or seem to stop. The heart reacts to strong emotion in such a way as to make us feel faint, or incredibly energized. In such moments, it's easy to attribute feeling to the muscular heart as it goes about its unique job of overseeing the rush of liquid blood.

When we are emotionally moved by something, our eyes often water. In the grip of either great sadness or sudden unexpected joy, we are apt to cry: liquid tears overflow our eyes and stream down our cheeks. When we are angry or frightened, we have a tendency to overwork our sweat glands; we begin to sweat excessively. Sexual arousal brings with it natural lubrication; juices flow. Within the human body, feeling and the creation/movement of liquid seem inextricably intertwined.

Intellectual discourse which fails to hold our interest, discourse which doesn't arouse in us either excitement or curiosity, which inspires in us neither appreciation for the beauty of the argument nor awe over the grandeur of the subject, is often characterized as "dry." This usage is reflected in dictionary definitions. The number one definition of the word *dry* is, of course: "1. free from moisture or excess moisture; not moist or wet . . ." Additional definitions: "17. dull, uninteresting . . . 18. expressed in a straight-faced, matter-of-fact way . . . 19. indifferent, cold, unemotional . . ."

What is dry inspires no emotional response in us. Dry = unemotional.

Not dry, ie, watery = emotional.

To restate our hypothesis: Water mirrors the emotional nature of human consciousness.

Evidence suggests that Earthly life began in water.
Newborn human beings have few of the intellectual skills they will later acquire; in fact, their brains are not yet sufficiently formed for these skills to be present. Human beings differ from lower animals primarily due to the neocortex, that part of the brain which controls coordination and higher mental activity. At birth this part of the brain, the neocortex, is barely developed; 85 percent of brain growth occurs after birth. Nevertheless, there is one brain function, one mental skill, at which the newborn is already expert: a newborn needs no lesson in how to *feel*.

Every living cell is dependent upon water for survival.
Life on our planet Earth expresses itself in many and varied ways. Life in all its forms exhibits a strong will to live. Even under the most adverse conditions, the majority of those who are alive show a tenacious desire to continue to exist. Human beings do not *think*

themselves into this desire to live, they *feel* it. And surely every living cell is dependent on this will to live, this influx of feeling, this flow, in order to survive.

The supply of water for living cells must be constantly replenished.

The will to live must continually renew itself or withering and death will soon follow.

Water as it becomes rigid and freezes into ice expands and grows lighter when, according to the natural Law that rules other substances, it ought to contract and grow heavier. This allows ice to float on water and life on Earth to continue.

As human feelings freeze into rigid patterns of bitterness, hate, resentment and despair, these feelings for all their rigidity and heaviness remain lighter than the basic will to live and therefore float atop that will. If this were not the case, if rigid feelings of bitterness and hatred began at the emotional core and froze outward, snapping off the will to live, life would not be the time extended, rich emotional learning experience that it is. Because emotional rigidity starts at the outer layers and freezes inward to the core, not vice versa, human beings can afford the luxury of negative feelings, a profoundly significant luxury.

The water molecule is a remarkably stable one, ie, extremely difficult to break into its constituent parts. The water molecule remains intact even when frozen or heated.

The human ego or self or personality, that part of us that has the capacity to feel, is a remarkably stable entity. Each human brain stores innummerable memory systems, yet somehow the mind achieves the miraculous feat of maintaining, in almost all cases, one single identifiable personality as possessor of all these uncounted memory systems. Even under the pressure of hot or cold emotions, most personalities remain intact.

As stable as the water molecule is, it can, with effort, be dissolved into its constituent elements.

> As stable as the human ego is, under sufficient pressure it *will* split into fragment personalities, each personality taking over its own brain-stored memory systems. While most of us are single personalities, as stable in our singularity as the water molecule, numerous cases of egos split into two or more personalities have been recorded.

Water molecules are held together through an electrical attraction they have for each other.

> Human beings have a herd instinct; societies are formed and held together by the natural attraction people feel for each other's company.

Water has an unusually high heat capacity, an exceptional ability to store latent heat.

> People have a remarkable capacity to store happy emotional memories which can be called up later to add life and warmth to colder days.

Water has an extremely high surface tension, that is, a great capacity to hold itself together and stick to itself. Because of this ability, it has an amazing ability to support weight.

> So has the human animal an amazing ability to hold itself together and support catastrophe.

In defiance of gravity, water molecules climb the walls of containers, pulling themselves up molecule after molecule.

> Most people accept the notion that Man started out on all fours before pulling himself into an upright positon. We have now climbed so high we have reached the Moon and are, we hope, on our way to the stars.

From ancient times to the present Mankind has harnessed water power to perform useful work.

> People are driven toward accomplishment by their feelings quite as much as water power drives machinery.

The restless movement of water vapor in our atmosphere creates climate and local weather.

> Our feelings determine the emotional climate in which we live.

Water is close to being the universal chemical solvent.

> Every thought in us dissolves away in a strong enough rush of feeling.

Water, for all its uniqueness, is the most common substance on Earth.

> In every quarter of the Earth, from the beginning of human life until tomorrow, perhaps until forever, human beings share one common heritage: they are *feeling* creatures. Language, beliefs, customs, lifestyles differ from one society to another, from one century to another, but what flows in our hearts is timeless and makes all human beings kin. Grief, hope, joy, despair, anger, fear, love—these feelings are and possibly always will be our most common shared experience.

Water sustains life, but in excess, when not under control, it becomes a destructive force which destroys everything in its path.

> Without feeling we would not be human, but feelings in excess, when not under control, become a destructive force destroying everything in their path.

Over time, water shapes everything to suit itself.

> Over time, our feelings shape everything in our lives.

Surely not all of the above outlined parallels are logical imperatives. A planet could conceivably have formed itself at an appropriate distance from the Sun to insure a moderate climate without also enjoying a superabundant water supply. On this theoretical planet, life could have begun on dry land (there's an outside chance it began on dry land on Earth but most of the evidence suggests otherwise). Two gases could have combined to form not a unique liquid but a unique gaseous compound, and life on our theoretical planet could have been based on carbon and this gaseous compound. Such a life, divorced from water, could have evolved into rich and complex forms possessing consciousness not only capable of thought but also of feeling. Such a life script is certainly conceivable but in our Solar System it did not happen that way. Life as we know it—flowing with feeling—evolved on a planet flowing with water. The only feeling life in the Solar System seems to have developed on the only physical body in the System abundantly supplied with liquid water.

Coincidence or reflection?

To help us decide, let's take a close look at the element that by weight is the major constitutent of water: oxygen.

8

THE BREATH OF LIFE
Where Would We Be, What Would We Be, Without Oxygen?

> And the Lord God formed man of the dust of the ground, and breathed into his nostrils the breath of life; and man became a living soul.
> Genesis 2:7
> Christian Bible

Conscious life on Earth is carbon and water based. To maintain itself in existence, its most immediate need is for oxygen.

Oxygen (Symbol O, atomic weight 15.9994, atomic number 8) is the most abundant element on Earth. It is found in the *lithosphere*, the rocky and mountainous crust of the Earth; in combination with silicon, aluminum and other elements, it forms sand, limestone and other rocks. It is found in the *hydrosphere,* the water sphere; by weight water is about 89 percent oxygen. It is found in the *atmosphere;* by volume air is about 21 percent oxygen. It is also found in the *biosphere,* the sphere of the living. Living matter is composed primarily of three elements: oxygen, carbon and hydrogen. By volume: oxygen 52 percent, carbon 39 percent, hydrogen 6.7 percent.

These four spheres—the lithosphere (*litho* from the Greek meaning *stone*), the hydrosphere (from the Greek, *hydro* =

water), atmosphere (*atmos* = *vapor,* Greek), and the biosphere (*bio* = *life,* from the Greek)—together form our entire environment, the *ecosphere* (Greek: *oikos* = *house*).

By volume oxygen is very nearly half—49.20 percent—of the ecosphere, nearly half of our entire Earthly environment.

Oxygen is a colorless, odorless, tasteless gas which is chemically very active, combining readily with other elements. In the atmosphere it is found in combination with itself, two atoms of O joining to form molecular oxygen, O_2. When electric sparks are passed through air or oxygen, three atoms of oxygen may combine to form ozone, O_3. In the upper atmosphere there is naturally occurring ozone, the ozone layer or ozonosphere, produced by the action of ultraviolet radiation from the Sun on molecular oxygen. This ozone layer provides an important chemical screen which limits the amount of high energy radiation that reaches the Earth's surface. As ultraviolet radiation is detrimental to plant and animal life, we owe thanks to the ozone layer and ought to show care not to destroy it.

Just as water has a natural cycle, so does oxygen.

The three substances most prominently involved in the oxygen cycle are water, carbon dioxide, and molecular oxygen.

The air that surrounds us is a mixture of gases. By volume it is mostly molecular nitrogen, N_2 (78.1 percent) and molecular oxygen, O_2 (21 percent), but carbon dioxide is also present as well as argon, neon, helium, krypton, and a variable amount of water vapor and dust.

Plants draw in carbon dioxide, CO_2, from the air and water from the soil for a process known as *photosynthesis. (Photo* from the Greek meaning *light; synthesis* from the Greek meaning *to place or put together.)*

Photosynthesis: "Biol. Biochem. (esp. in plants) the synthesis of complex organic materials, esp. carbohydrates, from carbon dioxide, water, and inorganic salts, using sunlight as the source of energy and with the aid of a catalyst, as chlorophyll."

One of the waste products of photosynthesis is molecular oxygen, which is released into the air. As this has been going on for millions of years, our air today is rich with molecular oxygen, a supply that is virtually inexhaustible as long as plant life on Earth continues to exist.

Plants, in addition to producing oxygen, also utilize it. Both animals and plants draw molecular oxygen in from the atmosphere to use in biological oxidation, the process by which food molecules are converted into carbon dioxide and water. The carbon dioxide and water are released into the air and hydrosphere, which keeps up a steady supply of each for the plants to use in photosynthesis whereby they replenish the molecular oxygen that animals need. Oceanic and land plants produce each year through photosynthesis approximately the same amount of oxygen that animals and plants then use up in biological oxidation so there is little if any net change in the oxygen content of the air.

It is through *biological oxidation* that animals are able to live and move and have their being. Plants use the energy of sunlight to convert carbon dioxide and water into carbohydrates and oxygen. Animals convert the carbohydrates and oxygen back into carbon dioxide and water, in the process releasing for their own use the energy of the Sun which the plant originally captured. All animal energy is derived from recycled sunlight.

Animal bodies are fuel burning machines and the fuel they burn is food. While plants can manufacture their own food, animals can't. This means that animals must obtain their food from outside sources, either from the plants that manufacture it or from other animals. As lord and master of the Earth, Man has free choice: he can eat his food firsthand in the form of plant life, or secondhand in the form of plant life that has previously been digested in the belly of some beast. In either case, in order to burn this food and obtain energy, oxygen is required.

Digestion is the process through which food is converted into energy or used for the manufacture of new cells. This process begins in the mouth, where the teeth chop up the food while it is being mixed with a juice called saliva. Once cut up and moistened, the food can be easily swallowed, that is, whisked down a transportation tube to the stomach. In the stomach the food is churned up some more and mixed with mucus and gastric juices. Turned into a thick liquid called *chyme,* it is sent on its way to the intestinal tract, where additional fluids from the liver, pancreas and the intestinal glands are poured into it. The small intestine is several feet long and by the time the diluted food has passed through it, almost everything of value has been absorbed out of it through the *villi,* the lining of the intestine, into the blood and lymph, which carry it to the cells where it is used for energy and new tissue for growth.

Food releases its energy through oxidation, that is, by combining with oxygen. Outside the body, oxidation often occurs very rapidly, as when a match is struck and flares into fire, but within the body oxidation occurs much more slowly. In this slow and steady burning, the sunlight originally captured by plant life is released in animal cells. The energy thus obtained can be used as heat, to accomplish work, or it can be stored for future use.

Any living body is a beehive of continual activity. Tissues are being broken down and replaced. The heart muscle works unceasingly and to accomplish this work requires energy. To supply this energy, oxygen must be drawn into the lungs. Heart action sends the oxygen through the bloodstream to every living cell. Without oxygen, the element which releases the energy of sunlight, the body, a highly complex organism, cannot function. Of all bodily needs, the most pressing is for oxygen. Pull the plug on any electric appliance and it will stop. Shut off the oxygen supply to a living body and it too will stop. Work is accomplished through energy—*energy:* "7. *Physics,* the capacity to do work"—and deprived of oxygen living cells have no energy. As activity ceases, so does life, in a very brief time.

Slow oxidation within the body keeps body temperature fairly constant. If the level of activity is stepped up, however, if we engage in energetic exercise, the body warms owing to the increased pace of oxidation. We literally burn up faster, and are very apt to pour water on the fire, that is, to start excreting a more than usual supply of watery fluid through the pores of the skin, in order to cool ourselves down again.

Bodily heat, like all other forms of heat, is measured in degrees of temperature. *Temperature:* "1. a measure of the warmth or coldness of an object or substance with reference to some standard value."

We all know what heat is: it's what's measured by temperature. We know that is so because everyone has agreed it's so. Apart from agreement as to how it's measured, heat, like light and life, has no simple, clear cut definition.

Water boils; it also freezes. The first temperature scales devised were based on these two naturally occurring material changes. Any one of us can touch a surface and know instantly whether it feels hot, cold or neutral to our touch. But how hot, or how cold? And how warm or cool is neutral? A more discerning instrument than the human skin was needed. That matter expands when heated and contracts when cooled was well known. The expansion/contraction of liquids or gases was far more pronounced than these changes in solid bodies, so one or the other would surely serve as an accurate gauge for the measurement of temperature changes.

A German physicist, Gabriel Daniel Fahrenheit (1686-1736), invented the mercury thermometer. Fahrenheit took for his two fixed points the freezing and boiling points of water at sea level. He divided the range between these two fixed points into 180 equal degrees. For zero he took the coldest temperature he could produce in his laboratory, which came from a mixture of salt, water and ice. A temperature 32 degrees higher than his zero proved to be the freezing point of water; 32 plus 180 gave him 212 degrees for water's boiling point. This scale, with mercury in a glass tube marked off into equal degrees, is still very much in use today, primarily in English speaking countries.

In the Celsius scale, devised by a Swedish astronomer Anders Celsius (1701-1744), formerly known as the Centigrade Scale, the temperature at which water freezes was set at $0°$ C. and the temperature at which it boils at $100°$ C. The range between was divided into one hundred equal divisions, hence the name centigrade: divided into one hundred degrees.

This scale too is still very widely in use, being the scale of choice in scientific work around the world.

In another early scale, French physicist and inventor Rene de Reamur (1683-1757) set the ice point at 0° and the steam point at 80°. This scale is still in use in Europe.

These various temperature scales—thermometers—helped immeasurably when it came to measuring heat. However, they failed to reveal what heat *is*.

We all know what heat is. We have experienced warmth and lack of warmth from earliest childhood. Yet like the mind, or love, or courage, heat cannot be seen, heard, or weighed. Temperatures fluctuate, we know, and heat can be easily transferred from one material object to another. Spill boiling water on the skin and the temperature of the skin rises precipitously: it *burns*. To stay out in sunlight too long uncovered is to risk reddened, sunburned skin. Not only contact with what is too hot can cause skin burns; so can contact with what is too cold, a fact that has been known for centuries.

Early physicists—Galileo Galilei (1564-1642), Robert Boyle (1627-1691), and Isaac Newton (1642-1727)—explained heat as due to the motion of tiny particles of which bodies are made. English philosopher John Locke (1632-1704) in his *Essay Concerning Human Understanding* published in 1690, ascribed heat to motion. In the 18th Century, however, this notion was discarded by Scientists in favor of the belief that heat was a material fluid, flowing from one substance to another. When two bodies with different temperatures are put in contact, they soon assume the same temperature; therefore heat is being transferred from the warmer to the colder. As heat flowed so readily, it was surely a fluid.

In 1798 an American born, English physicist Benjamin Thompson, later Count Rumford (1753-1814), revived the earlier belief that heat was a result of *kinetic* energy, the energy of motion, a theory of heat that was later proved by British physicist James P. Joule (1818-1889). Joule also proved the equivalence of heat and mechanical energy, a discovery which led to the First Law of Thermodynamics.

According to the First Law of Thermodynamics (*Law,* not theory or hypothesis), energy can be neither created nor destroyed. In all energy transactions, the same amount of energy comes out as went in. This "Law" holds true not only on Earth, but throughout the vast reaches of the universe, the Learned Ones tell us. Every drop of energy that existed at the beginning still exists and will exist until the end of time. This First Law of Thermodynamics is therefore known as the Law of Conservation.

A French physicist, Sadi Carnot (1796-1832), formulated a "principle" which later became known as the Second Law of Thermodynamics. According to this "Law," free energy, energy available to do work, constantly decreases, changing into bound or unavailable energy. This unavoidable loss of available energy—this *using up* of free energy—was given the name *entropy* by a German physicist, Rudolph Clausius (1822-1888). While energy cannot be destroyed, it is constantly degenerating into a bound state wherein it can no longer perform work. (Never mind that in physics, energy is defined as "the capacity to do work." Free energy can perform work, bound energy can't.) The Second Law of Thermodynamics proclaims that every time work is performed, energy in the free state is lost to the bound state, becoming unavilable for future work.

For example: Water flowing over a dam can be used to generate electricity or to move paddle wheels, but once it has fallen, its ability to perform useful work is over. The world, while gaining useful work, has suffered an increase in entropy.

This Second Law, like the First Law, is said to be in force not only here on Earth but throughout the universe, and if it is both a true Law and non repeatable, the universe is heading, some billions of years in the future, toward certain death. All free energy will have been used up, and inertness—non motion—death—will reign.

Once it was established that heat was due to kinetic energy—the energy of motion—and the equivalence of heat and mechanical energy had been proved, it was possible to devise a new kind of thermometer, one that was not dependent upon the expansion-contraction of some material substance, but instead had a measurement scale based on mechanical units (the force necessary to perform work, ie, move a material body through space). This was done by an English physicist, William Thomson, Lord Kelvin (1824-1907), who devised what he called the *thermodynamic* scale of temperature (*thermo* from the Greek meaning *heat; dynamic:* "*Physics* a. of or pertaining to force or power. b. of or pertaining to force related to motion."). In the Kelvin scale, absolute zero was set at zero and the degree intervals equaled those of the Celsius scale (0° Kelvin = $-273.16°$ Celsuis).

Another absolute scale was devised by a Scottish engineer and physicist William Rankine (1820-1870). On the Rankine scale absolute zero is set at zero and the degree intervals equal those on the Fahrenheit scale (0° Rankine = $-459.7°$ F).

Absolute zero: "*Physical Chem.* the lowest possible temperature that the nature of matter admits; the temperature at which the particles whose motion constitutes heat would be at rest, being a hypothetical point 273° below the zero of the Celsius scale."

As the dictionary definition attests, absolute zero is not a temperature which has ever been achieved on Earth. It is as yet a hypothetical one. No matter on Earth that we know of is ever completely, absolutely at rest.

Heat: "*Physics.* a nonmechanical energy transfer with reference to a temperature difference between a system and its surroundings or between two parts of the same system."

Heat flows—there is a nonmechanical energy transfer—in one direction only, from a higher temperature to a lower one.

Heat flows from higher to lower in three different ways: through conduction, convection, or radiation.

The flow of heat by *conduction* is similar to the flow of electricity. Kinetic energy—energy of motion—is passed along in a solid body from molecule to molecule. The faster moving nudge the slower moving until all molecules within the material are moving at the same rate, ie, have the same temperature.

The flow of heat by *convection* occurs in liquids and gases, and depends upon the movement of molecules in the gas or liquid being heated. All matter expands when heated. With lowered density there is a drop in weight per unit of mass, which means that warmer gas rises, as does warmer liquid. Put a kettle of water on to boil, and the water toward the bottom, which is nearer the flame, heats up first. As it heats, it expands, grows lighter and rises in the kettle while colder water from the top of the kettle moves down to become heated in its turn. This is heat flow through convection.

The third heat flow, radiation, is energy transmitted by waves through space.

All matter radiates energy. Hotter bodies radiate more, cooler bodies less. All bodies also receive radiation in a never ending interchange. If the temperature of a body stays constant, this means that the same amount of energy is being absorbed as is being radiated away.

Life on Earth depends on heat transfer through radiation from the Sun.

One form of nonmechanical energy transfer we are all familiar with comes from a blazing fire wherein wood or some other combustible burns itself into ashes and/or other residue as it radiates energy.

Fire: "n. 1. the state, process or instance of combustion in which ignited fuel or other material combines with oxygen, giving off light, heat, and flame."

According to myth, Prometheus stole fire from the Sun and gave it to Man, an impiety for which he was severely punished. Once Man tamed fire, godlike mastery of the Earth was sure to follow. Everything that happens happens due to the flow/transformation of energy. To control fire is to hold dominion over the world for heat is the most powerful of servants.

In the ancient world fire was seen as one of the four basic elements: Earth, air, water and fire. It wasn't until 1783 that there was an accurate reading of fire. In that year the French chemist Antonine Lavoisier (1743-1794), while investigating the properties of oxygen, showed that fire is due to *oxidation (Oxidize: "Chem. . . . 1. to convert (an element) into its oxide; combine with oxygen.")* Almost any substance will combine with oxygen given enough time. If the chemical combination with oxygen occurs rapidly, a flame will be produced. The flame results because heat—energetic motion—forces gas out of the burning substance, and this escaping gas combines with oxygen in the air. All fires require oxygen to continue burning. If no oxygen is available, they die out.

Fire warms our homes and cooks our food. Combustion engines—engines powered by the burning of fuel—run our cars, our trains, our planes, keep our factories humming, and send our manned and unmanned rockets into space. If we ever reach the stars, it will be because we have fire.

The colorless, odorless, tasteless gas oxygen is the most abundant element on Earth and the most essential to life.

There is no easy answer to the question, "What is life?" but the first dictionary definition is: *"Life:* "1. the condition that distinguishes animals and plants from inorganic objects and dead organisms, being manifested by growth through metabolism, reproduction, and the power of adaptation to environment through changes originating internally."

As far as we know—this may be simply another confession of our many-faceted ignorance—inorganic substances don't have consciousness. The degree to which plants possess consciousness is just now being explored, but it is universally agreed that as life moves upward—or downwards or sidewards—toward ever greater complexity, somewhere along the way consciousness is acquired.

Consciousness: "1. the state of being conscious; awareness."

Conscious: "1. aware of one's own existence, thoughts, surroundings, etc."

As life moves adventurously along, if it doesn't always have conscious awareness of itself, somewhere in its movement it acquires it.

For human beings, thinking occurs in the mind, and the mind in some fashion or other arises in the brain.

Of all the organs in the body, the brain is the most sensitive to oxygen deprivation. It must have a continual, uninterrupted supply of oxygen to function properly. Without this fresh, never ending supply of oxygen, brain damage followed by death occurs very rapidly.

Under normal circumstances we obtain our oxygen by breathing in the air which surrounds us. By volume this air is about 21 percent oxygen, and about 78.1 percent nitrogen.

Nitrogen (Symbol N, atomic weight 14.0067, atomic number 7) like hydrogen and oxygen is a colorless, odorless, tasteless gas. In the biosphere—the sphere of living organisms—nitrogen is the fourth most abundant element after carbon, hydrogen and oxygen. It is present in combined form in animal and vegetable tissues, in particular proteins, which are composed of nitrogen compounds. Nitrogen has a cycle of interchange through the ecosphere—the whole house sphere—just as carbon, hydrogen and oxygen do, and is used in the manufacture of ammonia, fertilizers, explosives, and cyanide.

In effect, nitrogen, the principle ingredient of air, is useful in keeping things cool and clean (ammonia is used in refrigeration and in household cleaners), in helping things grow (fertilizers), in blowing things up (explosives), or in extracting the precious metals, silver and gold from ore (cyanide process).

Nitrogen is not chemically active and is slow to combine with other elements. It slows down the action of oxygen in the body, and is expelled from the lungs unchanged. Protoplasm, the stuff of living cells, requires nitrogen in its formation, which means that all life is dependent on this colorless, odorless, tasteless gas.

Life is dependent on three gases, hydrogen, oxygen, nitrogen, all of which in their free state are without color, odor or taste. Life is also dependent upon carbon, the Dr. Jekyll and Mr. Hyde of the elements: in pure crystalline form, it's the sparkling diamond, in other forms it's as black as soot.

Put all of the above together, toss in a dash of this and that, and out comes life in all its diversity and complexity.

Man is a conscious being, and we all know what that means. It means that we as human beings think, feel, remember, etc.

In common parlance we speak as though the heart rules feeling while the mind rules thought, but expert opinion informs us that this does not reflect true physiological functioning. Both thought and feeling are today believed to originate in the mind, while the heart, we are told, is simply a hard working muscle with no more feeling than the liver. That thought and feeling have a common origin in the mind tends to verify experience, for we all know from years of conscious living how difficult it is to disentangle the two, to decide precisely where thoughts end and feelings begin or vice versa. Thought sparks feeling, feelings spark thought. Most of us are familiar with the term *stream of consciousness* which is defined as, "*Psychol.* thought regarded as a succession of states constantly moving forward in time," but we all know from experience that *pure* thought, thought unsullied by emotion, does not long endure. Feelings sneak in to muddy the stream. We think ourselves into or out of feeling—not feeling as done by the fingers but feelings/emotions/sensibilities.

However, we also think ourselves into most of the feelings done by the fingers, just as we think ourselves into a great number of actions. Much of the work of keeping a living body alive is done on automatic through the autonomic nervous system. We don't have to remind our hearts to keep beating, for example, or our lungs to keep breathing or our digestive system to stay on the job, though recent studies have shown that if we care to pay attention we have a good deal more control over these involuntary functions than was earlier believed by western medicine. Internally we are pretty much home thoughtless and free, but most of the activities with which we interact with the external world are under conscious control, wherein action is preceded by thought, no matter how brief and fleeting the thought.

Human beings are conscious creatures.

Consciousness depends on oxygen.

Within the human brain, oxygen gives birth to consciousness, to thought and feeling.

HYPOTHESIS:

Oxygen reflects the thinking aspect of consciousness: gaseous oxygen is a translation into the material world of thought.

****

Consider these parallels:

Oxygen, colorless, odorless, tasteless, is invisible to our eyes, undetectible by our senses of touch, taste, or smell.

> Thought, colorless, odorless, tasteless, is invisible to our eyes, undetectible by our senses of touch, taste or smell.

Air is 21 percent oxygen; we can often hear the rush or quick movement of air.

> If we pay the least attention, we can hear our own thoughts.

The air we breathe contains oxygen in molecular form, O_2, oxygen atoms joined together.

> A thought rarely comes to life on its own, unlinked to any other thought. One thought calls up another, the new thought calls up yet another, etc.

Oxygen enters our lungs accompanied by three to four times its volume in nitrogen (oxygen = 21.0 percent, nitrogen = 78.1 percent). Within the body nitrogen slows down combustion, slows down our internal burning. In the external world, nitrogen is used in cooling (refrigeration), cleaning (ammonia in household cleaners), fertilizers, explosives, and in the mining of precious ores.

> When a passing thought arises, there are several ways we can deal with it: we can

remain calm and cool, clean the thought up to make it more acceptable, grow from it, blow up about it, or extract insight from it.

Atomic oxygen combines with itself to form molecular oxygen, the form of oxygen we breathe, and combines with hydrogen to form water.

We speak of having thoughts and feelings as though the two were separate and distinct, but in truth it is all but impossible to disengage the two, and both arise from the same source: consciousness.

Almost all the work performed in the great world around us is accomplished through the transfer of the non mechanical form of energy known as heat, which is derived from combustion, ie, rapid oxidation.

Almost all of our actions are preceded by thought, given impetus and energy by thought, from the moment we wake up and decide to crawl out of bed until that moment hours later when we kick off our slippers and climb back into bed. If we are unconscious, unmotivated by thought, we lose our ability to deal actively with the external world.

In our inner reality, thought energizes. In the external world, energy is derived from combustion which is dependent on oxygen.

Oxygen is the most abundant element in our physical world; thought is the most common phenomenon of our mental world.

Surely these parallels between oxygen and thought are not logically imperative. It is easy to imagine a world wherein no such congruence exists. For example:

Thought is colorless, odorless, tasteless, invisible. So is oxygen. Earthlike life *could* have evolved dependent on a gas with color and taste, or on a gas with an odor such as ozone, chlorine, or fluorine. But it didn't.

Thoughts ordinarily come to life linked with other thoughts. Oxygen atoms join together to form molecular oxygen.

Earthlike life *could* have evolved dependent upon a gas which doesn't commonly combine with itself into molecular form. But it didn't.

Thoughts and feelings both arise in human consciousness and tend to be inextricably intermixed. Gaseous oxygen combines with hydrogen, another gas, to form the fluid upon which our lives depend. Earthlike life *could* have developed dependent upon a gas which was not the principle ingredient of a life-sustaining, essential fluid. But it didn't.

We are motivated—energized—by consciousness, by thought. Combusion, ie, rapid oxidation, performs almost all of the work in the world around us. Earthlike life *could* have developed dependent on a gas which did not also fuel energy exchanges in the external world. Living bodies could have one fueling system while the world around them runs by the grace of a different energy source. But that's not the way it is for us.

Thought, the most common phenomenon of our mental world, depends on oxygen, the most abundant element in our physical world. Earthlike life, life with consciousness, *could* have developed dependent on a relatively rare gas rather than on the most common element there is. But it didn't.

In effect, a universe containing life *could* have been created, or *could* have evolved, in which consciousness was not reflected. But such a universe is not the one in which we find ourselves.

In the universe as it exists—if it exists—to see our own reflection we have only to look.

9
THE FOUR FORCES
What Does Impersonal Nature Know Of The Personal Heart?

> It is the passions of man that both do and undo everything.—They are necessary to put everything in motion, though they often cause storms.—
> Bernard Le Bovier de Fontenelle (1657-1757)

There are today, we are told by the Learned Ones, four recognized ways of interacting in the universe. In old fashion parlance, there are four known *forces*. These four forces cover all known interations, with no need for any fifth force or fifth method of interacting.

These four forces given in order of *decreasing* strength are:

        Strong nuclear
        Electromagnetic
        Weak nuclear
        Gravitational

Gravity, like the poor, has always been with us as a recognized force, but not necessarily recognized as a way of interacting. What goes up must come down: this was known. The early Greeks postulated that bodies contained a force within them that propelled them downward. The Earth was flat and down was down. Obviously the Earth couldn't be round or occupied on the under surface because those poor benighted souls on the underside would promptly fall off.

Centuries later Isaac Newton (1642-1727) appeared and extended the well known Earth force, gravity, out into the Solar System and the force, or method of interacting, known as universal gravitation was born. Objects fall down upon the surface of the Earth because all objects in the world attract each other. A ball sailing through the air attracts the Earth just as the Earth attracts the ball, the power of the pull being proportional to mass and in inverse ratio to the square of the intervening distance. Due to relative mass, the Earth appears unmoved by the ball while the ball falls quickly back to Earth. Gravitation is the force, or method of interacting, that holds everything together, keeps all celestial bodies in their proper or at least their familiar places, the force that binds the universe.

Scientists were somewhat uneasy with this form of universal gravitation for how did this force act across distance? How can two bodies attract each other through empty space? Obviously some force was holding everything in place, but what was the mechanics behind the force? How did universal gravitation work?

Early in this century Albert Einstein (1879-1955) put before us a new curved universe in which he dispensed with the perplexing action-at-a-distance of Newton's universal gravitation. In Einstein's new relativistic universe, space and time are not separate and non-interchangeable as they have always been perceived as being. Rather they form a heretofore unsuspected unity, space-time, and mass has a heretofore unsuspected proclivity; it warps space-time. In the Solar System planets don't revolve around the Sun due to some mystical attraction She holds for them, but because the Sun, vastly more massive than her little brood of planets, warps space-time. Just as it is often easier to go around a mountain than to go up and over one, the planets circle the warp in curved space-time which the massive Sun creates because it's the easiest path available to them. In effect, gravitation is simply the geometry of curved surfaces.

Gravity as geometry apparently does not satisfy all our Learned Ones. Because the strong nuclear force and the electromagnetic force are explained in terms of the transfer of particles, the assumption has been made that the weak nuclear force and gravity also operate through some such exchange. The particle associated with gravity has been named, appropriately enough, the *graviton.* The graviton has been theoretically endowed with the properties it needs to do its job: it is electrically neutral, without mass (also without substance?), travels at the speed of light, is stable (that is, left alone it doesn't disintegrate), and has a spin of two. Although the graviton has been with us in name for over a decade, it has yet to be detected, or at any rate has not yet been detected under the proper auspices, with the proper scientific credentials. As of this writing, it remains elusive. It is still anybody's guess as to whether it in reality exists.

Although gravity is an old familiar friend (or enemy, as the case may be) and seems to rule the visible world with irresistible power, it is the weakest by far, we are told, of the four forces known to the Scientists.

The second weakest force: the weak nuclear.

The weak nuclear force operates, as its name implies, within the nucleus. It is the force held responsible for radioactivity.

In 1895 William Roentgen, a German physicist (1845-1923), while researching the effects of passing high-voltage electricity through various gases, discovered X-rays. *X-rays:* "a form of electromagnetic radiation similar to light but of shorter wavelength and capable of penetrating solids and of ionizing gases."

Roentgen's discovery of x-rays led to the invention of x-ray tubes. *X-ray tube:* "an electronic tube for producing x-rays, essentially a cathode-ray tube in which a metal target is bombarded with high-energy electrons."

Cathode-ray tube: "Electronics. a vacuum tube generating a focused beam of electrons that can be deflected by electric fields, magnetic fields or both. The terminus of the beam is visible as a spot or line luminescence caused by its impinging on a sensitized screen at one end of the tube."

Henri Becquerel, a French physicist (1852-1908), working with an x-ray tube noticed that the glass glowed with a greenish light while emitting the invisible radiation. He experimented with making various materials fluorescent to see if they too would emit an X-ray like radiation. (*Fluorescence: "Physics, Chem.* 1. the emission of radiation, esp. of visible light, by a substance during exposure to external radiation, as light or X-rays.")

One of the compounds he tried was a uranium salt. He found that this salt, whether or not it was made to glow, emitted some radiation. Every uranium compound he tried did the same. To radiate seemed a natural property of uranium.

Marie Curie (1867-1936), a Polish chemist and physicist working in France with her husband Pierre (1859-1906), found that pitchblende, a uranium ore, was four to five times as radioactive as pure uranium even after the uranium had been removed. Obviously the ore contained some other highly radioactive substance. The Curies worked to isolate this substance and in time discovered a hitherto unknown chemical element, four million times as radioactive as uranium. The element was given the name *radium* (Symbol RA, atomic weight 226, atomic number 88).

Other scientists were working to learn the nature of radioactivity. In 1899 an English physicist, Ernest Rutherford (1871-1937), found that uranium emitted three different kinds of radiation. He named the three rays: alpha, beta and gamma.

Beta rays, which experiment showed were negatively charged, turned out to be streams of electrons, while alpha rays, positively charged, turned out to be the nuclei of the inert gas helium (Symbol He, atomic weight 4.0026, atomic number 2). Gamma rays, with no electrical charge, turned out to be gamma rays. (*Gamma ray: "Physics.* a high-frequency, highly energetic, penetrating radiation emitted from the nucleus of a radioactive atom.")

Up until all of the above was discovered, atoms had been enshrined as the smallest units of matter. No more. Since alpha and beta particles and gamma rays were all tossed out from radioactive atoms, atoms could not be indivisible units. Clearly atoms were composed of parts, depriving Scientists of their bedrock unit out of which all of the physical universe was supposedly built. In return, however, this discovery gave our Learned Ones an invisible arena—the interior of the atom—in which they could allow their imaginations full reign.

In addition to radioactive decay, other forms of decay are believed to occur within atoms. Particles—it is said—flash in and out of existence, in a millionth or a billionth of a second or in even less time. The weak nuclear force presides over this disintegration of quantum particles and over radioactivity.

Because electromagnetism and the strong nuclear force both operate, it is believed, through the exchange of particles, it has been theorized that the weak nuclear force also has a particle exchange operating procedure. For this role as carrier of the weak force, a particle was proposed and named the W-particle. This particle, it was theorized, would be extremely short lived. It would also be massive—in subatomic terms—so massive that no existing accelerator had the energy to create one. Despite this negative prediction, it has since been reported that at CERN, the European Organization for Nuclear Research, which operates a nuclear laboratory near Geneva, Switzerland, researchers recorded one of their greatest achievements: the discovery of the elusive particle W, also a companion particle Z, the avidly sought particles believed to be the carriers of the weak nuclear force.

The third weakest or second strongest force in the world: electromagnetism.

The human race has had some familiarity with the electromagnetic force since long before Christ.

The ancient Greeks were aware that rubbing amber gave it an attractive power to pick up objects. Through rubbing the amber was *electrified.* Our English word "electricity" comes from the Greek word *elektron* meaning amber.

The ancient Greeks were also aware that certain iron ore had the power to attract light bits of iron. They called this iron ore *magne,* from deposits near the city of Magnesia in Asia Minor. From this is derived our English word *magnet.*

The two forces—the attractive power of electrified amber and the natural magnetism of some iron ore—were so similar that some relationship between the two was long suspected. In 1820 a Danish scientist, Hans Christian Oersted (1777-1851), tied the two together with proof that an electric current passed through a wire held north to south above a compass needle deflects the needle to east-west. An English physicist and chemist, Michael Faraday (1791-1867), in 1831 discovered electromagnetic induction: a magnet moved through a coil of wire produces a current of electricity. From this discovery came development of the electric generator, the heart of all modern electric power plants.

James Clerk Maxwell (1831-1879), a Scottish physicist, after a profound study of the work of Michael Faraday, reasoned that electromagnetism moved through space in waves. He calculated the velocity of the waves, discovered that it was the same as the velocity of light, and pronounced light waves electromagnetic in nature. He developed four simple field equations to express the fundamental workings of light, electricity and magnetism. Maxwell's field equations were accepted as fundamental Law of the universe along with Isaac Newton's Laws of motion and gravitation until the beginning of this century when the theory of relativity, quantum theory and wave mechanics shook up the established world view. Maxwell's equations still hold good in the macroscopic universe (*Macroscopic:* "visible to the naked eye") just as Newton's Laws of motion and gravitation are still used to explain the movement of visible bodies on Earth and bodies in the vast *out there.* It is only in the deep *in here* that new Laws have been devised.

So what is magnetism, what is electricity, what is electromagnetism, and how do they all work?

Magnetism:
Magnets or magnetized needles exert their force from around their ends, and experiments have shown that while the two ends of a magnet have equal power to attract, their attractive powers are not identical. One end of a magnet will attract the north-seeking end of a magnetized needle, the other end will repel it. This led to the designation of north pole end and south pole end on magnets and the rule that unlike poles attract while like poles repel.

If a bar magnet or magnetized needle is cut in two, new south and north poles come into being immediately in the cut off pieces. This happens no matter how often the magnet is cut in two. This led Scientists to believe that the magnetic power of the magnet resided in the smallest possible unit of it, that is, in a single molecule.

This simple molecular theory of magnetism failed to explain how the molecules of magnetic material exerted their attractive force. Modern theory explains it on the basis of the behavior of electrons within the atoms. Electrons are now believed to be in constant motion within the atomic structure. They are known to carry an electric charge. An electric charge in motion always creates a magnetic field.

Electrons are believed to have two kinds of motion, much as the Earth spins on its axis while revolving around the Sun. Within the atomic structure, electron revolutions ordinarily proceed in opposite directions, as do the spins, so each kind of motion is canceled out, canceling out the attendant magnetic fields.

Atoms of iron differ from this general rule. (*Iron:* Symbol Fe, atomic weight 55.847, atomic number 26). In the next to outermost shell of the iron atom there are five electrons sharing the same spin with only one electron of opposite spin. This five to one discrepancy creates a magnetic force which extends beyond the atom to give it a magnetic field.

Electricity:
In June 1752 the great Benjamin Franklin, American statesman, diplomat, author, inventor and scientist (1706-1790), flew a kite during a storm to test his belief that lightning is a discharge of electricity from the clouds. The

high flying kite sent a charge of electricity down its wet string. Franklin put his knuckle to a key tied on the string and saw an electric spark, proving his theory. He subsequently invented the lightning rod to protect physical structures from lightning bolts.

It had earlier been discovered by Sir William Watson, an English scientist, that electricity traveled almost instantaneously along a two mile long wire. In 1746 Watson suggested a "one fluid" theory of electricity. Before that it had been suggested that since there seemed to be two distinct types of electricity, perhaps there were two different electric fluids. Watson reduced these two to one fluid, of which there was either an excess (+) or a lack (−). Electricity would then be a flow of this fluid from + to −, neatly accounting for all known facts.

After Franklin flew his kite and brought electricity down to Earth from the sky, he accepted Watson's "one fluid" theory, which led to universal acceptance.

It has since been shown by the Scientists that what was considered a lack is actually an excess. Electrons, the moving force in electricity, are considered to have a negative charge while matter with a minus quotient of electrons is said to be positively charged. Thus the flow of current—the flow of electrical charges—goes from the negative to the positive, and not from the positive to the negative as originally supposed.

But what is it that flows? No one has ever seen a current of electricity. Electrons, which are crucially involved in electric current, have a mass, in grams, of 9.1×10^{-28} or 0.00000000000000000000000000091 grams, which makes them too small to be visible even under magnification. In dealing with such subatomic particles as the electron, physicists have to depend upon indirect methods of detection, from which they form imaginary models of what is actually taking place.

Electric current is commonly referred to as a flow of electrons, but nothing actually flows except force. To illustrate: Line billiard balls in a row. Apply force to the ball at one end and the ball at the other end will roll off while the other balls in the row scarcely move. Electric charge "flows" in this same way, with the force moving at the speed of light while individuals electrons move only slightly.

Electromagnetism:
Electromagnetism: "1. the phenomena associated with the relations between electric current and magnetism."

The electromagnetic force—the force that holds together oppositely charged particles—is considered to be the second strongest force in the world. All matter is held together by this force, which works on the atomic level to hold the orbiting electrons in proper place around the atomic nucleus. Currently the Scientists explain the workings of the electromagnetic force in this fashion: charged particles exert force on each other through the exchange of photons (*photon:* "a quantum of electromagnetic radiation," ie, the basic unit of light), not real photons but *virtual* ones (*virtual:* "1. being such in force or effect, though not actually or expressly such . . .")

This is the accepted script:

Nuclear protons shoot these virtual photons out toward the orbiting electrons, and the orbiting electrons shoot them back. Through this exchange of virtual photons two particles with opposite charges attract each other. The theory is that numerous virtual photons fly back and forth in this rapid-fire exchange, and the exchange is the source of attraction which keeps the orbiting electrons in proper orbit.

Physicists—or at least some physicists—concede that virtual particles, particles that are virtually particles but are not quite real particles, are a free creation of the human mind, may have nothing at all to do with the way Nature really is, but the theory has been found to work, rendering subatomic interactions predictable, which means it is virtually factual, at least, and the closest Scientists can come at the moment to actual, natural fact.

The strongest force in the world: the strong nuclear force.

Like electrical charges repel each other. This has been well established. Within all atomic nuclei other than hydrogen, there is more than one positively charged proton. If there weren't some force holding these protons together, the electromagnetic force would blow them apart.

It takes the strongest force known to hold atomic nuclei together, to where the positively charged protons can exist packed closely together in stable family atomic life. This force, or method of interaction, is known as the strong nuclear force. The energy released in atomic bombs taps into a very small fraction of this strongest of all known forces.

The current theory of the Learned Ones is that all force is mediated through the exchange of particles. The as yet undetected graviton is the carrier of gravity, the photon (the quantum of radiant energy) handles the electromagnetic force, the recently discovered W and Z particles mediate the weak force. Therefore there must be a fourth exchange particle to account for the strong nuclear force.

The properties of this exchange particle were theoretically outlined in 1935 by the Japanese physicist Hideki Yukawa (1907-1981). The particle contained energy, existed very briefly—just long enough to bounce back and forth between protons in the nucleus, in this fashion binding them together, but not long enough for this force to be felt outside the nucleus, where it is never felt—with a mass somewhere between the electron and the proton (protons are 1836 times more massive than electrons).

In 1936 a new particle was detected by an American physicist Carl David Anderson (born 1905) which was being occasionally knocked out of atomic nuclei by cosmic rays. The mass of the new particle, which Anderson named the *mesotron,* meaning intermediate, was right for the theoretically predicted Yukawa particle, but unfortunately in other ways the mesotron, a name quickly shortened to meson, failed to qualify as the sought after exchange particle. In 1947, a group of English physicists headed by Cecil Frank Powell (1903-1969), in the course of their studies of cosmic rays, detected another nuclear particle of intermediate mass. Anderson's previously detected particle was renamed the *mu-meson,* soon shortened to *muon,* and Powell's meson was dubbed the *pi-meson,* soon shortened to *pion.* The pion was awarded the crown as Yukawa's long sought exchange particle.

Later experiments brought the realization that the nucleus bustled with far more complicated life than was originally suspected. Experimental physicists working at Stanford University shot beams of high energy electrons at a proton target, studied the results of the collisions, and concluded that protons have internal structure and extension in space. Protons were not elementary particles after all, but were composed of smaller parts. These particle-parts were christened *quarks,* and once quarks were ushered onto the scene, *gluons* were sure to follow.

Quark: "any of three types of elementary particles that are believed by some physicists to form the basis of all matter in the universe." The three quarks have since expanded into five known ones and a suspected but as yet undetected number six. Some physicists theorize there may be as many as twelve. The name comes from *Finnegan's Wake* by Irish novelist James Joyce (1882-1941): "—Three quarks for Muster Mark!" *Quark* is a German word for a curd of cheese, and was first applied to the subatomic world by German physicist Murray Gell-Mann (born 1929).

Gluon: "an elementary particle that is conjectured to bind quarks together, thus forming most of the observable nuclear particles, such as protons, neutrons, pions, etc."

The latest on the four forces or four methods of interaction—as this is being written—stacks up something like this:

Gluons (from the word *glue*) carry the various forces or mediate interactions. In effect they are the stickiness that holds the world together.

In order of increasing strength:

Force	Gluon
Gravity	Graviton. Not yet detected; due to its nature may never be detected.
Weak nuclear	W^+, W^-, $Z°$. Reported to have been discovered at CERN (European Organization for Nuclear Research).

Force	Gluon
Electromagnetic	Photon, the basic unit of radiant energy, of visible light. Known and loved by all.
Strong nuclear	Colored gluons.

The strength of the interaction depends on the "stickiness" of the gluon. The strong nuclear force is the strongest of all known forces due to the super-stickiness of the eight colored gluons that bind the quarks together. Thus stickiness is the entire story, a story we needn't stick with any longer.

These four forces, or four methods of interaction, cover *all* interactions in the *physical* universe, we are told, or all *physical* interactions in the universe. When the Scientists describe these four interactions and make the statement that these four interactions cover everything, are they including every kind of *human* interaction?

For example, do they mean to include the interaction of romantic lovers? the interaction of parent with child? the forces that come into play when a human being contemplates or faces her own death or sure dismemberment? the forces that tie a man to his expensive new Mercedes or a woman to her prized fur coat? All of these are interactions, they all occur—*are they included?*

Certainly the human animal is not entirely excluded from the physical world described by the Physicists. Human bodies are subject to gravity, and to electromagnetic forces. A human body, like all other material in the universe, is composed of molecules, atoms, and the subatomic particles crowding the atomic nucleus. Therefore on an atomic or subatomic level the human body is presumably governed by the forces studied with such diligence by the Learned Ones. But what about those interactions in which the human psyche is involved, the human heart or the human mind? Are they covered too?

Which of the four forces binds a mother to her child? a man to his mate? either man or woman to some prized material possession? What force causes the fear of sickness? the fear of death? These are all realities, they *do* occur, and they occur within the confines of the physical universe. Yet in book after book dealing at length with the way these four forces work, with the way interactions occur, there isn't the least hint of how all of this applies to the human psyche or to human behavior. It's as though human beings somehow don't live in the same universe as the quarks and gluons, as though the human mind, the human heart, thoughts, emotions, dreams, have no place in the physical universe. If human interactions aren't covered by the four known forces, the four recognized methods of interaction, then the Learned Ones should stop claiming that their four recognized forces cover all interactions in the universe with no need for any fifth force.

If, as has been postulated earlier in this book, the physical universe is a projection or reflection of consciousness, then the four known physical forces, or four known methods of interaction, should be a fun house mirror image of the forces within human beings, the forces that govern their interactions both internally and with that which is or appears to be external.

If we look at the human condition, we will find, happily enough, that here again four is the magic number. All human behavior falls into one of four types of interaction, with no need for any fifth type.

Human beings interact 1) with their material environment; 2) with other living beings; 3) consciousness interacts with the physical body it inhabits; 4) consciousness interacts with itself.

We'll start with a translation chart, then proceed with a more in depth discussion of the claimed correlation:

Gravity	The attractive force between human beings and their material surroundings.
Weak nuclear	The drive in the human self or ego which supervises the growth (W^+),

	maintenance ($Z°$), and decay (W^-)of the physical body.
Electromagnetic	The attraction—love—between human beings in all its varied manifestations.
Strong Nuclear	The drive in the human self or ego to maintain itself, to preserve its integrity against any and all threats of disintegration.

In the physical world, two of these forces operate only within atomic nuclei while the other two are long range, operating over distances.

In our exchange chart, two of the forces oversee processes that occur *within* the individual being, the other two oversee interactions with what is external.

Let's consider the two forces that occur over a long range first.

Gravity:

In our day to day life, gravity does not seem like the superweak force it is. Rather it seems pretty close to all powerful. We learn in early childhood that what goes up will surely come down, and in later childhood are taught that gravity holds the Moon up there in the sky and keeps our Earth revolving around the Sun. For centuries we dreamed of flying but felt ourselves to be Earthbound, in the grip of irresistible gravitational force.

If we look around, we will see a force that seems pretty close to all powerful too: the attractive force between people and material objects. Greed seems rampant. We can scarcely glance at the morning paper or listen to a TV newscast without hearing of some new crime committed for material gain. People steal from each other on every side. Muggings, burglaries, car thefts, forgeries, embezzlements—the list seems endless. One would almost conclude that greed for money and material objects rules the human mind and heart quite as powerfully as gravity rules the physical body.

But is such rampant greed really the ruling power it appears at first glance?

Gravitation is such a weak and insignificant force it is scarcely more than a shadow in the universe. The strong nuclear force, the strongest known force, is 137 times stronger than electromagnetism, a hundred thousand times stronger than the weak force, but almost *a thousand trillion trillion trillion times stronger than gravity.*

Gravity—greed for matter or the material world—often seems a powerful ruling force, yet in reality it's extremely weak.

Compare the attraction the ego feels for material objects with the other interactions occurring, and the weakness of greed as a force becomes apparent.

While it is said of some people that they would push their grandmothers downstairs for a dime, this is not true of the vast majority of people. Those who are criminally greedy are still vastly outnumbered by those who are not. When it comes to those gray areas of petty pilfering where few are caught, many or most people who cheat a bit on their income taxes or help themselves to supplies owned by their employers would never consider stealing from their relatives or friends. For most people the attractive force that binds them to those they care about is far stronger than greed, just as the electromagnetic force is far stronger than gravity.

The other long range force—the other force that operates outside the ego or nucleus—is electromagnetism.

Electromagnetism:

References to romantic love are replete with similes and metaphors that tie into electromagnetic phenomena. The chemistry between lovers—ah, how important that is! Chemical behavior depends on electrons, leading us right into electromagnetism. Some people are said to be highly magnetic; looks can be charged, touches electrifying. Opposites attract, we are told, just as in the electrical world. For about 90 percent of the human race, physical attraction is inspired by sexual differences and leaps across sexual boundaries. In addition, attraction is often between the psychologically different, the extrovert attracting the introvert and vice versa. When we fall in love, we are falling under the spell of electromagnetic forces, and few people who have known this force would dispute its power, or deny that it is almost infinitely stronger than the attractive force between people and material things.

Romantic love, no matter how thrilling and special, is not the only kind of love, of course. Parental love may be even stronger, or brotherly love, or love of the good or God. In each case an attractive force is at work, a force mirrored in the electromagnetic force inherent in Nature.

Two of the four known forces operate only within atomic nuclei: the weak and the strong nuclear forces.

The weak nuclear force:

The weak nuclear force, far stronger than gravity but a hundred thousand billion times weaker than the strong force, operates only within the constricted world of the nucleus, overseeing particle exchanges and radioactive decay.

This force mirrors a force that operates strictly within the individual self: that part of the self that oversees the growth, maintenance and aging of the physical body.

While we tend to feel little tension at the loss of renewable parts, such as hair and nails, when it comes to our non renewable assets, like arms, legs, eyes, etc., there is a drive within us to hold on and not part with what we've got. This drive is rarely as strong as the force that binds us to the ones we love. Most of us would risk loss of limb and sometimes even loss of life for those we love. But the drive to maintain our physical bodies and not give up any irreplaceable parts is commonly far stronger than the attractive force most of us feel toward material objects. Few of us would part with an arm in exchange for a new Mercedes or give up a leg for a new fur coat. When we say we'd give an arm or leg for something, generally we are kidding. Asked to put up, we would shut up.

The strong nuclear force:

The fourth and final force, the strongest known force in the universe, like the weak nuclear force operates solely within atomic nuclei.

This mirrors a drive occurring solely within the individual: the drive of the mind or ego to maintain itself, to keep its integrity intact.

Self preservation is the first Law of Nature, we are told. Yet many of us, under the dictates of love, would and do sacrifice our lives for others: parent for child, brother for brother, lover for loved one. However, if we were asked to sacrifice not our lives but our *egos,* our sense of self, most of us would not know how. Asleep and dreaming or awake, we are aware of a deep sense of *I,* and few of us have any idea how to let go of this sense, how to dissolve it away. Each of us has been a distinct *I* all of her life and we don't know how to stop being one. The force that keeps the ego intact, that keeps each individual *I* intact, is the strongest force in the world, and is mirrored by the super-stickiness of the gluons which hold the tiniest bits of matter together in atomic nuclei.

If the universe we live in is a reflection of consciousness, then the four known physical methods of interaction should mirror the way we human beings interact with ourselves, with others and with the material world.

The four known forces *do* mirror exactly that.

For additional evidence of this, let's take a more careful look into the innards of the atom to see what's there to see.

10

THE ATOMIC WONDERLAND
Who Would Have Thought the Tiny Old Atom Had So Much Stuff In It?

> All nature is a vast symbolism; every material fact has sheathed within it a spiritual truth.
> Edwin Chapin (1814-1880)

That matter has an atomic structure was first suggested, so far as historical accounts have come down to us, by a Greek philosopher, Democritus, the Laughing Philosopher (c460-370 BC). All substances, according to the theory of Democritus, were composed of tiny, invisible particles suspended in empty space.

This theory, which ran counter to the accepted notion of a material continuum, was rejected for over two thousand years. But experimental observations during the late 18th Century forced Scientists away from their cherished notions of continuity, and in 1805 an English chemist and physicist, John Dalton (1766-1844), proposed the first formal atomic theory.

All matter is composed of tiny, discrete particles, Dalton theorized. He named these particles *atoms,* from the Greek word, *atomos,* meaning "indivisible." The types of atoms are limited by the number of elements: each element has its own kind of atom.

In 1911 an English physicist, Ernest Rutherford (1871-1937), on the basis of results from experiments with alpha particles, gave the world a picture of the internal structure of the "indivisible" atom: most of the mass of the atom was concentrated in a small sphere which was positively charged, and this core or nucleus was surrounded by a large cloud of negatively charged electrons, which were of very small mass. Thus the atom was similar to a miniature Solar System: a massive nucleus surrounded by its family of tiny electrons, the system held together by electrical forces rather than by gravity.

There was only one serious flaw in this picture. According to classical physics, such an atom could not be stable. The orbiting electrons would radiate away their energy and collapse into the nucleus.

A Danish physicist, Niels Bohr (1885-1962), rode grandly to the rescue. Atoms are stable in defiance of electrodynamic Law because such Law did not apply to the atomic world, Bohr declared. Electrons in orbit do not radiate light; the light emitted by atoms comes from some other source. Bohr postulated that there are specific orbits for the revolving electrons and declared that there is an innermost orbit beyond which no electron can fall, thus insuring stability.

Most of us still visualize the atom according to the Bohr model: a microscopic Solar System in which tiny electron-planets revolve in set orbits around the massive nuclear Sun.

Once it was shown that atoms had internal structure, they could no longer be considered the fundamental building blocks of the material universe.

In 1879 an English physicist, Sir Joseph J. Thomson (1856-1940), had discovered a particle much smaller than the atom, and this tiny particle was named the *electron* (from the Greek *elektron,* meaning amber).

In 1919 Ernest Rutherford, bombarding the atomic nucleus to break it into its constituent parts, discovered the *proton,* a particle 1836 times as massive as the electron, with a positive charge equal to the negative charge of the electron.

In 1932 an English physicist, James Chadwick (1891-1974), discovered a particle which was slightly more massive than the proton and electrically neutral. This particle was named the *neutron*. In time the two massive nuclear particles, the proton and the neutron, came to be called the *nucleons*. Except for the fact the proton has a charge and the neutron has none, they are practically identical.

The atom was now explained: protons and neutrons inhabited the tightly packed nucleus, and the number of protons, which were positively charged, equaled the number of negatively charged electrons which revolved around the nucleus in their specified orbits. The total of protons and neutrons, the nucleons, determined the atomic weight.

One primary problem immediately emerged: if the electrons weren't sprinkled around, through and among the protons, neutralizing their electric charges, how did atoms exist? Like charges repel. The protons, instead of living in closely packed harmony, should explode away from each other in mutual repulsion. Matter could not exist, except for hydrogen with its single proton. Yet matter *did* exist, or seemed to anyway, in stubborn disregard of well established scientific Law.

This problem was soon solved. A force was needed to hold the nucleus together, a force strong enough to overcome the electromagnetic repulsion. In such wise the strong nuclear force was born. The strong force operates right where it should, within the nucleus, and doesn't go roving out where it isn't needed and doesn't belong, outside the nucleus. In this fashion matter was saved and the universe as we know it awarded the scientific seal of approval.

Once the Learned Ones had become this learned, they were naturally interested in knowing whether the three particles they had identified—the electron, the proton and the neutron—were fundamental particles or whether they too were composed of even smaller particles. They craved assurance that their latest picture of the internal structure of the atom was the last word on it. In pursuit of final truth, they kept prodding at and probing their invisible prey. Under constant bombardment, continually forced to scatter, the world of the quanta, the subatomic world, had what a non-scientist can only describe as a nervous breakdown.

How many angels can dance on the point of a pin?
Solemn arguments once raged on this question. Those debating were dealing with invisibles to whom they ascribed unseen properties. In today's scientific world, the subatomic Physicists are dealing with invisibles, to which they ascribe unseen properties in the well established tradition of those Learned Ones of the Middle Ages.

To gain some notion of how tiny an atom is consider this: one linear centimeter of solid material (centimeter = cm = .3937 inches) is said to contain *50 million atoms.* The typical atom has a radius of 10^{-8} cm (.00000001 cm), most of this empty space. As minuscule as the atom is, the diameter of the atom is ten thousand times greater than the diameter of the nucleus, which measures no more than 10^{-12} cm (.000000000001 cm). As the nucleus contains about 99.95% of the mass of the atom, nuclear matter is considered to be incredibly dense, at least one million billion times the density of water.

Within this too-small-to-be microscopic bit of incredibly dense nuclear mass, the subatomic particles are found.

As there is no way directly to observe a particle which is no bigger than 1/10,000,000,000,000 of a centimeter across, some other mode of gaining information must be devised. The method used by our Learned Ones is scattering. Through electromagnetic means, particles are sped up to great speed, then thrown at other particles and the results of the collisions studied.

Two types of equipment are needed for this kind of experiment. First there must be some form of accelerator to send the projectile particles hurtling on their way. Then there must be some kind of detecting devise to record the results of the collisions.

Modern accelerators come in two shapes: straight linear or circular. The straight linear are used for start-up purposes even with the circular accelerators, which are called *synchrotons.* Once the particles have been given an initial velocity by the linear accelerators, they are fed into synchrotons for greater acceleration. The particles are sent circling around by powerful magnetic fields; they can make the round trip over and over, with each circling gaining a boost in speed and energy. Finally they are speeding fast enough to throw them at their targets, much as high speed chases in movies finally end in some spectacular collision.

At Stanford University in Palo Alto, California, there is a linear accelerator for electrons which is two miles long. The two largest proton synchrotons are located at Fermilab outside Chicago, Illinois, and at CERN—European Organization for Nuclear Research—near Geneva, Switzerland.

After the projectile targets have been sufficiently speeded up, they can be used in two ways. They can be made to collide with a fixed target, or they can be used to interact with a second beam of high speed, projectile particles. In the latter case, each beam of particles contributes enormous energy, which of course makes for more breath-taking collisions, as we all know from watching high speed car crashes in movies.

Once the collision has taken place, some means for detecting the results is required. One of the earliest means used was devised by a Scottish physicist and meteorologist, C. T. R. Wilson (1869-1959), working at Cambridge University in England. It became known as the Wilson cloud chamber. The cloud chamber contained cooled water vapor on the point of condensation. A speeding particle moving through the vapor ionizes some of the atoms it rushes by and at these sites tiny drops of water condense. Through these droplets of water the particle leaves a visible trail of its movements.

The early cloud chamber has since been replaced by a more sophisticated detecting device: the bubble chamber. Instead of containing a vapor about to condense, these chambers employ a liquid about to boil. This liquid serves not only as a detector but also as a target, for the collisions studied occur between the projectile particles and the particles making up the liquid. Tracks are left in the rather dense liquid of the chamber, and from this the experimenters can deduce all manner of wondrous things.

There other forms of detector devices which are based on electronic monitoring. These electronic devices have the advantage of being able to handle a greater number of interactions at a time, but the disadvantage of providing less information about any given transaction. Both types of detectors are considered important to modern subatomic physics and on occasion are used in concert. The electronic device is used to select an interesting interaction, then the bubble chamber is used to zero in on it.

Photographs are taken of the tracks left in the detector devices and these are studied to determine the nature of the particles leaving the tracks.

Through their cloud and bubble chambers, the subatomic Physicists have spread before us a fabulously rich cast of atomic characters. Through their tracks we do know them.

What began as a rather small cast of characters when the atom was first split—protons and neutrons within the nucleus, electrons in fixed orbits outside the nucleus—quickly proliferated into a dizzying and somewhat embarrassing array of particles. Today the Physicists claim they have detected the existence of thousands of subatomic particles, and still counting. Theoretical Physicists have suggested that there may be an infinity of them. Most of these particles flash in and out of existence in life spans of a millionth or a billionth of a second, or even less time. Some live just long enough to leave tracks in the bubble chambers, while others don't live even that long—Physicists *deduce* the existence of these unstable ones from the stable ones which live long enough to leave tracks. Bubble chambers, along with the experimenters who study the tracks within them, have created a veritable particle zoo.

The story is that only four of these thousands of particles are stable, that is, left to themselves they do not disintegrate. into these four stable ones. The four stable particles are: the proton, the electron, the photon, and the neutrino.

Up until the last few years it was assumed that these four stable particles, left undisturbed, would exist undecayed throughout eternity, but recently Science has pounced on the proton and is currently expending great effort and expense to prove that it isn't infinitely stable after all. If protons are infinitely stable, then the universe of matter that Science says we live in shouldn't exist. Right after the Big Bang there must have been—Science says—as much antimatter produced as matter. (Why? Because, that's why. Why should the Bang have favored the creation of matter over antimatter? It isn't scientifically right for Bangs to play favorites.) The matter and antimatter would have collided, annihilating each other, and the universe today wouldn't have galaxies, stars, planets and satellites composed of matter; it would be nothing more than a thin, lumpless soup.

Instead of this soupy universe, we have one containing matter.

To explain our matter-filled universe, it has been conjectured that the Big Bang created a hypothetical particle called X, which then decayed asymmetrically. Two physicists, James Cronin and Val Fitch, showed that a particle known as the $K°_L$ (K-zero-long) meson decayed asymmetrically in the laboratory, decaying slightly more often into a set of particles containing a positron than into a set of particles containing an electron. Therefore the hypothetical particle X may also have decayed asymmetrically (this now being allowed, due to the asymmetrical behavior of the $K°_L$ meson), decaying with slightly greater frequency into matter than into antimatter.

(Moral: Bangs can't play favorites but hypothetical X particles can.)

In time annihilation would eliminate all the antimatter, leaving a residue of matter to create our universe.

This scenario neatly (or rather arbitrarily?) explains our matter universe, but one of its mathematically built in features calls for proton decay.

Science has another reason for wanting the proton to be unstable. Today there are four recognized forces. Four is too many to satisfy the esthetic sense of Science. At the instant after the Big Bang, the four forces were surely one. Three theoreticians, Abdus Salam, Sheldon Glashow, and Steven Weinberg, have successfully unified two of the forces, the electromagnetic and the weak nuclear, into a single force, the electroweak. There is a concerted drive on the part of Science to add yet another of the forces, the strong nuclear, into a unification scheme. (Gravity, the weakest of the forces, remains at this point odd force out.) Theoretical mathematicians are hot on the trail of Grand Unification Theories, or GUT's. One of the predictions of the various GUT's is proton decay.

The proton has until recently been considered stable due to its extremely long life. The usual measure of a particle's stability is its half-life, the estimated time it takes for half the atoms in a given radioactive sample to decay. The best estimate of the proton's half-life, or average lifetime, is somewhere between 10^{31} to 10^{33} years, which is an almost inconceivably long time. The present age of the universe, estimated at about 17 billion years, is less than an eye-blink compared to the proton's theoretical half-life. This extended lifespan makes it extremely difficult to detect proton decay, if it exists. It's scarcely possible to fasten on a given proton, then wait around 10^{33} years (1000000000000000000000000000000000 years) to see whether or not it decays. (Even if it were possible, Science wouldn't want to wait that long.) But if the proton's average lifespan is 10^{33} years, then in a mass containing 10^{33} protons, *one* of the protons should decay each year.

One thousand tons of water contain 10^{33} protons. Therefore five thousand tons of water should give experimenters a chance to catch some protons in the act of decaying.

To block out cosmic ray interference, the Scientists have gone far underground with their huge tanks of purified water—ordinary water won't do—tanks lined with detecting devices which will, they hope, detect the tiny flashes of light the decaying protons give off.

Nobody knows exactly what a proton will decay into, but the decay products will be swiftly moving and electrically charged, according to the Scientists. And if proton decay *does* occur, if it can be proved to occur, this will be exciting and profoundly important news.

If protons decay, this will lead to the eventual death of the universe. Proton decay, if it occurs, signals a rotting process of matter itself. Goodbye, dear old material world.

However, even if protons are shown to decay, there's no need to rush off in immediate, panicky search of the antimatter universe the Learned Ones theorize may exist. There is loads of time. The ultimate decay of matter, if the proton *does* prove to be unstable, is not forecast for a thousand billion billion times the present age of the universe.

So far no suspicions have been cast upon the stability of the other three elementary particles: the electron, the photon, and the neutrino. All will exist as is throughout eternity, we are told.

Once subatomic particles are detected, various properties are ascribed to them. Such properties include, for starters, mass, charge and spin, these properties being designated by given numbers called quantum numbers.

In 1928 a brilliant young English physicist, Paul Dirac (born 1902), imposed the demands of relativity on quantum theory. His mathematical formulations insisted upon the existence of a particle no more massive than the electron but with a positive rather than a negative charge. In 1932 an American physicist, Carl Anderson (born 1905), who had not yet heard of Dirac's theory, discovered a particle which fit the specifications, named it the *positron,* and antimatter was born.

It is now believed that every particle has its antiparticle, a particle that is its counterpart in some respects and its exact opposite in other respects. Exceptions are those particles considered to be their own antiparticles.

As an example of how all of this works out, here is a breakdown on the four stable particles:

The proton is a fairly massive particle, being 1836 times more massive than the electron. It has a positive charge, a spin of ½, and its antiparticle is the antiproton (discovered at Berkeley in 1955).

The electron is a lightweight particle carrying a negative charge. It has a spin of 1, and its antiparticle is the positron. The stability of the electron is considered absolute, for this reason: it is the lightest known particle to carry a charge and cannot decay into anything lighter for no particle that was lighter could carry away its charge. Its decay would therefore violate the Law of the Conservation of Electrical Energy, a Law which countenances no violations, even in the generally liberal subatomic world.

The photon, which is the basic unit of light, is said to be massless. It travels at the speed of light, of course, which works out just fine. If it had any mass, that mass would become infinite at the speed at which the photon travels, according to Einstein's relativity theory. Even though the photon is massless, its lightning speed allows it to acquire energy and momentum. It is electrically neutral, has a spin of 1, and is considered to be its own antiparticle.

Don't ask what is spinning if the photon has no mass. Nonmaterialized energy is spinning. Photons are considered to be infinitely stable, yet if two photons collide, the energy is great enough to create mass and the collision results in the creation of an electron and a positron. If electron and positron collide, they annihilate into two photons, mass dissolving into pure energy. As Einstein showed the world, mass and energy are not distinct and separate, but are interchangeable, mass being a frozen form of energy, energy a liberated form of mass. In the high speed, massless photon, energy has spin.

The fourth infinitely stable particle, the neutrino, was predicted to exist before it was detected. In the 1930s it was found that in the decay of radioactive nuclei there wasn't enough energy left following the disintegration. Some mass-energy that had been there to start with wasn't accounted for, in blatant disregard of the Law of Conservation of Mass-Energy. An Austrian physicist working in the United States, Wolfgang Pauli (1900-1958), hypothesized that some undetected particle was carrying off the extra energy. This suggestion seemed rather too pat when it was made, but the elusive little fellow was soon detected. It carries no charge and therefore was named the neutrino, "neutral little one," by Enrico Fermi, an Italian physicist working in the United States (1901-1954).

The neutrino turned out to be uniquely fascinating. It is lighter than the electron and may be massless. On the other hand, it may have an extremely small mass. It is now believed to be so abundant that if it has any mass at all, the estimate is that neutrinos would account for 90 percent of the mass of the universe. They would become the dominant feature in this best of all possible worlds, with all visible matter in the form of galaxies, stars, planets, moons, etc., containing the other 10 percent of matter, relegated to a supporting role.

This superabundance of neutrinos stems from the fact that they are routinely produced in the decay of other particles. Stars radiate due to nuclear reactions deep within them which give off neutrinos, thus pouring these "neutral little ones" into space. Neutrinos remain neutrinos as they engage in only extremely weak interactions with other particles. Once a neutrino, always a neutrino—almost. Estimates are that it would take eight solid *light years* of lead to stop *half* the neutrinos given off in nuclear decay. They whiz through matter unaffected. Neutrinos are pouring through our bodies right this instant, it is said, yet the chances that a single one will interact with the nuclei of our tissues is slim to none.

To the surprise of Physicists, it was discovered there are two kinds of neutrinos: one neutrino is associated with the electron, the other with a particle known as the *muon*. Another surprise: neutrinos are left-handed. Whereas most quanta come in roughly equal mixtures of right and left-handed ones, neutrinos are exclusively left-handed.

How can a particle which may not have mass have either right or left-handedness? In this fashion: Neutrinos have a spin of ½. The axis of rotation is considered to be along the path of motion. Around this axis the spin can be clockwise or counterclockwise. Clockwise rotation is right-handedness, counterclockwise rotation is left-handedness. The counterclockwise spin of the neutrino makes it a leftie.

The elusive neutrino has been so tamed that Physicists can now produce and control beams of them. These beams have been used to penetrate deep within the structure of protons and neutrons, and much has been learned through these neutrino probes.

Classification of subatomic particles is simple and sensible. First there is the photon, the light-bearer, classy enough to start off alone in its group. More recently, this group has been expanded to include all gluons (all forms of glue) which mediate interactions, those detected and those merely surmised: the graviton (gravitation), the photon (electromagnetism), the W^+, W^- and $Z^°$ particles (weak nuclear force), and the colored gluons (strong nuclear force). Another name for these four mediators is *boson*.

The second group of particles: the *leptons*. Prime example: the electron. At first it was assumed that all leptons would be lightweight particles like the electron and neutrino, but in time leptons were discovered with embarrassingly large mass. For example: the *muon*, with a mass 207 times that of the electron, and the *tau*, with a mass 3536 times that of the electron. These heavy particles are classified as leptons despite their large mass because, like electrons, they engage in no strong interactions.

The third group: the *hadrons*. This group includes the protons and neutrons.

The word *hadron* comes from a Greek word for large. Hadrons are massive particles which participate in strong interactions. Hadrons are broken down into two primary groups according to spin: the *mesons*, with zero or integral spin, and the *baryons*, with 1/2 or 3/2 or other non integral spin.

To sum up this classification system:

Group 1: the gluons. They mediate interactions.

Group 2: the leptons. They engage in weak interactions but not in strong interactions.

Group 3: the hadrons. They participate in strong interactions.

In addition to mass, charge and spin, quantum particles are said to have a property called *statistics*. This property is related to behavior in a group. Some particles are sociable and enjoy being together. Other particles fall under the exclusion principle propounded by Wolfgang Pauli. Under the exclusion principle, the presence of one particle in a state excludes all others from this state.

There is a classification system based on this characteristic of statistics.

The particles which are sociable are called *bosons*, in honor of Indian physicist Satyendra Nath Bose (1894-1974), while those which abide by the Pauli exclusion principle are called *fermions*, in honor of Italian physicist Enrico Fermi (1901-1954).

It was found that all particles with an integral spin (a spin of 0, 1 or 2, etc.) are bosons, while all particles with half-odd-integral spins (a spin of 1/2, 3/2, etc.) are fermions. Photons are bosons, while electrons, protons and neutrons are fermions.

The bosons are carriers of force; the fermions are particles affected by force.

Under constant bombardment, the subatomic world broke down and a discouraging and embarrassing assortment of new hadrons sprang forth. To keep these particles sorted out, a new property was assigned: *strangeness*. Particles formed through strong interactions which decay through weak interactions have a strangeness quantum number, either positive or negative. Strangeness is conserved in strong interactions but not in weak interactions. Fortunately neither the proton nor the neutron have strangeness and their quantum strangeness number is zero.

Even this addition did not suffice to sort out the hadron particle zoo, so Physicists began to doubt they had reached the elementary level of particles. Hadrons were possibly composed of yet more fundamental particles. Probes of protons detected a graininess. Quarks were born.

Quarks, named after a word in James Joyce's book, *Finnegan's Wake*, were first hypothesized by a German physicist, Murray Gell-Mann, in 1964. What are quarks?

They are the substance from which hadrons are made. At first it was thought that three types of quarks would do the trick, explain all the different hadrons, and these three types were theorized to have *flavor: up, down* and *strange* or *sideways* (or chocolate, vanilla and strawberry, which of course have nothing to do with chocolate, vanilla and strawberry as we know those flavors). Letters were assigned as follows: *u* for up, *d* for down, and *s* for strange or sideways. Anti-quarks (everything must have an antiparticle) are denoted by the same letters with a bar across the top: $\bar{u}$, $\bar{d}$ and $\bar{s}$.

Hadrons are, we are told, very simply built out of quarks. The baryons, hadrons with 1/2, 3/2 or other non integral spin, are composed of any three quarks. The mesons, that other group of hadrons, are composed of quarks and anti-quarks. Quarks have integer electrical charge of 0, plus or minus 1, plus or minus 2, so that when the three quarks combine the right charge is present on the hadron.

In time it was found that three quark flavors couldn't handle the job of explaining the hadron zoo after all, so new quarks were hypothesized. In the early 1960's three theoretical physicists, Steven Weinberg, Abdus Salam and Sheldon Glashow, put forth an elegant theory which demanded the existence of exactly six quarks. The six quark flavors were designated as: *up, down, strange, charm, bottom* and *top*. The first five named were detected, it was claimed, but the sixth quark, the *top*, proved more elusive: accelerators did not generate sufficient energy to create collisions powerful enough for the *top* quark to be detected.

However, a recent newspaper article (Los Angeles Times, July 7, 1984) reports that physicists at CERN have now found the sixth and perhaps last of the quarks, the massive *top*. Beams of protons and antiprotons were set up to collide at extremely high energies. When matter (protons) and antimatter (antiprotons) collide, they annihilate each other, producing a tiny fireball of pure energy in which elementary particles are formed. Quarks cannot be isolated, so their existence must be inferred. The proton-antiproton collision occurs, the Physicists add up the momenta of the subatomic particles which spring out of the decay and from this estimate the mass of the original particle. After checking the debris of over 100 million collisions, experimenters claim to have found *six* fireball showers in which the *top* quark had been involved.

Quarks have never been isolated as free particles. Currently it is feared that all quarks have this one property in common: they are, apparently, permanently confined within hadrons.

The *top* quark is massive, much heavier than any of the other quarks. Both the u and d quarks are very light, while the s, the *strange* quark, is, like the *top*, rather massive. No one knows why. But this massiveness explains why strange hadrons, which must contain at least one *strange* quark, are heavier than non-strange hadrons.

The two nucleons, the proton and the neutron, not being strange themselves, naturally contain no *strange* quarks. The proton consists of two *up* quarks and one *down* quark, the neutron of one *up* quark and two *down* quarks.

The confinement of quarks within hadrons is so unbreakable a rule—at least so far—that when hadrons are split apart, quarks aren't freed; instead more hadrons are produced. The energy used in an attempt to separate the quarks creates new quarks trapped within another hadron.

Does this mean that Scientists, in detecting the quarks, have at last arrived at the ultimate building blocks of matter? that they have reached rock bottom? that the trapped quarks are *it*, the basic constituents of all that is?

No one knows, or at least if anyone knows she isn't saying.

Along with quarks came the *gluons*, the mediators that cause the quantum particles to stick to one another. The stickiest of all gluons are of course the ones that keep quarks bound inside their hadron prisons: the colored gluons.

With the emergence of quarks and gluons, radioactivity is explained. What happens is this: the weak gluons, in charge of radioactive decay, change the flavor of quarks. Strange hadrons by definition contain a *strange* quark. The weak gluons change the flavor of this *strange* quark into an *up* or *down* quark. They also change the flavor of *charmed* quarks into the non charming *up* and *down* quarks. In this way radioactivity becomes clear: it is the leaking away, through the mediation of the weak gluons, of strangeness and charm.

If the material universe mirrors consciousness, as is being contended herein, then this atomic wonderland must reflect basic aspects of consciousness.

To see whether there is any resemblance between subatomic matter and mind, let's first take a brief look at the structure and functioning of the human brain, the organ of mind.

The brain is the greatest challenge Scientists face. It is the most complex and highly specialized of all our organs. More than any other organ, it depends on an uninterrupted supply of nourishment. Brain cells, like all living cells, produce energy with which to function through the oxidation of glucose. Having few reserves, the brain *must* have a constantly renewed supply. It is the body's most sensitive organ in this regard. Deprived of nutrients, brain cells will suffer permanent damage very quickly. If the blood supply is cut off, loss of consciousness occurs within seconds. If deprivation continues, coma follows, then death.

Although the brain accounts for only about two percent of the total adult body weight, it consumes twenty to twenty-five percent of the glucose the body requires. To supply this disproportionate amount of nourishment, one-fifth of the output of the heart passes through the brain.

The brain is an information center processing sensory data. This data pours into the brain via electrical impulse. The brain has been mapped so that it is now known which area of the brain oversees which function: where memory is stored, which area controls bodily movement from the toes, ankles, knees, etc., right around to the jaw, tongue and swallowing; the area that oversees visual perception; the auditory area that oversees hearing; the area that oversees bodily sensation, etc. There are also "silent" areas in the brain, an *anterior silent area* and a *posterior silent area,* areas that are believed not to receive messages or initiate outgoing impulses. The posterior silent area is believed to be a clearinghouse where incoming information is organized, while thinking and planning may be carried out in the anterior silent area. This remains educated guesswork as it is not yet known precisely how the physical brain, an accumulation of grey and white cells, gives rise to—as it is assumed to do—an associated *mind,* to consciousness.

The first dictionary definition of mind is: "1. the agency or part in a human or other conscious being that reasons, understands, wills, perceives, experiences emotions, etc."

The mind is what *thinks;* it also *feels.* We all know what *thinking* is, just as we know what light is, and what life is and what death, as viewed from the plane of the living is. Just as with these other well known, commonly experienced phenomena, there is no precise definition of *thinking,* but it can be loosely defined as "whatever goes on in the brain" (though *thinking* may turn out to be a good bit more than this and far less tied to the physical brain than is commonly supposed). *Individual consciousness* can be defined as the sum total of what has gone on in a given brain (or its associated mind) from its birth to the present moment. Whether there is such a thing as *universal consciousness* remains as of this moment an open question.

The human brain is a marvel: three pounds of wrinkled, pink-grey porridge-like tissue capable of storing more information than all the computers and libraries in the world. The mind associated with the brain is equally or possibly even more marvelous. Sensory data pour into the brain, calling upon the mind to organize and respond to this input, with the power of choice as to which data it will pay attention to and bring into consciousness.

Despite the astounding storage capacity of the brain, the mind remains highly selective about which electric impulses pouring in it will honor with its notice. Every mother knows that there is more truth than fiction to the oft told tale that she can sleep through an alarm, a raging storm, a shrieking siren, yet if her baby whimpers in sleep in another room she will be instantly awake and alert.

Most of us have had this experience: we suddenly hear something—a ringing telephone, a knock on the door, someone calling our name—and as we hear it we *know* that the sound has been reaching us for some time without catching our attention enough to be consciously recorded. The brain has heard but the mind has not.

Many of us have also had this experience. We can stand talking with someone for several minutes, looking directly at the person, yet when the conversation ends and we turn away, we may have little or no idea what color hair the person had, what color eyes, what color and type of clothing. The sensory data poured in but simply did not register. The mind was not sufficiently interested to convert information into thought, to store the information as conscious memory.

Experiments have shown that much information which is lost to conscious recall can be brought back and expressed under hypnosis, when the masterminding conscious mind is put to sleep and communication established with other levels of mind. Such experiments have also shown that we store quite a lot of information perceived below the level of conscious awareness. To some impulses the mind pays attention and these will be brought into consciousness, converted into thought, and stored in memory. Other impulses, while they have the potential to become thought, will remain virtual only; they will virtually be thought, but not quite thought.

The stable constituents of the material atom are the negatively charged electron and the positively charged proton. They are attracted to each other—remain attached to each other—*associate* with each other—through the electromagnetic force, which force is expressed, the Physicists tell us, through the rapid fire exchange of *virtual* photons, photons that are not real but are virtual only. If enough additional energy is added to the charged particle, however—that is, if the electron becomes excited enough—the *virtual* photon becomes a *real* photon, capable of all the behavior of other real photons. It becomes a bearer of awareness, a bringer of light.

The mind is an associate of the physical brain. Their association is expressed through the rapid fire exchange of information, carried on electric impulse. Much of the exchange does not lead to real thought, it leads only to *virtual* thought, thought which has the potential to become real but remains virtual. However, if the mind reacts to incoming information with sufficient interest—energy—excitement—*virtual* thought becomes *real* thought, with conscious awareness. The thought comes to life—sees the light of day—within the mind.

We live in the age of drugs, an age when mind-altering chemicals are commonly ingested. This is nothing new. Every known society has partaken of some form of mind-altering drug, from the wine and beer of the Romans to the "magic" mushroom and peyote of American Indians. In late 20th Century United States society there is a wide choice of such drugs, from LSD through PCP to heroin, cocaine, marijuana, whiskey, gin, rum, vodka, wine, beer, which doesn't begin to name everything available. Many of us have had some experience, if only second hand in movies or books, with the hallucinations seen by those in the throes of the DT's. Those who have taken LSD talk and write of their wondrous "trips" through unfamiliar terrain. When the mind is altered, perceptions change, moods change, the familiar old world spins and sparkles or grows slow and static, becomes dazzling or nightmarish. Ordinary reality is escaped and a new reality emerges, brought on through the chemical and electric changes occuring in the brain. The brain is drugged and the mind succumbs.

The emerging new reality described above is drug-induced and its relationship with ordinary, non drug-induced reality is tenuous at best.

How much *ordinary* reality does a drug-induced *reality* have? How *real* is it? how meaningful? how permanent?

The atomic Physicists tell us that they have now detected thousands upon thousands of subatomic particles. Some Physicists suggest there may be an infinity of them. Most are detected from tracks they leave in bubble chambers, but some particles don't live long enough to leave tracks so their existence is indirectly deduced. The lifespans of most of these particles are almost infinitesimally small. The average lifetime of the charged pion, for example, is believed to be 26 *billionths* of a second. This is considered one of the more stable particles due to its long lifespan. The neutral pion, also considered relatively stable, only exists for 80 *quintillionths* of a second. Others flash in and out of existence even more quickly, or so the Physicists tell us.

As we read of this wild and wondrous subatomic world, we should keep one fact very strongly in mind. Over and over the nuclear Scientists remind us that the world of the subatomic, the quantum world with which they deal, *is an observer created world.* The type of experiment set up determines what properties are revealed. High energy collisions are arranged in order to *create* particles, and repeatedly the hope is voiced that once even higher energies are obtainable, additional particles will be created.

Heinz R. Pagels, in his fascinating book *The Cosmic Code* (Simon & Shuster, New York: 1982), puts it this way: "... most theoretical physicists are convinced that all these hypothetical particles will be discovered once accelerators with the energy capable of creating them are built."

Certain particles such as the weak gluons have not yet been detected because they are "extremely massive, so massive that no existing accelerator has the energy to create them." (Heinz R. Pagels, *The Cosmic Code.*)

First the Scientists *create* these exotic particles, *then* they detect them, thus proving their existence. When creation *by* human beings *precedes* detection by human beings, we are clearly not dealing with anything that resembles wholly objective—without human involvement—reality. Rather we are dealing with, as the Scientists very readily admit, *an experiment-induced reality.*

Physicists have proved it's possible to create a new, mind-boggling world. LSD enthusiasts have proved the same thing. Both proofs occurred at about the same time. Does the reality of one induced world mirror the reality of the other?

A user of LSD could boast that as soon as an even more powerful drug is produced, he will be able to take even wilder and weirder trips.

As soon as the Scientists have the power to create an even wilder and weirder subatomic world, they assure us they will do so. There is no reason to doubt their word.

According to current scientific belief, there are three infinitely stable particles: the photon, the electron and the neutrino. A fourth particle, the proton, enjoys either an infinite lifespan or an average lifespan trillions of times longer than the current estimated age of our universe. A fifth particle, the neutron, is under most circumstances also stable. When released from nuclear confinement, the neutron undergoes slow decay, disintegrating in about twelve minutes—a very slow process, by subatomic standards—into a proton, an electron and a neutrino. In the nucleus of radioactive elements neutron particles also decay. When safely confined in the nuclei of non radioactive elements, however, neutrons are stable.

If any subatomic particles have objective reality, these five would seem to be the ones: the proton, the neutron, the electron, the photon and the neutrino.

If the physical world mirrors consciousness, as is being argued herein, then these five particles must possess a reflective truth about the basic human condition.

A discussion of the way in which they do so is offered in the following chapter.

11

SHADOW AND SUBSTANCE

A Shadow Is — Does It Have Substance?

> If we begin with certainties, we shall end in doubt; but if we begin with doubts, and are patient in them, we shall end in certainties.
> Francis Bacon (1561-1626)

If the material world mirrors consciousness, then the basic, stable elements of matter must reflect basic, stable aspects of consciousness.

What are the basic, stable aspects of consciousness?

What do we know about consciousness, its basic nature and manifestations?

The first—and from our viewpoint the most significant—thing we know about consciousness is that we partake of it. We are conscious and we are here—whoever "we" are, wherever "here" is—and we, conscious creatures that we are, are here in the flesh. We are, or perceive ourselves as being, material creatures, and materialized life abounds on all sides around us. Weeds, grass, flowers spring up in every crack and cranny while animals are driven to reproduce, life flinging itself into matter with what seems to be total dedication and wild abandon.

Yet existing right alongside, or possibly within, this impulse toward life and growth there exists an impulse toward aging, decay and death. Cells age and die, to be replaced by new cells. This is a continuous process in all forms of life. It is so continuous within the human body that, according to the latest biological report, not a single molecule from the face I had six months ago survives in the face I have today. Yet even as my face and body continually renew themselves, casting off old cells and building new, I continue to be recognizable, both to myself and to others. Some organizing principle manages to rebuild the same old face and body, even aging it in the process, despite the disadvantage of having to achieve this with a constant supply of newly created, very young cells. This organizing principle seems driven by an impulse toward aging, decay and death.

Our bodies live and grow, they age and die.

Clearly there is a drive *toward* materialization and also a drive *away from* materialization.

The evidence indicates that every human being who has ever lived (excluding gods who may have taken on human form) has already died or in time will die. Therefore the drive toward aging and death has to be at least as strong as the instinct for survival. Yet life is everywhere, springing up in the unlikeliest and least welcoming places, indicating there is a drive at least as strong as the drive toward death which brings material life into being. Nothing can die that has not first been born, yet everything that is born eventually dies, so the two opposing drives—toward and away from materialization—achieve a standoff and appear to be equal.

According to the Physicists, there are three infinitely stable particles: the electron, the photon and the neutrino. A fourth, the proton, may also be infinitely stable or it may not be. In any case, its extended lifespan makes it stable enough for material purposes. A fifth particle, the neutron, is stable under most circumstances.

Three of these particles—the electron, the proton and the neutron—are the basic building blocks of matter.

The colorless, odorless, flammable gas hydrogen is believed to be the most abundant element in the universe. In its commonest form, it is composed of only two particles, an electron and a proton, held together by the electromagnetic force, an interaction mediated, we are told, by the rapid fire exchange of virtual photons.

The tiny electron is the smallest known unit to carry a charge.

The proton is 1836 times more massive than the electron.

The electron and the proton carry an equal but opposite charge.

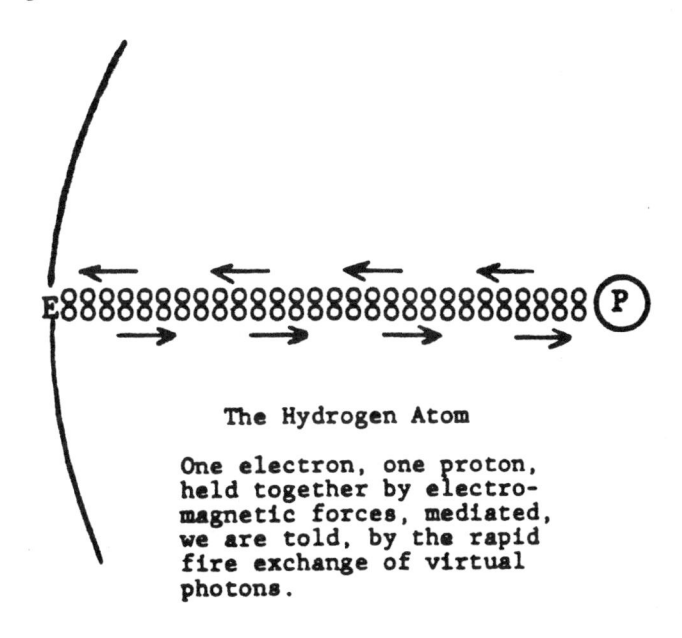

The Hydrogen Atom

One electron, one proton, held together by electromagnetic forces, mediated, we are told, by the rapid fire exchange of virtual photons.

The positive charge of the massive proton can be viewed as a successful drive *toward* materialization, toward life in material form.

The negative charge of the tiny electron can be viewed as a drive *away from* materialization, from life in material form, ie, a drive toward aging, decay and death of the physical body.

HYPOTHESIS:

Once upon a time a bit of energy wandered into the great ocean of materialization. A part—particle—cried out, "Oh,

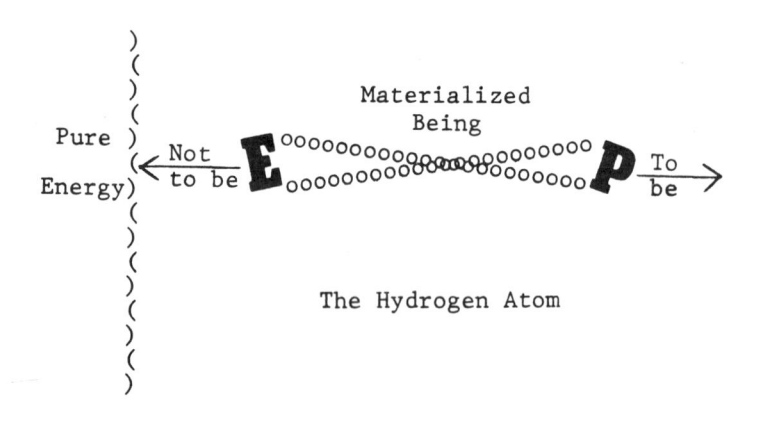

```
       )
       (
       )
       (                Materialized
 Pure  )                   Being
       (  ← Not  E°°°°°°°°°°°°°°°°°°°° P → To
Energy)    to be   °°°°°°°°°°°°°°°°°°°°     be
       (
       )
       (
       )
       (              The Hydrogen Atom
       )
       (
       )
```

I love it, I want more, more, more!" Another part—particle—snapped back, "I hate it, I want out!" and the battle was on.

Hydrogen—one proton, one electron tied together through electromagnetic force—is a highly flammable gas. *Flammable:* "Easily set on fire."

The electromagnetic force which holds electrons and protons together is mediated, the Scientists tell us, through the rapid fire exchange of photons.

The photon is the basic unit of electromagnetic radiation, a portion of which is visible light.

The exchange of photons within the atom could be considered the tossing back and forth of insight, or awareness, a basic atomic game of "To be or not to be, that is the question," a game being played in every cell of our body from the day of our birth until the day of our death.

****

The first glimpse inside the atom was given to the world by a New Zealand born, English physicist, Ernest Rutherford (1871-1937). Rutherford described an atom modeled after the Solar System: a massive, Sunlike nucleus with tiny electron planets in orbit about it, the system held together by electric force in place of Newton's gravitational force. Unfortunately there was a major problem with this picture: such an atom would not be stable. According to classical physics, the orbiting electrons would radiate away their energy and collapse into the nucleus.

A Danish physicist Niels Bohr (1885-1962) saved the day by making a daring, intuitive leap: electrons in orbit are *not* subject to the laws of classical physics and are *not* the source of the light radiated from atoms.

Photons, the basic quanta of light, are massless.

Electrons do *not* radiate away—do not reject—masslessness.

If an electron is a drive *away from* materialization, it would embrace masslessness, not reject it.

Picture again, if you will, the electron and proton within the atom tossing virtual photons—massless light—back and forth in what we have described as an endless atomic game of *To be or not to be.*

To *add* masslessness to the atom is to give the electron what it craves, strengthening its argument or position.

To *subtract* masslessness is to side with the proton, weakening the electron's argument or position.

Light—masslessness—is *emitted* from the atom as an electron falls from an outer to an inner orbit. The electron has temporarily lost the argument and has been drawn closer to the massive nucleus, toward the materialization the proton wants. Masslessness is lost in the process.

As light—masslessness—is *absorbed* by the atom, the electron, its argument strengthened, jumps from an inner to an outer orbit, moving farther away from the materialization of the proton in the massive nucleus.

Consider one ramification of the above argument that electrons have a drive *away from* materialization, a yearning *for* the masslessness of the photon, the quantum of light.

Scientists have now learned how to harness and put to use this moving drive within electrons. We now have artificially generated light, produced by electricity, the movement of electrons.

Very recently, in the high powered world of subatomic physics, the question has arisen as to whether the massive proton is in fact infinitely stable. The suggestion is that possibly the proton does decay—after a lifetime one thousand times longer than ten billion billion billion years. If this is so, according to the Physicists, goodbye material universe.

Proton = drive toward materialization.

If over a very long time, a time billions of years times billions of years, the drive toward materialization dies away—if life no longer feels any urge to fling itself into matter—there'll be no more animation in a non existent universe.

All matter shares a rather unique property: inertia. The dictionary definition of *inertia* is: "2. *Physics,* the property of matter by which it retains its state of rest or its velocity along a straight line so long as it is not acted upon by an external force."

The Solar System is not held together by gravitation alone, regardless of what gravitation is or how it works. The System is also held together by this basic property of matter, inertia. Once a material body is put into motion, it will remain in motion at uniform speed along a straight line forever unless some outside force acts to deflect or inhibit it.

Planets circle the Sun not only because the Sun, as a massive body, warps space-time, but also because, once bodies are set in motion, it takes an external force to stop that motion. Without the force of gravitation, the space-time warp holding them to the Sun, the planets would take off in a straight line toward outer space. Without inertia, the property that keeps material bodies in motion once they start moving, the planets would stop moving and would collapse into the nearest warp. Inertia—sluggishness—habit—keeps everything rumbling along in the same old rut, either in uniform motion or at rest.

Once life has begun, habit takes over, and self preservation becomes the number one law. In most of us inhabiting material form there is, under most conditions, no matter how adverse those conditions are, a sluggish unwillingness to climb out of the rut. Inertia—habit—keeps us jogging alone, even if the inner drive toward decay and death is so close to winning that we are little more than half alive. Most of us are pretty sure there is no way of getting out of this life alive, yet the instinct for survival within us keeps us trying.

Except in hydrogen, the lightest and simplest of all atoms, protons come accompanied by neutrons in atomic nuclei.

Neutrons are electrically neutral and somewhat more massive than protons. Within the nucleus they are stable, but released from confinement they disintegrate, a decay supervised by the weak force.

In matter, a massive neutral body—the neutron—accompanies the proton.

In life, the successful drive toward materialization brings with it an instinct to stay the course, to stay in motion, the instinct for self preservation, habit, inertia.

The proton, the electron and the neutron are the three basic constituents of atoms, out of which the material universe is built.

Proton   = the drive toward materialization.
Electron = the drive away from materialization.
Neutron = the inertia that accompanies all life/matter.

These three particles reflect the surge into material life, the sure pull of material death, the instinct that keeps life going once it has experienced birth into matter.

While the will to live, even under adverse conditions, is strong in most of us, there are those among us in whom this will is weak, or non existent, which can result in suicide.

While the neutron is stable in most nuclei, in the nuclei of radioactive elements, it isn't stable: it decays.

Radioactive elements radiate their substance away. *Radioactivity:* "*Physics, Chem.* the phenomenon exhibited by certain elements spontaneously emitting radiation as a result of changes in the nuclei of atoms of the element."

Suicide: "1. the intentional taking of one's own life."

Most elements are stable, but a minority of elements are radioactive and spontaneously destroy themselves.

The neutron is stable in non suicidal elements, but decays in suicidal ones.

Habit—inertia—the will to live—is strong and stable in most of us, but in a minority of cases is subject to decay and suicidal impulses emerge.

With the discovery of quarks and gluons, Scientists can now explain radioactivity. This is how it occurs: the weak gluons, in charge of radioactive decay, change the flavor of quarks. *Strange* quarks are changed into *up* or *down* quarks. Radioactivity occurs, under the guidance of the weak gluons, when strangeness and charm leak away.

Gluon = glue = the stickiness that holds things together.

In mirror-like fashion, suicides occur, under the aegis of weak stick-to-it-iveness, when strangeness/novelty and charm have leaked out of living, leaving materialized beings with no wish to continue in material form.

Released from confinement in the nucleus—released from its close association with the proton—the neutron is subject to a slow decay. It disintegrates into a proton, an electron and a neutrino.

When the neutron is released from confinement, from close association with the proton, it no longer has any drive toward materialization to accompany and protect. Its job is over, or can no longer be performed, so—just as with people who find all their usefulness at an end—slow disintegration follows.

While possibly not infinitely stable, for all practical purposes the proton is stable enough. No aspersions have yet been cast upon the infinite stability of the electron. The other two particles which are currently believed to be infinitely stable are the photon and the neutrino.

The photon, the quantum of light, has a zero rest mass, a spin of 1, is electrically neutral and is its own antiparticle.

Few of us have any close acquaintance with consciousness divorced from matter. Our own consciousness has been inhabiting matter as far back as our memories go (for most of us at least), and contacts with disembodied spirits are rare and extremely hard to verify. So it is difficult to state with any degree of certainty what aspect of consciousness the massless photon reflects. To shed light on the matter we'd almost have to go to the mystics. Forswearing such a course, we'll settle for conjecture.

Light *is*. Without solar radiation we would not be here. We could not see, could not be as keenly aware, could not be enlightened. The basic unit of light, we are told, is massless.

Consciousness *is*. Without consciousness we would not be what we are. We could not see, could not be as keenly aware, could not be enlightened. As far as we know, consciousness too is massless.

There is a strong temptation to suggest that light mirrors consciousness, and that the infinite stability of the massless photon mirrors the stability and infinite life of consciousness released from mass. But this is conjecture only. I know of no way at present to prove it, or to disprove it.

The fifth and final stable particle is the neutrino, the "little neutral one."

The neutrino has no charge, travels at the speed of light, has a spin of 1/2, and for some reason baffling to the Scientists is always left handed.

The universe is pervaded by neutrinos, according to current scientific belief. They flood space and stream through matter, minding their own business, interacting with the greatest rarity, all the while spinning only counter-clockwise to the direction of their motion, making them incurably left handed.

Why no right handed neutrinos?

The subatomic Physicists cannot say. Such left handed exclusiveness violates a "Law" they have set up, the Law of Parity Conservation, which says that if a particle exists so must its mirror image. This means that if a left handed neutrino exists, so should a right handed one. But no such right handed neutrino has ever been detected, and two Chinese-American physicists, Chen Yang and Tsung Dao Lee, working at Columbia University, set up an experiment to prove that parity violation *did* occur. In the world of the neutrinos, there is no parity. A mirror image of this stable particle, the little neutral one, is no longer believed to exist.

As previously mentioned, there is more than one kind of neutrino, according to the Scientists.

There is the neutrino associated with that well known lepton, the electron: the electron neutrino. (Leptons, as the reader will recall, are elementary particles which engage in weak interactions but not in strong interactions.)

There is also a neutrino associated with the little known lepton, the muon. The muon is said to be a fat electron, a particle 207 times as massive as the electron with a life span of 2.2 millionths of a second. The muon neutrino, like the electron neutrino, is considered to have an infinite lifetime.

Physicists presume there is one other neutrino: the tau neutrino. The tau is another lepton even more massive than the muon; it is said to be 3491 times as massive as the electron. The assumption is that because the other leptons, the electron and the muon, have associated neutrinos (which are also considered to be leptons), that the tau has its neutrino too. As the tau neutrino has not yet been discovered or created, it is not known what kind of life span it enjoys, whether it shares in the infinite stability of the other two neutrinos.

What basic, stable aspect of consciousness does the neutrino reflect?

Mind as it exists in *Homo sapiens* has been divided, for practical purposes, into two subdivisions: the conscious mind, those thoughts, feelings, etc., of which we are aware; and the unconscious mind, those thoughts, feelings, etc., of which we are not aware.

The unconscious mind has been shown to serve as a receptacle for frightening thoughts that the conscious mind pushes out of awareness.

Psychic phenomena have shown that there is another aspect of mind which is frequently not under any kind of conscious control: that aspect of mind which seems free, at least on occasion, of all limitations imposed by space and by time, a mind capable of extrasensory awareness, an aspect of mind which could be called super- or supraconscious, above or beyond the ordinarily experienced conscious mind.

Some aspect of mind also creates and orchestrates dreams. This may be a distinct aspect of mind or dreaming may be handled by the unconscious aspects of mind mentioned above.

To sum up: there may be two distinct aspects of the unconscious mind, or there may be three.

Massless photons, the quanta of electromagnetic radiation, stream to us from their source, the Sun, traveling at top legal speed.

Massless neutrinos stream to us from their source, the Sun, traveling at top legal speed.

Photons are visible to us as light.

Neutrinos are not visible to us.

HYPOTHESIS:

Light allows us to see. Light = awareness. The massless photon, the quantum of light, reflects the *conscious,* aware aspect of mind.

Neutrinos—both of them, or all three of them if there are three—reflect the *unconscious* aspect of mind.

****

Massless photons can spin either clockwise or counterclockwise (can be either right or left handed) and are considered to be their own antiparticles.

Massless neutrinos are always left handed, while the *antineutrino* (the neutrino's antiparticle) spins the opposite way and is always *right handed.*

Ordinarily when particle and antiparticle collide, they annihilate each other, producing photons. No one is sure precisely what the neutrino and antineutrino, if they were to collide, would annihilate into as they are already, like the photon, massless energy.

Some decay processes produce both a neutrino and an antineutrino, but the two don't collide to annihilate each other. Instead they shoot off in opposite directions at the speed of light.

Matter, as the reader will recall, has three primary building blocks: the electron, the proton, and the neutron.

Neutrons are stable within the nuclei of non radioactive elements and are composed, according to the subatomic Physicists, of three quarks: one *up* quark and two *down* quarks. However, when the neutron is released from the nucleus and undergoes a slow decay, three quarks don't emerge. Rather a neutron free of confinement decays into a proton, an electron, and an *antineutrino*.

In its stable, confined existence within the atomic nucleus, the neutron is not believed to be a conglomerate of these three particles. The theory is that, undergoing decay, it dissolves into energy and this energy then creates the decay products: the electron, the proton and the antineutrino.

Theoretically any process which occurs can be reversed. If the neutron decays into three particles, then the three should be able to get back together to reform the neutron. To illustrate:

Neutron → Proton + Electron + Antineutrino.
Therefore:
Proton + Electron + Antineutrino → Neutron.

If this were Nature's way of producing neutrons, the material universe would be in serious trouble for neutrinos (a designation often used to refer to both neutrinos and antineutrinos) react with matter with such rarity that it would take billions of encounters of these three particles (the proton, the electron and the antineutrino) to produce a single neutron. There would scarcely be time enough in all of eternity to produce a cupful of matter, much less the material cosmos we presently find ourselves living in.

Fortunately, neutron construction doesn't wait on this highly improbable event. *A proton can change itself into a neutron by capturing an electron and emitting a neutrino.*

Proton + Electron → Neutron + Neutrino.
To recapitulate:

The particle emitted during neutron *decay* is the *antineutrino*.

The particle emitted during neutron *construction* is the *neutrino*.

Protons, electrons and neutrons are the building blocks of matter.

If there weren't any neutrons, the universe as we know it would not exist. Only lightweight, colorless, odorless atoms of the flammable gas hydrogen can come into existence without the added weight of neutrons.

Neutrons come into existence when a proton captures an electron, emitting a neutrino.

Therefore to build the material universe all we need are protons and electrons and the rejection of neutrinos.

However, to allow the proton to capture the electron we need the electromagnetic force, which means we need the carrier of that force, the photon.

To construct our material universe we must have: protons, electrons and photons, while we reject that massless bit of left handed energy, the little neutral one.

Life on Earth depends upon the electromagnetic radiation which streams to us from our Sun. This radiation is believed to originate in nuclear fusion in the Sun's core. Nuclear fusion can occur there due to the extremely high temperature, believed to be as high as $15,000,000°$ K. (At this temperature, there are no atoms; there are only particles.) Even at this temperature, the fusion of hydrogen into helium occurs at an extremely slow rate. According to current scientific belief, a proton in the core of the Sun will collide and rebound from other protons an average of 40 trillion trillion times before it will successfully fuse with another proton following collision.

Once the fusing of two hydrogen nuclei (two protons) has occurred, the rest of the chain reaction occurs somewhat more rapidly. The proton-proton chain is believed to produce helium in this fashion:

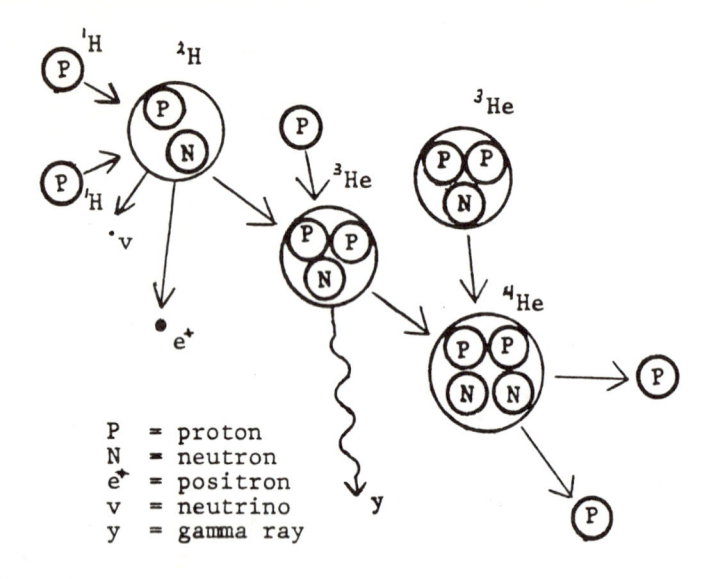

P = proton
N = neutron
e⁺ = positron
v = neutrino
y = gamma ray

 Two protons fuse to form deuterium, or heavy hydrogen, with a nucleus containing a neutron as well as a proton; a positron and a neutrino are emitted. A third proton is quickly captured, on the average within six seconds, and a lightweight helium nucleus (^{3}He) is formed containing two protons and one neutron, with the emission of a gamma ray. Two lightweight helium nuclei then fuse, in about one million years, to form the ordinary helium nucleus containing two protons and two neutrons, with two protons left over to initiate the process all over again.
 Of the various particles emitted, the positron soon collides with an electron and the two annihilate each other, creating photons in the form of gamma rays, electromagnetic radiation with extremely short wavelength and high energy. The neutrino, which interacts with practically nothing, traveling at the speed of light zips right through to the Sun's surface in about 2⅓ seconds, then streams off into space at the same speed. In contrast, the gamma rays emitted travel a tortuous path, being constantly absorbed and reemitted by the solar material through which they pass. As the radiation moves outward, through cooler and cooler layers, the wavelength lengthens as the energy is lessened. The original gamma rays

change into x-rays, then into ultraviolet rays, and finally, as they approach the surface some ten million years later, visible light.

Despite the slowness of the original fusion process, the Sun is believed to process about 700 million tons of hydrogen every second, converting it into helium. During this nuclear "burning," about five million tons of matter are transformed and released as pure energy.

Where does this energy come from? From the *binding energy* that holds nuclei together. The ordinary helium nucleus contains two protons, two neutrons. However, the sum of the masses of two neutrons and two protons when measured as separate particles is larger than the mass of a helium nucleus. The difference is small—0.7 percent. But this small difference in mass which is lost when two neutrons and two protons fuse into a helium nucleus is released as enormous energy under the highly favorable exchange rate of $E = MC^2$ (Energy = Mass Times the Speed of Light Squared).

On this transformation of matter into radiant energy our Earthly lives depend.

The reader noted perhaps that here on Earth a neutron is produced when a proton *captures* an electron and emits a neutrino, while at the Sun's core a neutron is produced when two protons get together and emit a neutrino *and* a positron (the antiparticle of the electron).

This is in effect the same process, for the *addition* of a particle is considered to be the same thing as the *subtraction* (emission) of its antiparticle.

This won't seem strange if we keep in mind that matter is considered to be a plus, antimatter a minus, and that the two cancel each other out much as a plus number and a minus number of the same amount add up to zero.

To illustrate:
  In neutron production on Earth:
    Proton + Electron = Neutron + Neutrino.
  In neutron production at the Sun's core:

Proton + Proton = Proton + Neutron + Positron + Neutrino

Subtract a proton from each side of the Sun's equation:
Proton = Neutron + Positron + Neutrino.

Now if we add an electron to each side:
Proton + Electron = Neutron + (Positron + Electron) + Neutrino.

The positron and electron cancel each other out and we have the same equation we started with for neutron production on Earth:

Proton + Electron = Neutron + Neutrino.

Once there were neutrons, the universe as we know it could come into being.

HYPOTHESIS:

Once upon a time there was only consciousness. At one point a bit of it grew rather sluggish and began to cast a shadow, ie, it clothed itself in matter. A part—particle—was delighted with this and cried out, "Oh I love it, I want even more!" while another part—particle—snapped back, "I hate it! I want to return to the freedom of massless energy!" and the battle was on.

The war being waged heated up to where the two combatants overcame the consciousness unifying them (the photons, carriers of the electromagnetic force) and parted company. The drive toward materialization (the proton) did what any intelligent fighter does: it hastened to enlist an ally. Two protons fused, producing inertia (the neutron). Upon acquiring inertia, the sluggish unwillingness to be moved, there was no turning back. Again the proton did what any intelligent, agressive fighter does: it went on the rampage, rejecting neutrality (the neutrino) and purging itself of all traces of the enemy within itself (the positron).

Once this was accomplished, the pro-material life force began adding to its size and strength, first by enlisting those of its own persuasion, later by capturing enemy particles (electrons) and forcing them into servitude as it formed itself into heavier and heavier nuclei (protons + electrons =

neutrons + neutrinos). The combat was so heated, and so distasteful to pure energy, that pure energy escaped and shot away from the battle scene at the speed of light (neutrinos and gamma rays).

The neutrino—the left handed, neutral one—never paused to look back, wanting nothing to do with matter. The photon, however, which can spin either way, allowed itself to get involved. Like a compassionate, impartial judge, it brought the contestants back together into atoms, the victory swollen protons massively occupying center stage, the tiny, non victorious electrons circling warily around outside. The pros and cons of the debate still rage, mediated by photons, with material beings here but never here to stay.

As material beings we are here, but for how much longer?

****

The left handed neutrinos want nothing to do with matter and interact with it only with the greatest rarity. But what of the right handed antineutrinos?

As we have seen, when neutrons decay, they decay into protons, electrons and antineutrinos. Theoretically this process is reversible: these three particles could combine to make a neutron. This event would be extremely improbable, we are told, but somewhere within the neutron an antineutrino, or at the very least a potential antineutrino, must lurk for when the neutron decays, one is released.

If it had been left up to left handed neutrinos, there would be no material universe beyond the simplest, lightweight hydrogen gas. But the right handed antineutrino, a component of the essential neutron, pitched in to construct our material world.

The four stable particles, into which all others decay, and the aspects of consciousness they represent:

The proton = the drive toward material being that brings us into life and growth.

The electron = the drive toward non material being that carries us toward aging and death.

The neutrino = the unconscious mind, an aspect of which brings together the contradictory pro and con drives to create our material world.

The photon = the conscious mind which holds it all together.

Why is the neutrino that completely spurns interaction with matter left handed and the neutrino that pitched in to build our material world right handed?

In recent years Scientists have discovered DNA: *"Biochem.* any of the class of nucleic acids that contains deoxyribose, found chiefly in the nucleus of cells: responsible for transmitting hereditary characteristics and for the building of proteins . . ."

DNA, we are told, is life's master builder. Cells in human bodies manufacture proteins unique to human bodies because that's what they've been instructed to do by DNA blueprints. DNA is the carrier of genetic information and without it we wouldn't be who we are. Life on Earth wouldn't be what it is without DNA.

DNA is right handed. No particular Law says it has to be right handed, but it is. Life on Earth developed on right handed DNA.

The material universe was constructed through the agency of right handed antineutrinos.

Why are our bodies and the material universe both built through the agency of right handed forces?

Recent study has assigned differing roles to the two hemispheres of our brain. The left hemisphere is said to oversee verbal skills and abstract reasoning while the right deals with spatial concepts and is, it is suggested, not only the site of feeling but also the site of dreaming and the unconscious.

It has also been found that we are for the most part crosswired. The left hemisphere of the brain oversees the activity of the right side of the body while the right hemisphere oversees the activity of the body's left side.

The right hemisphere—the hemisphere believed to deal with spatial concepts, also to be the site of intuition, dreaming and the unconscious—oversees the activity of the left hand.

Mirrors reflect but reverse the image. *Mirror image:* "an image of an object, as it would appear if viewed in a mirror, with right and left reversed."

The right brain oversees the left hand. In a reflection the left hand becomes the right.

Why are our bodies and the material universe both built through the agency of right handed forces?

Because 1) the right brain is our creative brain, 2) we are cross wired for spheres of influence, 3) mirrors reverse right and left, left and right.

Also for the same reason that the Sun and the Moon form the same size disc in our sky: because consciousness, as it plays throughout eternity creating the Creation, likes to drop boulder size clues in our path here and there so that sooner or later we will stumble upon them.

So why is the right brain our creative brain?
Maybe because it's right to create.

Do neutrinos have mass?

Recently Science has been striving to answer this question, for if neutrinos have any mass at all they could account for the "missing mass" of the universe.

For almost five decades, Astronomers have been stewing about the mass they consider missing. This "missing mass" is Cosmology's "dire secret," according to astronomer Joseph Silk of the University of California at Berkeley. Up to 97% of the mass that Science feels *ought* to be *out there* isn't.

Studies of the heavens beginning half a century ago indicated that all was not well *out there.* The stars were not playing according to Hoyle. A certain galaxy cluster known as the Coma cluster, located some 300 million light-years from Earth, stubbornly sticks together when, according to

Earthly Laws, there isn't enough visible matter in it to bind it together and it should be flying apart. Closer to home, our own dearly beloved galaxy, the Milky Way, is interacting with our neighbor galaxy, Andromeda, as though it has a mass almost ten times greater than Astronomers have attributed to it. The Milky Way is also falling toward a cluster of galaxies known as the Virgo cluster at a rate Science can explain only by assuming that the universe has far more mass than its output of light reveals.

None of this led Science to question its method: the application of Earthly Laws to the great *out there*. Instead it reacted by feeling perplexed and embarrassed. The "missing mass" or "dark matter" must be there, but where is it hiding?

Various theories have been spun and are being spun to account for the "missing mass," but no theory has yet won universal scientific acceptance. The "missing mass" may not be made out of ordinary matter, it is argued, for if all the luminous matter in the heavens is added up, it accounts for just about all the matter created in the current Big Bang Scenario, and no one wants to upset that theory by jamming in thirty to forty times as much matter into the script. This makes the elusive little neutrino a prime suspect: if only it has a tiny mass, it can be made to account for all that is missing.

Science has another reason for attempting to pin mass onto the elusive neutrino.

At the moment it appears to the Learned Ones that it took a little something in the way of infused energy to create the universe.

There is the *positive* mass-energy of all the material particles the universe contains.

There is the *potential* energy represented by positioning: the distance between stars within galaxies and the distance between the galaxies themselves.

It takes energy to pull masses away from each other, to put distance between them, ie, it took energy to put the stars and galaxies into the positions they're now in. Therefore potential energy goes down as a *negative* on the how-did-it-all-begin balance sheet.

Add the negative to the positive and the negative wins. There is more negative energy, according to this reckoning, than positive, which the Scientists don't relish.

If only there were more mass, which would add to the value of the positive, the two—negative and positive—could come out equal. To achieve this equality, the Cosmologists are searching for more mass, enough to make their energy total come out zero (thus excusing any outside force, such as a force called God, from participating in the Creation).

If perchance the elusive neutrino isn't completely massless, like the photon, if by chance it has even a fraction of the mass of the tiny electron, this would supply enough additional mass and the energy balance sheet of the universe would add up to a delightful zero, doing away with any need for a Creator of the creation.

According to the Cosmologists, if neutrinos supply the necessary mass, or if enough mass is located somewhere else, then the universe came out of nothing, is equivalent to nothing, and represents nothingness.

On the other hand, if the neutrinos don't have mass, if they aren't the possessors of the sought after mass, and if this necessary additional mass can't be found anywhere else, then the energy equations won't quite balance, and way back in the beginning it may have taken an infusion of creative energy to set the universe Big-Banging on its way. In this case, the material universe may be the equivalent of something more than nothing.

If the Cosmologists find the mass they are seeking, if their mathematical formulas then "prove" that the universe created itself out of a slightly unstable vacuum, is equivalent to nothing and represents nothingness, what are they telling us?

How close to non existent is nothingness?

If neutrinos, as has been suggested herein, are a reflection or mirror-image of the unconscious mind, do they have mass?

In their basic nature, do they belong to the reflective world of matter, or are they an aspect of the creative world of mind?

My own best guess is that they are both: that some aspects of the unconscious mind belong to the world of matter, other aspects belong to the world of mind.

This translates into the prediction that neutrinos will be found to have mass some of the time but not all of the time, that in time experiments will reveal the neutrino to be the first known massless particle which at times possesses mass, that in its fundamental nature it is both possessed of mass and massless.

If the material world is but a shadow or reflection of consciousness, as this book is arguing, then regardless of which direction we peer, whether into the microscopic world of the subatomic or out into the vast reaches of the cosmos, we are in fact peering into the mind of man.

Science is moving toward a realization of the linkage of these two, the macroscopic and the microscopic. In an article, "Missing: 97% of the Universe," (Science Digest, December 1983) author Marcia Bartusiak sums up:

> The search for the missing mass... has produced a strange and wondrous marriage between astronomy and particle physics. For the first time in the history of physics, the two ends of the universal scale are linking up.

Only one small step remains and that is for Science to realize that, no matter in which direction it trains its instruments, it is gazing at its own consciousness.

12

A LOOKING GLASS WORLD

Mirror, Mirror in the Sky, Aren't You Proof We'll Never Die?

> Narcissus, a beautiful youth, spurned the love of the nymph Echo. Aphrodite, the Goddess of Love, to punish Narcissus cast a spell upon him under which he fell in love with his own image. Gazing longingly at his own reflection in a pool of clear water, Narcissus pined away and died.
>
> Greek Myth

Is the material universe we seem to live in objectively real?

Do we have any real need for an objectively real universe?

The subatomic world put before us by the Learned Ones, the microscopic world out of which the visible universe is made, is a weird one, as those who tell us of this world are frank to admit. For example, in his fascinating book *The Cosmic Code* (Simon and Schuster, New York: 1982), author Heinz R. Pagels writes:

> These properties of the quantum world—its lack of objectivity, its indeterminacy, and the observer

created reality—which distinguish it from the ordinary world perceived by our senses I refer to as "quantum weirdness."

This weird quantum world—a world of flash-in-the-bubble particles and antiparticles, of quarks and gluons, a world in which massless bits of energy (photons) behave as though they process information and communicate with one another—is weird in a way that distinguishes it from the ordinary visible world of our senses, Pagels claims.

But is this weird quantum world really so different from the visible world?

If we put our minds to it, even for a moment, we will realize that there is something very like this weird world of the subatomic in the visible world around us. In an experiment any one of us can duplicate almost at will, we can familiarize ourselves with the conditions which Pagels refers to as proving "quantum weirdness."

The properties he mentions are, as a glance above will remind you:
1. Lack of objectivity
2. Indeterminacy.
3. Observer created reality.

To duplicate these conditions in the visible world you need only stand in such a way as to cast a shadow.

If you remove yourself from the scene, your shadow ceases to exist. Clearly it lacks an independent existence; without you it has no "external reality." *It lacks objectivity.*

Try to measure the shadow which you cast while standing. As you bend down to measure it, your standing shadow is no longer there. To measure your standing shadow, you have to remain standing and settle for an estimated measurement. *Indeterminacy.*

As you bend down in a vain attempt to accurately measure your standing shadow, your shadow changes. Your movement changes it. In dealing with your shadow, you are dealing with an *observer created reality.*

The "weirdness" of the subatomic world is duplicated in the everyday common visible world of shadows.

Dare we conclude that the subatomic world exists solely as the shadow of something?

In the shadowy world of the subatomic there are a few stable particles, we are told. These particles—photons, electrons, etc.—really *do* have material existence, it is claimed, even though it is not possible to determine in the same experiment their position and their momentum. With these properties in limbo, waiting to be observed, particles exist as *waves*. Waves of what? Probability waves, until the experimenter intrudes and creates a "reality."

Is it possible to build a visible world which is objectively real out of this shadowy underworld of observer created reality?

Some of our Scientists, in accepting the subjective nature of the microworld, give up any notion of an objective macroworld. If the invisible is observer created, then the visible which is built up out of the invisible must in some way be observer created too. This makes sense. It also leaves us with a visible universe which shares the weirdness, all of the indeterminate unreality, of the subatomic world. A world created by the observer—as a shadow of herself?

Other Scientists can't quite give up an objective visible world, regardless of the shadowy nature out of which it is made. Somewhere between the visible and the invisible a line can be drawn, they claim, beyond which the weirdness need not be extended. Logically it *can* be extended, but it *need not* be: the material universe around us *can* exist without being observed, without a consciousness observing it. Reality *need not* spring into existence only when and as it is observed, it can in truth be there all the time, objectively real, independent of observation. All it takes to achieve this view is to toss in a few arguments and decree it is so. Presto, substance comes into being out of shadow.

Atlas, a material being, no longer carries the weight of the sky on his shoulders. Probability waves now carry the weight of the world.

How objectively real—how divorced from the subjective, from conscious observation—is the material universe?

Quantum Physicists of our day admit that their mathematical constructions pertaining to the invisible world may have nothing to do with reality, whatever reality is, but this is of little concern, they say, as long as their constructions lead to a greater understanding and control, as they do. Pragmatically speaking, their theories work, and that alone is more than enough to give them value. That there is no way to prove their intrinsic truth does not matter.

The Big Bang Creation Story enjoys the same uncertain relationship to reality, though the Cosmologists seem unwilling to admit it. Books are written purporting to tell what happened to within split-split-split microseconds following the Bang with no acknowledgment that all calculations are based upon not just unproved but unprovable assumptions. In both the microscopic and the macroscopic worlds, Science is serving up myths.

This is nothing new. Since the dawn of human history, conscious beings have spun elaborate creation theories. There is no very compelling reason to believe that the current version of the story is the sole, or unique, possessor of truth. Is it truly more credible—or more meaningful—to say that the universe began with the gigantic explosion of an egg and is built up out of probability waves than to say that it began when two gods mated and rests on the broad, strong shoulders of the Titan, Atlas?

To each century its own peculiar myths.

Myth: "1. a traditional or legendary story, usually concerned with deities or demigods and the creation of the world and its inhabitants. 2. a story or belief that attempts to express or explain a basic truth; an allegory or parable. 3. a belief or a subject of belief whose truth or reality is accepted uncritically."

Myths can be charming, amusing, a lot of fun. But the Big Bang myth is none of these. When a myth is as pernicious as this one, it deserves to be challenged.

If there were any proof that the Big Bang Creation Story is the truth of the universe, then there would be little to do but face up to it like the courageous race of beings we are. But theories do not a universe make. Science must have its theories, admittedly, must believe that the universe obeys certain Laws and therein becomes intelligible, or the scientific world would have little choice but to fold up its tents and steal silently away. As this must be avoided at all costs—the driving curiosity of the scientific spirit is surely one of the most precious of our gifts—I do not suggest a turning away from the old myth without in the same breath offering a new myth in its place, to wit:

The material universe exists as a reflection of consciousness, a shadow of consciousness, a mirror image of consciousness.

This myth, like all the myths preceding it, may not reflect the final reality. There may be underlayers of even more intense reality. But as a working hypothesis, viewed pragmatically, what kind of value might such a theory have for us? How well would it work?

First, and importantly, such an hypothesis would immediately restore Man, with his creative consciousness, to a central position in the scheme of things. Any notion that *Homo sapiens* emerged by accident in a universe hostile toward him or at best indifferent to him becomes errant nonsense. An unsophisticated child in the dark can find his own shadow frightening, but with age and knowledge such a fear is seen for the foolishness it is. If the world does not even exist apart from consciousness, then we human beings who possess it should stand tall, confident of our own importance.

This sense of our own importance has been hard to come by in recent times. As Cosmologists found, or deluded themselves into thinking they had found, an incredibly vast, expanding universe, human life on Earth seemed to shrink into ever greater meaninglessness. The view of the universe created in the astronomical observatories of this world spilled out onto the landscape, inundating classrooms on every level, to where there is scarcely a child living in the so-called civilized world who doesn't have intimations of how big and impersonal the universe is and how tiny and insignificant she is. In the last several decades, bombarded constantly by new scientific "discoveries," human beings have absorbed a frightening lesson and have absorbed it well: we are, Science tells us, a chance-born excrescence of nothingness in a frighteningly vast universe of something, a universe completely indifferent to us, a universe in which we are incidental and accidental. In such a universe, there is little wonder we have increasingly suffered from cold, lonely feelings of alienation and isolation. Regardless of the material security many of us now enjoy, the comfortable environment Science in the last few centuries has provided for us, the exciting new toys that technology spews out to us, underlying everything else, deep within our hearts, lives the uneasy feeling that perhaps we don't really belong, the universe may not really feel hospitably toward us. If we just accidently came into being, like an unwelcome oil spill, we may be rubbed out for good any time.

This damaging, fear-laden self-assessment has been based on a scientific myth, nothing more, and it's time we understood this. On occasion the truth may hurt or prove upsetting, but there is no reason to allow ourselves to be emotionally crippled or diminished by what will be revealed in time as one more outmoded, outworn, outgrown myth.

Secondly, if we accept the material universe as a mirror of consciousness, we throw wide the doors to a wondrous new understanding of both ourselves and our world.

The earliest known mirrors were natural ones: the still surface of a lake or a woodland pond. Mirrors were closely related to magic, for the reflection or image seen in the water was believed by many primitive people to be the soul. The soul could exist separately from the body, as long as it didn't wander too far away and was careful not to get caught by evil spirits, and the image seen in a mirror was this out-of-the-body soul. Among the ancient Greeks, to dream of seeing one's image in water was an omen of death, for if the image-soul was caught by the water spirits and dragged into the dark depths below, the body bereft of its soul would perish.

The belief in mirror-magic circled the globe, from the homes of China where small mirrors were hung to scare away evil spirits, through the Middle East where a magic mirror appears in the *Arabian Nights*, to the Camelot of King Arthur where Merlin had a magic mirror, to Chaucer's *Canterbury Tales,* wherein a magic mirror foretells misfortune. Divination by mirror was practiced in England at least until the second half of the 19th Century, and to this day the superstition persists that to shatter a mirror is bad luck.

Another visible form of the soul, in primitive belief, is the shadow. In a number of languages, one word signifies both *shadow* and *soul*. The shadow-soul can and often does exist apart from the body, and a body can be killed by spearing, stabbing, hacking, or otherwise inflicting fatal injury on the shadow. The shadow as it wandered could be stolen and then woe betide its owner. In Greece and some other southeastern European countries, shadows were commonly stolen to enhance the durability of new buildings. The unsuspecting victim was maneuvered into a position where the building's foundation stone could be laid on his shadow. This ensured the stability of the new construction, at the expense of the poor body whose shadow-soul had been stolen—within forty days he'd be dead. Earlier in history, living bodies had been immured in the walls of new buildings or buried alive under the foundation stones. When this practice died down, shadow-souls were substituted. Theft of his shadow still brought death to the victim, but in a somewhat more subtle and less messy way.

These beliefs about the shadow, like the similar belief about magical mirrors, circled the globe. In China it was thought dangerous to stand too close to a coffin during a funeral; one's shadow might fall across it and get trapped inside. Chinese gravediggers protected themselves against this occupational hazard by tying their shadows to their bodies with cloth. In European folklore, when someone makes a pact with the Devil she loses her shadow. To this day the superstition persists in many parts of Great Britain that to walk or trample on a shadow will doom its owner to bad luck.

If the material universe is the reflection of consciousness, the mirror image or shadow of consciousness, are we as tied to its well being as the body, according to worldwide superstition, is tied to the health and well-being of its mirror image or shadow?

Obviously we are. If water dried up or otherwise altered its behavior, if oxygen went up in smoke or otherwise were stolen from us, if carbon stopped freely sharing itself, *if, if, if,* our material existence would be doomed.

This parallel, while it exists, obviously proves nothing. We have evolved in response to the material world—according to scientific theory—and naturally have adapted to the world as we found it. Given a different world, elements which behaved in a different fashion, we would have evolved, if we existed at all, along entirely different lines. As we were fashioned by the way things are, adapting to the environment in which we found ourselves, naturally our existence depends upon a continuation of the status quo.

This is the scientific view—which may have as much validity as the widespread primitive beliefs about mirror-images and shadow-souls.

We know today—or think we know today—that the shadow is a natural phenomenon, caused by the interception of light, that it has nothing to do with the soul, if we have a soul, that a shadow cannot be stolen, and that to stab or spear a shadow as a means of causing harm to its owner is superstitious nonsense.

Scientific belief holds that the environment shaped, or controlled the evolutionary pathways, of life.

This may be attributing power to a shadow that a shadow does not truly have.

Primitive belief: the shadow-soul controlled the destiny of its owner.

Current scientific belief: the physical environment shaped/controlled the destiny of evolving life.

Current scientific belief may be nothing more than the old superstition in modern dress: the shadow controlling the life of the one casting it.

Quite possibly it is the other way around: life—consciousness—may exist without form. Existing without form, it casts a shadow of itself, a reflective physical environment.

In this scenario, the environment, a shadow, does not shape or control Man.

Man, possessor of consciousness, shapes and controls his shadow, the material world.

The earliest recognized mirrors were, as noted, still water ones. As civilization grew more sophisticated, pieces of polished brass, gold or silver served as mirrors. In the 17th Century the use of plate glass came into vogue: the front surface was highly polished while a metallic reflecting film was applied to the rear surface. This is the kind of mirror still widely used today.

Quite apart from their once reputed now disputed magical properties, mirrors serve any number of useful purposes. In the home they help us to locate and cleanse smudges on our cheeks and chins, allow us to check the fit of our clothing, help us arrange our coiffures in a manner to please, shock or amuse one another. Automobiles, buses and other vehicles are equipped with rear view mirrors to help us navigate traffic. Specially designed mirrors are used by doctors and dentists. In factories mirrors are frequently used as safety devices, for it is often possible to see something reflected in a mirror that the human eye cannot look at directly. Color television cameras, reflecting telescopes and microscopes all make use of mirrors.

To sum up: mirrors help us see ourselves, help us navigate among moving objects, help us stay physically well, help us work safely, allow us to bring the world in full living color into our homes, also allow us to see objects too distant to be seen by the unaided eye as well as objects too small for the naked eye to perceive. All in all, without mirrors we would scarcely recognize ourselves.

If the material universe is a mirror image of consciousness, it ought to offer us aid, comfort and enlightenment in very much the same way that our other mirrors do.

The universe as a mirror-image would give us a rich new way to learn about ourselves. It is a difficult if not impossible task to see our own faces without some reflecting surface. To see our backsides is almost as difficult. If the material universe reflects the consciousness with which we are so magically blessed, what a grand and enticing image in which to find ourselves.

If we postulate that the universe is a shadow of consciousness, we bring within reach ever greater and surer knowledge. We can study the shadow to learn about ourselves, or we can, in learning about ourselves, increase our knowledge of the shadow. In time we might even learn how to bring under conscious control the process by which we change the universe—our shadow—by changing ourselves.

Mirrors work, of course, by reflecting light. A flat mirror forms a true image while a curved mirror forms a distorted one.

If there is such a thing as objective space, it is curved, according to Einstein's well established relativity theory. If objective space does not exist, if space is simply an organizing principle of mind, this organizing principle is apparently curvaceous in nature or its reflection in the material world would not be curved. Therefore, a mirror-image cast by consciousness would not be a true one but a distorted one.

This distortion should not deter us. Distortion has its purposes, and curved mirrors which form distorted images are not without use. In any case, the distortion may be no more than is required for translation into a different medium. Two gases—oxygen and hydrogen—combine to form a new and distorted form, fluid water. In much the same way, consciousness in casting a material image of itself may distort only in the way required for translation from one medium to another.

After Einstein had revolutionized scientific thought with his Special and General Theories of Relativity, he spent the remainder of his life trying to formulate a unified theory, one that would explain the existence of all matter, all energy and all forces in the universe. When his search began, there were only two forces known, the two forces that had been known for centuries: the electromagnetic force and the force of gravity. Though he put thirty years into the effort, he did not achieve his goal.

In the 1920s Physicists decided that two more fundamental forces were needed to explain the quantum world. The two forces were tagged the strong nuclear force and the weak nuclear force. The strong nuclear—the strongest force in the universe, we are told—binds quarks together into protons and neutrons, allowing the nuclei of atoms to exist, and the weak nuclear force oversees decay.

Three of these forces—the electromagnetic force, the weak and strong nuclear forces—have now been mathematically unified by Physicists. Experimentally they are somewhat behind theory, but ghostly particles have been discovered, they claim, which carry the weak force, proving that the electromagnetic force and the weak force are different aspects of a single electroweak force. To incorporate the strong force into this scheme, however, though it has been accomplished in theory, presents possibly insurmountable problems when it comes to experimental proof, for this reason: the energies at which, theoretically, the strong and electroweak forces merge are currently beyond the wildest dreams of accelerator builders. In effect, the Physicists haven't yet figured out how to create the particles which they will then use to prove their point about the universe which they do not believe is their own creation.

To unify the fourth force, the well known and commonly experienced force of gravity, in actual experiment seems even farther out of reach. The energy level at which gravity theoretically unites with the other forces is ten thousand times greater than the out-of-reach energies needed to prove the unity of the strong force with the electroweak force. Gravity remains, in physical theory, the embarrassing and dismay provoking, odd force out.

Let's take a closer look at these latest developments with the mirror-image concept in mind, recalling an earlier reflection system suggested:

Gravity = the attractive force between human beings and their material surroundings.

Weak nuclear = the drive of the mind or ego which oversees the growth/maintenance/decay of the physical body.

Electromagnetic = the attraction (love) between human beings in all its varied manifestations.

Strong nuclear = the drive of the mind or ego to maintain itself, to maintain its integrity against any threat of disintegration.

There has now been experimental proof, we are told, that the weak nuclear and the electromagnetic are aspects of the same force.

Seen as a mirror image, this translates to:

The force within the body that oversees its health and well being is experimentally allied with the force of attraction we feel toward others. On a high enough energy level these two become aspects of the same force.

To care about our own bodies is to find other bodies attractive. On a high enough energy level, it is to care for those other bodies as we care for our own.

To incorporate the strong nuclear force into this unity presents experimental problems the nuclear Physicists have not yet been able to solve.

The drive of the mind to maintain its own integrity—the strongest force in the world if it equates, as suggested, to the strong nuclear force—theoretically unites with our concern for our own bodies and other bodies, but it is so much stronger a force that to achieve its unification with the other forces takes more energy than is currently available to us. We may willingly sacrifice a limb to insure our own physical survival or the survival of someone we love, we may on occasion even sacrifice our physical lives, but to give up the mind, the ego, the sense of self, is something that most of us simply cannot do. We haven't the energy or the know-how. The grip that the ego has on us is a life/death grip, one that we don't know how to relinquish. As long as we are alive most of us don't know how to give up who we are, though death of course may teach us.

In this regard, we should look at the attempts to split hadrons into quarks.

As the reader will recall, the proton and the neutron—the stable hadrons which are the basic building blocks of matter—are composed of three quarks each. Attempts have been made to split these hadrons to get at the quarks, but the confinement of the quarks within hadrons has so far proved unbreakable. When energy is applied, the quarks aren't freed. Instead the energy supplied creates new quarks trapped within another hadron.

In similar fashion, when a human personality, under enormous stress, splits apart, we do not wind up with fragments freed from the tyranny of an ego. Rather we wind up with an additional ego. If the personality who knows herself as May splits apart, she does not then view herself as two partial personalities, one half Ma and the other half aY, or two thirds Ma and one third Y. Rather she now knows herself to be an intact personality known as May, and a second intact personality who may call herself Anne. Even with further splits, we do not meet up with fragment personalities (quarks freed from a hadron?). If under severe emotional stress, May splinters further, she still doesn't split into fragment personalities. Instead she gives birth to new personalities Jon and Ruth and Tim and Sandra. Each of these personalities will see herself/himself as complete and intact, even though in only partial possession of the physical body. This deep sense of selfhood continues no matter how many personalities emerge to share the body, and no matter how spotty the time sequence memory of each split off personality. Though May splits herself in two dozen ways, at no time do we meet up with fragments M and A and Y.

This fact of experience leads one to the speculative question: At our present stage of development, is the human ego, the deep sense of *I am I,* the basic building block of consciousness as the nucleons (the stable hadrons: the protons and neutrons) are the basic building blocks of matter?

If so, we have an intriguing situation. Hadrons have been found to consist of three trapped quarks. Throughout much of human history, Man has been seen as a unity composed of three aspects: body, mind and spirit or soul.

The quarks within the proton and neutron have been designated as the *up* and the *down*. The proton is composed of two *up* quarks and one *down*, the neutron of one *up* and two *down*. What a ball a free-spirited spirit could have with this! Mind and soul are *up*, yes, and body *down?* Or are body and mind both *down* and only spirit *up?* Or is the body an *upper* and mind and spirit dismal *downers?* Or can the individual ego choose, in any given life, which will be *up* and which *down?*

Gravity, the odd man out for the Physicists, is the one force as yet for the most part completely unsubdued. Einstein did away with gravitational attraction and ascribed all movements to geometry: matter following a curved path simply takes the easiest course around other chunks of matter in a space-time warpage. Physicists trying for total unification have to work this or some other theory of gravitation into their equations, but this has proved all but impossible to do. Gravitation remains resistant to all efforts to back it into a corner and tie it up.

Gravity = the attraction between consciousness (human beings possessing consciousness) and matter (the material universe).

With gravity, we come to the basic cosmic question: Why does consciousness feel such an attraction for matter that it takes on material form? Why is there such a thing as life? Why was Man ever born? When we have an answer to this, the ultimate mystery, we will know what gravity is and the way in which it unites with the other known forces. We will, in effect, have precisely what the Physicists are searching for: a grand and glorious unification theory, an answer to the question of why we are here.

One of the problems with various Grand Unification Theories which mathematically unite the strong force with the electroweak force is that the numbers in them are far too big and unwieldly to suit theoretical purists. In addition, ratios aren't explained. Why should the electromagnetic force be only 1/137 the strength of the strong force while the weak force is even weaker, being only 10^{-5} (.00001) as strong as the strong force? Bring in gravity, currently measured at 6×10^{-39} (6 x .000000000000000000000000000000000000001) the strength of the strong force, and everything really falls off the board. Such a vast difference in relative strength is viewed as outlandish. A good theory should explain the ratio between the forces and not contain any number so big it's ungainly. Another problem with the GUTs (Grand Unification Theories) thus far expounded is that they set no limit on the number of elementary particles and fail to predict the mass of these particles. A really *grand* unification theory, even without the inclusion of gravity, has to do better than this.

Here again, if we take into account our mirror-image postulate, we are dealing with very basic questions. Once conscious life evolved, why did it split or seem to split into such a wide variety of forms? Is there no limit on the material bodies which now possess or will in future possess consciousness? And what of the mass these bodies possess? Is variety of form limitless?

As for the ratio between forces, here we can offer speculative answers:

Why is the strong force more than a hundred times stronger than electromagnetism?

> Because the drive of the ego to maintain itself is far stronger than love.

Why is electromagnetism almost a thousand times stronger than the weak force?

> Because love is the strongest force in the world apart from the need/drive of the ego to maintain itself, and lovers will sacrifice life and limb for love. Consider the way young men have gone marching off to possible injury or death in war throughout the centuries for

whatever cause is placed before them: love of creed or country, or infatuation with notions of honor and glory.
Why is gravity such an absurdly weak force?
Apparently because the drive of consciousness to incorporate itself is extremely weak; possibly no such drive exists at all and consciousness simply falls into a material expression of itself—casts a shadow of itself—as Planets fall into orbits around the Sun. In any case, the drive is so weak that everyone born into material being in time overcomes it and dies.

Recent attempts to unify all four known forces have resulted in a postulated Supergravity, a force mediated by the *graviton,* which is part wave, part particle, and travels at the speed of light. In more advanced versions of Supergravity, the universe has eleven dimensions, and in the eleven dimensional universe, the only fundamental particle is the eleven-dimensional supergraviton.

Supergravity developed out of a suggested one-to-one correspondence between what quantum Physicists have now set up as the two fundamental particle species in the universe: the *bosons,* which carry forces, and the *fermions,* the particles affected by the forces.

Bosons are sociable by nature, fermions are loners. The best known boson is the photon, the quantum of light, while one of the better known fermions is the electron. Two Physicists, Bruno Zumino, who at the time was working at CERN, and Julius Wess, University of Karlsruhe, Germany, showed that fermions could be turned into bosons and vice versa by a simple mathematical transformation, which indicated that possibly in the earliest moments of the Big Bang there was only one species of particle, and that fermions and bosons are simply different aspects of that one and only particle.

In the theory of Supergravity, every particle must naturally have a superpartner of the opposite species, very much as in the ordinary quantum world every particle has an antiparticle. In the quantum world, the well known photon and the postulated graviton are both considered to be their own antiparticles, but in the theoretical world of Supergravity, these particles are no longer doomed to wave alone. For the three known bosons—the photon, the W and the Z—three superpartners have been stipulated and given these appropriate names: the photino, the wino and the zino. The as yet undiscovered gravitino is partnered with the equally undiscovered graviton. The fermions, naturally enough, also have superpartners, the superpartner of the electron being the slectron and of the quark, out of which protons and neutrons are made, the squark. American Physicists have now requested that the federal government finance a multi-billion dollar particle accelerator—dubbed the Superconducting Super Collider—so they can test out and possibly confirm Supergravity. The Superconducting Super Collider—the SSC—would be twenty to forty times more powerful than the mightiest accelerator in existence today, and would allow experimenters to smash particles together at energies of forty trillion electron volts, in imitation of how things were moments after the Big Bang. In this way they can possibly create the particles upon which the theory of Supergravity rests.

The intricate mathematical equations of Supergravity explain space, time and matter, plus all the forces of the universe, as manifestations of a single force which existed immediately after the Big Bang. As such, it offers what many have sought throughout the centuries: an ultimate theory of the universe. On paper the theory is beautiful. All that needs still to be done is to find some confirmation that it is true, that it has some valid relationship to the way things actually were or are.

It is intriguing to speculate about the eleven dimensional framework of Supergravity. Possibly, in time, this will always be written as a number (11) with a colon included: 1:1. The eleven dimensions may dissolve into a $1 = 1$ situation: one reality, one shadow.

In their speculations, Scientists seem addicted to symmetry. In the quantum world, each particle has an antiparticle, though some, like the photon, are their own antiparticles. In the theoretical world of Supergravity, the same symmetry is postulated; everything has its mirror twin. As a final triumph of symmetry, Science may in time reach the theory offered in this book: Only consciousness exists, partnered by the shadow it casts, the material universe.

If we look closely at the latest scientific word on particles—that they are divided into two species, those that carry forces and those that are affected by forces—we will see the same old dichotomy that Man has been aware of since the dawn of history: the split between mind and body, or spirit and body.

Primitive man saw his spirit as so distinct from his body that it could wander freely away from the body at will, yet if harm befell the wandering spirit, the body was doomed. The spirit-force gave the body energy and life. The material body deprived of spirit, deprived of a force acting within it or upon it, quickly died.

This primitive belief in the ability of the spirit to exist apart from the body has been substantiated throughout the centuries by those who report out-of-body experiences, adventures in which the mind/consciousness temporarily departs from the body, often staying nearby, frequently hovering just overhead, but on other occasions suddenly finding itself, in what seems instantaneous time, a vast distance away from the body/brain with which it associates. In keeping with primitive belief, the evidence indicates that for the body to continue living the mind/consciousness has to find its way back and reinhabit the body/brain. Not everyone has personally experienced this type of out-of-body occurrence, but reports of them abound in the literature and it is not difficult for anyone who tries to locate someone who will offer first hand witness to such an experience. All indications are that primitive man was right and that the mind/spirit/consciousness can on occasion leave the body to wander freely. (There are those who claim this happens nightly to all who dream as they sleep. It is also claimed that everyone dreams.)

To recapitulate:

The latest word from the quantum world is that there are two basic particles, the bosons and the fermions, but back at the start of things these were two aspects of the same particle.

The massless bosons are the carriers of force.

The fermions, endowed with mass, are acted upon by the bosons.

Mind/consciousness, carrier of the force of life, apparently is as massless as the bosons.

The material body has mass and is affected by the mind/consciousness in much the same way that fermions, endowed with mass, are affected by the massless bosons.

The dichotomy in the quantum world seems to equate with the dichotomy in the macroworld in this fashion:

The massless bosons, carriers of force = mind/consciousness.

The fermions, endowed with mass, affected by forces = material bodies.

Back at the beginning, if Supergravity proves out and the analogy holds up, mind/consciousness and material being were different aspects of the same thing.

This book argues that this was not only true at the beginning, it is still true today, that mind and body, consciousness and the material universe, are nothing more nor less than different aspects of the same thing, that one exists solely as a mirror image or shadow of the other.

Did material being come first, casting a shadow that is consciousness?

Or did mind/consciousness come first, casting a shadow that is the material universe?

The latter seems more likely, also more appealing, but this may be nothing more than late 20th Century bias. Activating force seems more powerful, therefore more creative and fundamental, than inert matter. The evidence indicates that when the mind/consciousness departs the body and goes aroaming, it retains full possession of its senses and faculties. The discarded body, in contrast, seems able only to sleep or sink into a coma while the mind which activates it is away learning or playing.

If the theory of Supergravity proves out, we may have an answer as to why we were born. If gravity in the theory is as super as it sounds, mind/consciousness in the beginning may have felt irresistibly drawn toward materialization. In essense, material life may have come into being because—under the influence of Supergravity—we could not resist being born.

The fermions, endowed with mass, are loners. One of the best known fermions, the electron, is so unsociable that its aloneness has been formulated into a rule known as the *Pauli exclusion principle* (named after the physicist who formulated the rule, an Austrian by birth who worked in the U.S., Wolfgang Pauli, 1900-1958). Under this principle, no two electrons in a given atom can share the same quantum numbers; each must have its own unique set. This keeps two electrons from sitting on top of each other, ie, from occupying the same spot at the same time.

Material bodies appear to be loners too, separate from each other, each one unique. Some kind of exclusion principle—similar to the Pauli exclusion principle mentioned above—seems to operate in the macroworld much as it does in the microworld, a principle that goes something like this: no material body shall occupy the same space as, or share precisely the same characteristics of, any other material body.

While the fermions, endowed with mass, are loners, the bosons, massless, are sociable.

This fact—that bosons are sociable and willingly mingle with each other—could conceivably teach us something about the fundamental nature of consciousness.

While minds, like bodies, on first acquaintance may seem to be separate and alone, there is ample evidence to show that this is not true of all minds under all conditions. Some minds break down the barriers of individual consciousness and tune into the consciousness of others. Researchers have suggested that there is a threshold above which or below which or beyond which the individual consciousness loses its ordinary boundaries, following which it can find itself flooded with sensation/information which is not arriving through the body's five sense channels. Most of us have experienced this at least once in our lives. Such experiences may indicate that mind-mingling is natural for consciousness, in a way that space sharing and precise duplication does not seem to be natural for material bodies, and that we all have the ability to turn on and tune in to others if we wish to develop it.

The physical universe is built up out of probability waves, we are told. Waves, as we know, wave as they move, that is, they have crests (high points) and troughs (low points). Wave motion can be easily charted on a graph. The highest point is called the wave amplitude. While it is never possible to know exactly where a given particle, the electron for example, will be found, the amplitude of the wave helps the experimenter know where it *probably* will be found. The amplitude of the wave, squared, gives the *probability* for finding the particle at that particular point.

Until the particle is found, it is considered to exist only as a probability wave, not as a material body.

If the material world is really built in this fashion, out of probability waves, and if the material world is a reflection, shadow or mirror image of consciousness as is being argued herein, then this fundamental process by which matter comes into being out of probability waves must offer a basic truth about how individual minds spring into being out of consciousness.

For instance (constructing the original from the outlines of its shadow):

HYPOTHESIS:

Consciousness is a sociable wave that occasionally, in its wave amplitude, reaches such a peak of intensity that it coalesces into being, into a sense of individuality, a sense of *I am I*. Consciousness in coalescing (as an ego) becomes distinct enough to cast a shadow of itself, the material body, with which it then associates, for a time. As the intensity, after peaking, flows down into the wavy sea of consciousness again, consciousness loses the distinct sense of self it briefly assumed, and the shadow-body it cast dissolves back into the probability-potential/nothingness out of which it came.

****

If such a reading of life and the universe leaves you less than breathlesly thrilled, have no fear: the probability is overwhelming that it is not the final script. What the Scientists of today proclaim as their most profound understanding and truth, the Science of tomorrow sweeps out with the trash. The material world is quite possibly built out of something more substantial than probability waves. Probability may be just another name for: We don't yet know. Particles may exist even before they are found; minds may continue to experience individuality even after they rejoin the sociable wave that is consciousness.

> "The world is an illusion created by a conspiracy of our senses that make it seem three-dimensional."
> ("Spinning New Realities,"
> by Robert L. Forward,
> Science 80, December issue.)

The above are the opening words of an article about the work of Roger Penrose, theoretical mathematician, Oxford University, England.

For most of us, the three dimensional world of our senses is the only world we know and we're content to leave it at that. Not so the theoretical Physicists. Early in this century, Albert Einstein put before us a four dimensional space-time continuum. Now Roger Penrose is expanding this into a multi-dimensional universe constructed out of basic building blocks he calls *twistors*.

In math there are *real* numbers, the numbers we are all familiar with, the digits one through nine plus zero, with a placement system indicating value: 1, 10, 100, 1,000, etc.

In math there are also *imaginary* numbers, numbers invented by mathematicians which are not believed to have any counterpart in the real world. Descartes, Newton and Euler, early mathematicians, needed a number which defined the square root of a negative number. No real number multiplied by itself will produce a negative number; in math two negatives multiplied produce a positive. Therefore there can be no *real* number which is the square root of a negative number. To overcome this lack, mathematicians *invented* a number, designated as *i,* the square root of minus one. In so doing they created a whole new set of numbers for anything that the number 1 can do, *i* can do also. It can go to any positive size, can be negative to any value, can fractionate into fractions, etc. This set of numbers is considered non-real or imaginary, ie, having no corresponding reality in the material world.

Einstein gave us a four dimensional world using only *real* numbers, but when Science began to peer into the subatomic world, something weird happened. To solve the complicated equations of quantum theory, real numbers proved inadequate. Something new had to be used.

A new set of numbers—*complex* numbers—came into being. Complex numbers are *a mix of real numbers with imaginary numbers,* and are used to solve the equations of the subatomic world.

This being so, theoretical mathematician Roger Penrose feels that *all* calculations about the universe should be made using complex rather than real numbers. If the world is constructed of particles whose behavior can only be adequately described through complex numbers, then the universe built of these particles must also require complex numbers for its accurate description. To toss out the Einsteinian universe based on real numbers and construct a new one based on complex numbers would mean a thorough overhaul of all major physical laws, but Penrose theorizes that our understanding of the universe will be incomplete until this is done.

The space-time world we're familiar with may be no more than an illusion in a far more intricate world.

In Penrose's theoretical universe, built out of complex numbers, there is an eight-dimensional twistor space. As fate or luck would have it, this eight-dimensional twistor space is controlled by numbers in such a way that only one kind of space-time is allowed to exist: the four dimensional space-time we perceive.

In this theoretical twistor universe, space ceases to be the fundamental Science has always assumed it to be. Instead it is reduced to something derived from the true fundamental: the twistor. As space and time have already dissolved into space-time, time would apparently also cease to be fundamental. In the Penrose universe, twistors are the fundamental building blocks.

So what are twistors?

First, things that twistors are said *not* to be. They are not particles. They are not points in space-time. They exist somewhere between these two concepts, somewhere between being a particle and being a point. It is suggested that a twistor can be thought of as a "fuzzy" particle, but not as the same thing as a particle. Mathematically a twistor is close to being the square root of a particle. Theoretically it is closer to being an undivided point.

Twistors combine to produce objects which behave like elementary particles, according to Penrose and his associates. A single twistor can produce a massless particle like the photon or neutrino traveling at the speed of light, two twistor combinations can bring forth an electron-like particle, and three twistors, in theory, can combine to produce the nucleons, the protons and neutrons out of which all atomic nuclei are built.

Twistors cannot be seen. We become aware only of that part of their behavior which is described by real numbers, but in reality, according to Penrose, real-world behavior is controlled by the hidden complex number structure.

Complex numbers—real numbers combined with imaginary numbers—work to describe the universe for this reason:

the behavior of the *real* part of the number is controlled by the *imaginary* part of the number and vice versa.

The twistor universe currently being constructed by Roger Penrose and the students working with him is purely theoretical as of this writing. Yet there are indications, we are told, that Penrose may be heading in the right direction. The model he puts forth is highly intriguing.

To review:

Real numbers describe the Newton-Einstein world of space-time.

Real numbers were found to be inadequate when it came to describing the subatomic world, out of which is built the Newton-Einstein world. It takes complex numbers to describe this world.

Complex numbers are numbers using a mix of real numbers with imaginary ones.

In mathematics, it took a marriage of the real with the imaginary to create numbers which could adequately describe the quantum world.

If the reality of the microscopic world can only be described mathematically with complex numbers, it is only logical to assume, as Penrose does, that the macroscopic universe built up out of the microscopic world also requires such numbers for its proper description.

Real + imaginary = accurate description of the universe.

One reality + one image = the universe we live in.

Complex numbers—numbers combining the real and the imaginary—are said to work because the behavior of the *real* part of the number is controlled by the *imaginary* part and vice versa.

The *real* behavior we observe—like the forward motion of a train or plane—is controlled by a hidden complexity.

Mirror images are also controlled, as are shadows.

The fundamental of Penrose's theoretical universe is the twistor. The first definition of *twist* is *to intertwine.* Another definition: *to contort.* Another: *to distort or pervert.* Another: *to warp.*

How intertwined, contorted, distorted, perverted or warped does a reflection have to be before we cease to recognize it as an image?

Imaginary numbers may be necessary for the adequate description of the world because we are dealing with an image.

The theoretical twistor universe of Roger Penrose, constructed with complex numbers, is said to have eight dimensions.

We ordinarily see ourselves as living in a four dimensional world: three spatial dimensions, plus a fourth dimension, time.

One four dimensional world casting an image of itself would yield eight dimensions.

Complex numbers (real numbers mixed with imaginary ones) yield an eight dimensional universe.

Four dimensions of reality, plus four dimensions of image?

Human consciousness is constructed in such a way that regardless of what the mathematicians tell us about our world, we perceive it as possessing three dimensions of space, plus one of time. We do not seem mentally equipped to visualize additional dimensions. Given a fourth spatial dimension, where do we put it? in what direction? We've already used up all the directions we can imagine. Five, six, seven, eight dimensions—as far as our ability to visualize these dimensions, forget it. We can't.

We seem quite as thoroughly trapped in our perceptions of time, unable to escape an intuitive sense that time flows, and flows in one direction only, forward, with one *now* instant flowing after another after another, ad infinitum. It's hard to imagine not moving forward with this flow. Even in fictional time travels, no one moves backwards moment by moment through the flow of time or darts about in the flow. Fictional creations simply jump from one part of the time flow to an earlier or later part. Once plunged into the new stream, they again live in time's flow.

Is it possible to imagine not moving forward with this flow? How would it work to live time backwards, or to jump around here and there in time? It's easy enough to visualize oneself in the time stream suddenly swinging around to live time backwards—like a movie reel set to run in reverse—but the moment this visualization is effected, problems set in. Imagine yourself in this position and you soon realize that you are still not moving backwards in time. Regardless of the direction in which time may be flowing for all those around you, if you've kept your head, time is still flowing forward for you. In your private imaginary world, all you've accomplished is to reverse the previous direction of flow. You are still living in a succession of *now* moments, one *now* instant following after another. Even if you imagine yourself jumping around in what seems disconnected time, as we often do in dreams, you are still experiencing yourself and your reality in an unending flow of *now* moments. Just as we can't imagine where to put a fourth spatial dimension, we can't imagine our own existence apart from a forward movement in time, however slow, speeded up, jerky or jumpy the movement is.

We live within these limits. Human consciousness, in its normal waking state, is now, and as far as we know always has been, incurably four dimensional.

If a four dimensional consciousness casts an image of itself, creating a four dimensional mirror-universe, we have four plus four, the eight dimensional universe theorized by Roger Penrose, composed of the real plus the imaginary.

To sum up:
Advantages of the suggested new myth: the universe as a mirror of consciousness:
1) It will restore to us our dignity and pride, based on a solid sense of our own worth.
2) It offers us a rich new way to learn about ourselves.

There is a third advantage, the most important of all.
Once we fully realize our pivotal place in the scheme of things, and feel the full, surging force of our own creativity, we can surely avoid the fate of Narcissus, can stop ourselves

from falling so slavishly and jealousy in love with our own image, the material world, that, fastening all our attention on it, yearning for it, craving it, on occasion even lying, stealing or killing to grab onto a piece of it, lacking proper nourishment we pine away and die.